Classic Boat
Seamanship

Other titles of interest

See also page 181

Gaff Rig: 2nd edition *John Leather*
ISBN 0 229 11844 5
In John Leather's definitive study he examines both the history of gaff rigged craft and the practical aspects of handling them. Two new chapters survey French and Baltic rigs, and the more technical details of the vessels, their working practices and the characters who sailed them.

Spritsails and lugsails: *John Leather*
ISBN 0 229 11517 9
John Leather evokes tales of a hundred years ago as he traces the evolution of two of the world's oldest rigs.

Surveying and Restoring Classic Boats: *J C Winters*
ISBN 0 7136 3611 4
This book is intended to guide potential buyers of derelict classic boats through the traps and pitfalls, as well as advising on the rewards or potential bankruptcies of embarking on a restoration project.

Laurent Giles: An evolution of yacht design: *Adrian Lee and Ruby Philpott*
ISBN 0 7136 3322 0
Jack Laurent Giles' reputation is based on a successful series of cruising, racing and motor yachts which are known throughout the yachting fraternity. From over 800 designs produced between 1927 and 1982 the authors have selected 45 of his most famous craft which are described in detail with photographs and the original lines plans.

Effective Skippering: *John Myatt*
ISBN 0 7136 3560 X
A complete manual for yacht owners covering every aspect of yacht management. John Myatt addresses the problems of skippering and takes the reader a long way towards the elusive goal of yacht mastery.

Cruising Under Sail: *Eric Hiscock*
ISBN 0 7136 3564 9
This book has for many years enjoyed a considerable reputation as a major work covering every practical aspect of cruising for the beginner and expert alike.

Heavy Weather Sailing: 4th edition *K Adlard Coles Revised by Peter Bruce*
ISBN 0 7136 3431 6
Heavy Weather Sailing has long been the established authority on the subject of handling sailing and motor vessels in gales and storm conditions. This new edition includes recent worldwide accounts of those who have overcome unusually fearsome weather conditions.

Fitting Out: Preparing for sea: 4th edition *J D Sleightholme*
ISBN 0 7136 3558 4
This book covers every aspect of preparing a boat for sea. From the bare essentials needed to make a safe delivery passage, to a total fit-out, it's all here.

Boat Electrical Systems: *Dag Pike*
ISBN 0 7136 3451 0
In this very practical straightforward guide to small boat electrics Dag Pike demystifies the subject for the average owner wishing to fit out a boat, install new electronic equipment or simply sort out an annoying electrical problem.

Laying Up Your Boat: *H Janssen*
ISBN 0 7136 3456 1
In this book the pros and cons, risks and costs are analysed carefully, and advice is given on a whole range of matters in a straightforward manner to help anxious owners lay up their boats safely and without problems.

Classic Boat Seamanship

MARTIN TREGONING

ADLARD COLES NAUTICAL
London

To the crew

Jacky, Hannah and Jenna
who lost their husband and father
beneath a mound of paper

Published by Adlard Coles Nautical
an imprint of A & C Black (Publishers) Ltd
35 Bedford Row, London WC1R 4JH

Copyright © Martin Tregoning 1992

First edition 1992

ISBN 0-7136-3606-8

A CIP catalogue record for this book is available from the British Library.

Typeset in Palatino by
Rowland Phototypesetting Ltd, Bury St Edmunds, Suffolk
Printed and bound in Great Britain by
Butler and Tanner Ltd,
Frome and London

CONTENTS

ACKNOWLEDGEMENTS

The author of any book of this nature attempts to give thanks to those who have directly or indirectly contributed to its completion. I, like those who have gone before me, am equally indebted to those without whom this book would never have reached the publishers.

Firstly, to Pete Greenfield publisher of *The Yachtsman* and *The Boatman*, who first convinced me that such things were possible, and to Janet Murphy at Adlard Coles Nautical whose patience and advice sustained my efforts.

To Harry Aitken, Vice President of the Cornwall area of the OGA as well as to the other members.

To my good friend Jean-Jacque Guillou who introduced me to Chasse Marée and showed me that a mutual love affair with sail bridges an ignorance of each other's language.

To Peter Keeling of Cornish Crabbers, and Martin and Janet Heard of Gaffers and Luggers, both builders of fine boats in the old tradition.

Special thanks to Peter Garnier who, despite a preference for high speeds on four wheels, also cherished a lifetime's love of saltwater and converted a sailor's ramblings into readable English.

Finally, to all those seamen and craftsmen who have gone before, without whom we would have neither the tradition nor many of the wooden craft still afloat today.

To
One and All

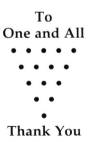

Thank You

Martin Tregoning
Penzance 1992

INTRODUCTION

One of the objectives in writing this book is to remove some of the mystique that seems to have grown up in recent years associated with the sailing of gaffers and other traditionally rigged craft. The hope is to reawaken interest in these lovely boats, to demonstrate the present day value of some of the rapidly vanishing skills of yesterday's seamen – and to do this before the skills are lost for ever. In the following pages it will become evident that sailing these craft is not really very difficult; sailing a gaffer requires neither the rope-swinging agility of Errol Flynn, nor a detailed knowledge of every part of a fully rigged three-masted ship.

The title can be read in two ways as 'Seamanship for Classic Boats' or 'Classic Seamanship for Boats', both equally valid. So perhaps I should start by explaining what I mean by the title. Classic comes from the Latin and means 'first class', so when considered with more modern interpretations such as 'model, enduring or polished', then its true meaning is perhaps clearer. Classic is often used to imply 'perfection', of which two further significant definitions are 'watertight' or 'seaworthy'.

Good seamanship is the performance of a whole range of individual duties and tasks afloat, while having regard at all times for the safety not only of your own boat, but other vessels and their crews. So defining seamanship presents a more complex problem because it encompasses the proper management and navigation of a ship at sea. The definition that I prefer comes from the title page of *A Manual of Practical Seamanship*, first published in the middle of the nineteenth century, which says that seamanship includes: 'everything necessary to be known by the seaman of the present day'. *Classic Boat Seamanship*, then, can perhaps best be described as using the age-old skills of the seaman amidst the materials and equipment of today and yesterday.

Good seamen must be versatile and adaptable if they are to survive in their chosen environment. Their world is changing continuously around them, sometimes dramatically, but the one characteristic which distinguishes good seamen is that nothing should happen for which they are unprepared.

Much of the development of yachts and their equipment has been as a direct result of industry or customer-led fashion. The speed of modern boat production coupled with the apparent ease of maintenance has seen GRP, stainless steel and aluminium replace wood, brass, copper and iron as the principal construction materials.

Simpler rigs, reefing systems and better winches, together with more reliable engines and tougher sail cloths, have resulted in smaller crews. This has enabled owners to sail by themselves and in greater comfort and more spacious accommodation. To attract the potentially large 'family' market, designers have increased below-deck space, thereby changing hull shape and sailing characteristics, while to some extent sacrificing overall seaworthiness.

The introduction of modern designs and the conveniences that they bring has demanded new skills from those on board, requiring a different level of awareness. Consequently the skills of our forebears have steadily been lost or have fallen into disuse as they have been overtaken by these changes in sailing techniques, and advances in technology. The new techniques are perfectly valid and will continue as further advances in development are made. Nevertheless the very strong re-surgence of popularity and interest in traditional rigs and boats also demands the revival of the old methods.

The owners of Thames Barges, Bristol Pilot Cutters or Brixham Trawlers, along with the members of the Old Gaffers Association, will rightly claim that this interest has never died. These groups have naturally tended to attract like-minded owners, but until recently they have found it difficult to encourage a wider interest in traditional sail.

The greater public awareness of all things old (and therefore perhaps valuable) has spread into just about every area of human activity. The consequence for sailing is that it has seen a steadily increasing appreciation of traditionally rigged craft. Initially, this grew from a love of the yachts themselves, but the recent heightened popularity of these boats, almost to the point of speculation, has in some cases increased their prices beyond the enthusiast's ability to buy.

Demand for these older vessels – yachts and working boats alike – has spawned a flourishing industry in boatyards all over the country. Craft which, at one time, would have been considered irreparable are being restored, or modern materials are being used to build traditional interpretations and replicas. Although the purist will despise such craft, for many people this is the only way they can sail or own a traditionally rigged craft.

Classic Boat Seamanship concentrates more on gaff rig and the smaller lugsails set aboard the small day boat or tender, rather than some of the other older rigs. The resurgence of traditionally rigged yachts has not persuaded the new generation of owners to forsake all the comforts of today, however; there are few modern owners who will forgo the pleasure of a cabin with standing headroom for a canvas tent rigged over an open boat. Neither will today's sailor suffer the hard work involved in handling the yards of a large lugger each time she is tacked.

The learning curve becomes less steep with experience, so that new skills may differ from old only by the manner and place in which they were acquired. The tasks performed aboard a Hurley 18 or Whitbread Maxi may be the same, but their practical application will, of course, be totally different.

Plenty of experience is the only real answer to learning the everyday skills used by our seafaring forefathers which can be translated to the present-day breed of classic boat. Today's new owner must look to a variety of sources for advice and guidance in this area.

The owner who is fortunate enough to have the time to visit the boatyard during the final days before the boat is handed over will learn much from the builder. Unfortunately, with the increasing move to mass production, this link between craftsman and owner has dwindled, and the new owner may simply receive a set of instructions to accompany the boat.

Books are, of course, an obvious source of information, but their greatest value is in pointing the owner in the right direction and then explaining what might go wrong. The only real solution is to get out there on the water and to start sailing your boat. Whether you choose to take the first tentative steps with a sailing instructor, a friend, or on your own, will depend upon your personal confidence balanced against caution.

Few yacht brokers, salesmen or even builders, for that matter, pay as much attention as they should to their customers' welfare once the sale is complete. This is not a reflection on their aftersales service but rather a warning that while new craft do not come cheaply, neither do they include all that is necessary for safe cruising. Yachts often described as 'sail away' usually lack such basic items as life jackets, flares and safety harnesses while, in some cases, even fire extinguishers or an anchor are not included.

The experienced owner will usually have clear ideas of what is needed; the novice on the other hand will have to seek advice. The new owner should first obtain a full inventory of what is supplied with the yacht from the builder and then ask for a second list of safety recommendations plus other essential items. Books providing valuable advice for the beginner can also be used as a source of impartial information.

Everyone has their own ideas on what constitutes the ideal yacht. In order to decide which is the most suitable yacht for you, it is as well to understand the evolution that developed the various rigs which still regularly sail around the coasts of the United Kingdom.

CHAPTER 1

Sailing rigs: the origin of the species

From the moment the very first sailing boat was launched it has never ceased to undergo change. As both the water in which it floats and the wind which blows across it remain the same, why this almost continuous process of evolution?

Early efforts concentrated on the need to stay upright and keep the water on the outside rather than the inside of the hull. Boats were required for trading, fishing, carrying freight and passengers, and for travel and exploration; vessels were designed to meet the specific requirements of their task; their designs were also dictated by various factors such as the waters they sailed and the materials available for their construction. The twentieth century, and the decades following the Second World War in particular, has seen significant changes, with the growth of sailing as a means of recreation and the development of yachts suitable for these pursuits. The substitution of the bermudian rig for the gaff, coupled with the arrival of glass reinforced plastic (GRP) and other rapid advances in technology, resulted in bermudian sloops being launched from production lines in large numbers: the public, it seemed, expected a modern rig to accompany the new construction material, but the desire for a simpler form of rigging together with attractively low costs were probably also a strong influence on the change.

The increase in leisure time for the masses created a demand during the 1950s and 1960s for boats of all sizes which were easily handled and easy to maintain. This boom in plastic or tupperware craft, as their detractors called them, meant that they soon rapidly outnumbered older craft. Many small gaffers and luggers were soon considered uneconomical and impractical; they were abandoned and left to rot in yards all over the country. Perhaps inevitably, those still preferring wood and more traditional rigs are considered somewhat eccentric. The reasons are all too obvious: wood boats are heavier, frequently slower, require hours of painstaking maintenance and their sail plans are not always as efficient as they should be.

Gaff or lug rigged boats did not become extinct, although large numbers had already vanished because of neglect during the war years, followed by an overall depletion in their numbers caused by the emergence of the new material, GRP, during the 1950s, hastening the transition from older gaff rig to sleek bermudian rigged hulls. The founding of the Old Gaffers Association and many other similar groups, both large and small, halted this slide into oblivion. Annual OGA events held all round the country began to attract a respectable number of entrants, which in turn generated more public attention than the sight of a single old gaffer. The introduction of the Tall Ships' Races and formation of the Sail Training Association also not only helped to keep interest alive, but also broadened appeal by introducing the enjoyment of traditional sail to a much younger generation. This combination finally brought about a more general interest in, and awareness of, the country's rich fleet of traditional boats.

The wider prosperity of the 1960s and 1970s brought with it a tentative interest in the older rigs without a commitment to the laborious and demanding maintenance. The awakening interest was quickly fuelled when attractive craft like the Cornish Crabber, Tamarisk and Itchen Ferry were all launched in GRP. These rigs compromised the original large sail area but reintroduced gaff rig to a much wider and receptive purchasing market. At the same time Gaffers and Luggers at Mylor in Cornwall started producing a GRP hull for the commercial oystermen of the Fal estuary who can only fish under sail. The later decline in that fishery is a good example of the evolutionary process, resulting in the strong, seaworthy cruising yacht that is now built on exactly the same hull.

Today, the wheel has turned full circle, with many people introduced to or attracted back to the older rigs now demanding craft and equipment closer in appearance to the original. The influence of the older values has caused a number of builders to offer cutter rigged versions of their standard bermudian sloops in an attempt to meet growing public demand. This short-cut approach was inevitable, and their efforts are only too conspicuous, with a tiny staysail squeezed between a conventional genoa and the mainmast. Nevertheless, amongst all this 'engineering' are a number of true attempts at restating the advantages of the more classical styles of rig.

The gaff cutter is the rig most frequently adopted by the restorer or replica builder; it is, after all, ideal for most applications aboard boats up to 40 feet (13 metres). Once the deck exceeds that sort of length then the mainsail and its associated gear starts to become too large and cumbersome to handle. I am a great believer in making full use of blocks and tackles to reduce effort to sensible proportions but the principle can be taken too far.

Evolution of the rigs

It was not until the nineteenth century that sailing craft were designed and built in any great numbers to sail for solely recreational purposes. Certainly people had sailed for pleasure as far back as the sixteenth and seventeenth centuries but then, as in even earlier times, it had been the prerogative of kings and nobles. Any attempt by lesser mortals to emulate their betters would probably have been aboard some form of working craft, a small fishing boat or a ship's boat with sail rigged.

Early yachts were either scaled-down versions of much grander craft or modified working boats of one sort or another. It is for this reason that, until comparatively recently, yachts continued to display marked similarities with the working boats of the area where they were built.

The sea conditions and type of work that a boat was used for dictated its shape and freeboard. Boats along the East Coast, for example, achieved their stability through beam rather than deep draft: there is little point in building a long-keeled hull if the local waters are shallow and strewn with mud banks. Thus the working and sailing environment did, in most respects, dictate the overall design and ultimate performance of a boat, performance being crucial in fishing and trading where the first boat home with the catch or cargo snatched the best price.

There are obvious practical reasons for following the lines of a working hull, not least that the men who built them had experience of building strong, heavy work boats. Strength and reliability were seen as benefits in withstanding the power of the sea rather than disadvantages in the effort to increase speed by reducing weight. The substantial integral strength of the working boat hull was more than able to cope with the needs of the leisure yachtsman. However, it was when the interior came to be fitted and, later, as the rig was put aboard that these builders would be breaking new ground, because in this respect the demands of the working boat and yacht are very different.

It was the gear required on the working boat – fishing vessels in particular – which tended to force the evolution of different sailing rigs. Fishing boats setting huge seine or drift nets which stretched across the sea for miles needed as much deck space as possible from which to work their gear without risk of it fouling on structure or rigging. The West Country Lugger is a good example of a two-masted vessel striving for the maximum working space on deck. Their builders consequently stepped their masts as far forward and aft as they possibly could, so leaving a huge well amidships for tending the nets and fish.

Not all designs were born on beaches, in coves or the small ports and harbours around the coast. The larger hulls in particular were strongly influenced by whatever was the current fashion in naval and commercial dockyards. The customs men also strived to be at the forefront of sailing technology, endeavouring to carry as much canvas as possible on every point of sailing; whilst those they sought to capture had no choice but to do everything possible to increase their speed in order to beat the revenue cutter. In fact the smugglers became so successful at building faster craft that the boot was frequently on the other foot, with the customs even resorting to using captured blockade runners in their efforts to catch their quarry. It was perhaps natural that those who could afford to do so built copies of whichever design was in front when a fast yacht was needed.

The Bristol Channel Pilot Cutter is a typical example of how the evolutionary process created a large, purpose-built craft which was almost totally unsuited to any other kind of work. A fast, deep-keeled hull with wide side decks, shallow cockpit and first rate sea-keeping qualities, she could remain on station waiting for ships in all weathers. Her simple yet powerful rig was set on a single mast carrying a huge mainsail which probably reached the limits of what a short-handed crew could handle. Once this maximum was reached, any larger sail area had to be split between two masts; consequently some performance had to be sacrificed in favour of retaining a small, commercially economical crew.

The yawl and ketch were two solutions to the problem of retaining a large sail area without increasing the size of the crew or making the rig too tall. The ketch's origins appear to have been the older of the two, perhaps evolving from the two-masted lugger. It has been suggested that the yawl was a development of a cutter, firstly reducing the length of the main boom and then stepping a short mast at the stern. The ketch keeps most of her gear inboard which makes the whole craft much easier to rig and handle, whereas with the yawl's mizzen set so far aft, a bumkin is usually needed.

The use of ketch, yawl and even schooner rig aboard small craft is a fairly recent phenomenon brought about by the enjoyment of sailing rather than by a desire to travel efficiently between one point and another. Our forefathers were, after all, practical, and would see no rhyme or reason in increasing the number of masts and complexity of rigging unless there was a logical benefit.

Sloop

This term is commonly misused to define a bermudian rigged yacht. In fact, it simply refers to a single-masted vessel rigged fore-and-aft, setting just one headsail, regardless of whether her main is gaff or bermudian. The term sloop was once used to describe small naval vessels which did not conform to the established class of warship. It would have had two and occasionally three masts and been square rigged on all.

The single-masted modern configuration is a very popular rig, especially in smaller craft and open boats, but it suffers as the size of the boat increases. The mast becomes excessively tall, requiring complex rigging arrangements to maintain its rigidity, and at the same time the sails and in particular the foresail become too large.

Cutter

This term applies to any craft flying a jib and staysail forward of the mast, whether she has a bowsprit or not. There has been a tendency in recent years to fit a slightly cut down genoa and to squeeze a small staysail between it and the mast and call the result a cutter. While strictly true, I suppose, it is more an attempt to pander to an apparent fashion than any serious attempt to change to cutter from sloop rig.

Lug

The origins of the lugsail are unclear. It may have evolved from the lanteen or perhaps started out as a downwind square sail set athwartships, which gradually became a high-peaked, quadrilateral shaped sail. The sail is laced on to a yard which is then hoisted up the mast by a single halyard and traveller; the yard and the

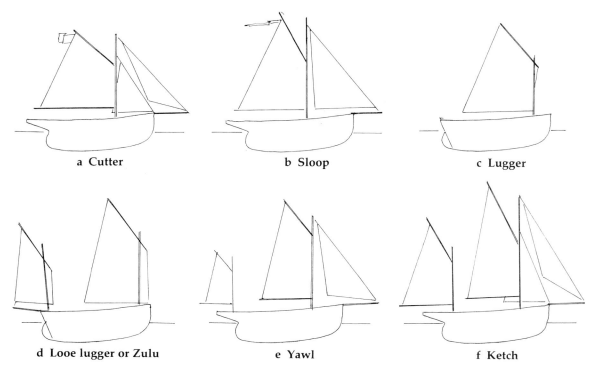

FIG 1 The six most common traditional rigs, indicating the differences in sails and masts in a stylised form. The gaff cutter (a) has two headsails while the gaff sloop (b) has only one, the standing lug (c) is more usually set in small craft, the two masted rig (d) is typical of a Looe lugger or Scottish Zulu, and the difference between the yawl (e) and the ketch (f) is the position of the mizzen, being aft of the sternpost in the yawl and forward on the ketch.

small portion of the sail that it supports extend forward of the mast. The sail is cut in such a way that the tension in the luff keeps the peak of the sail fully raised. The lug is usually a loose-footed sail, although there is a less common variant called the balanced lug where the foot of the sail is laced on to a boom.

The most common examples are either the dipping or the standing lug. Although their masts are stepped in similar positions, they differ from each other in two ways. The most obvious feature to recognise is the proportion of sail area which is set forward of the mast as a consequence of where the luff of the sail is tacked down in the fore part of the boat.

The tack of the standing lug sail is made fast to the mast so that the yard is peaked much higher and as a result only a small amount of sail is carried forward of the mast. The dipping lug on the other hand has the tack of the sail secured to the stemhead with a significant portion of the total sail area set forward of the mast.

Any lug rigged craft sails closer to the wind if the yard is set to leeward of the mast and it is in achieving this that the second difference appears. Each time a vessel with a dipping lug sail wants to change tack, her sail and yard have to be dipped. This means that the yard and sail must be lowered into the boat, the yard passed around the mast on to the leeward side and then rehoisted.

As the name standing lug implies, the sail and yard remain set all the time. So that the yard can move to the opposite side of the mast after each tack, the luff must be hauled aft so that the yard can slide around the mast. The sliding gunter is a type of standing lug, although the end of the yard has jaws or a saddle like the gaff and does not therefore need to be dipped.

The lug is often regarded as an outdated, unsophisticated and rather crude rig, fit only for fishing boats and some poor quality yachts. This is in fact doing the rig a grave injustice, as during the nineteenth century luggers from both sides of the Channel proved to be more than a match for many supposedly more efficient craft.

To my eyes, the epitome of the classic lugger was the rig aboard the French Chasse Maree, used to beat the blockade imposed by the Royal Navy during the Napoleonic Wars. These boats, which in the final stages of their development were lug rigged on all three raked masts, also had a long bowsprit. In order to squeeze in the maximum sail-carrying capacity, the two fore masts often had lug topsails while the mizzen mast was stepped hard up against the transom.

Not least amongst the British equivalents were the Scottish Zulus or the Mounts Bay luggers. The latter so impressed Dixon Kemp that he included them in his *Manual of Yacht and Boat Sailing*. Certainly it is a testimony to their seaworthiness that a 30 foot half-decked boat was able to sail from Cornwall to Australia so that its five-man crew could join in the Gold Rush.

Gaffer

The terms sloop or cutter both refer to the headsail configuration, but the more important and significant portion of any fore-and-aft rig is the type of mainsail it carries. It determines much about the character and performance of a yacht as well as identifying it, for example gaff sloop or bermudian cutter.

The commonest traditional mainsail is probably the gaff – either sloop or cutter rigged. The former tends to be on small craft where the size of the foresail is so small that splitting it into two creates more problems than it solves. The modern gaff sail is four-sided and is laced on to the gaff from which it takes its name. How the sail evolved as a mainsail in its own right is difficult to say; there are several schools of thought. One suggestion is that it could have developed from the lugsail or alternatively have originated from the lateen sail set upon the mizzen mast aboard the Carrack and Caravel, naval and trading ships common in western Europe during the sixteenth century. Another theory is that a dipping lugsail was split into a standing lug and jib because the single sail had become too large to handle. Then a crude gaff saddle was fitted to increase the size of the mainsail without imposing too much strain on its luff.

There is little doubt that during the first half of the eighteenth century the loose-footed lateen sail, set upon the mizzen mast, lost that part of the sail which extended forward of the mast. By the end of the century the balancing portion of the yard which projected forward of the mast was gone also – the gaff sail had arrived.

A varied selection of traditional rigs. Left to right: a gaff cutter with black and white yard topsail; gaff cutter with tan sails and a top mast but no topsail; a gaff sloop with white yard topsail; a dipping lug sailing hard on the wind (note that the sail is tacked on the stem and sheeted right aft); and a three masted French lugger, the Bisquine or Chasse Marée, possibly the finest lug rigged vessel ever built, here complete with topsails on both fore and mainmast. It can be seen that the sails are set on alternate sides of the mast to balance her performance both on and off the wind. *Photograph: Peter Chesworth*

It is more than probable that sailmakers and riggers followed parallel development paths with either the lug or lateen. Whether working on the beach or in the naval dockyard, each improved and adapted the ideas of the other.

Lug and lateen sails were loose-footed and consequently gaff sails followed this trend by initially being rigged without a boom; but later, as both crews and builders gained experience, the additional spar was fitted.

The size of any loose-footed sail is limited by the length of the deck along which it can be sheeted; while bumkins can extend the overall length, their effect is limited.

The fitting of a boom gave greater control and allowed larger sails to be set, extending beyond the stern.

The gaff sail was a more complex arrangement than its predecessors, being more controllable and giving better performance. The sail and its spars were hoisted by a twin halyard arrangement, with one made fast to the jaws of the gaff to set the luff and a second halyard raising the gaff itself. The luff of the sail is held against the mast in a number of ways, by lacing, hoops or even line and parrel balls.

Two-masted rigs

The attraction of two-masted sailing rigs is difficult to define. While there is the obvious aesthetic appeal, the extra work is not always a benefit. Some sailors enjoy the advantages of sailing and handling such a vessel while others are perhaps just seeking the link with the sailing traditions of the past. Sailing vessels adopted two-masted rigs for very practical reasons, principally that the sail area could be reduced into more manageable sizes, and that moving the mast away from the centre of the boat towards the ends increased the open working space.

The economics of sea trade demanded that the largest and fastest ship possible, carrying her maximum cargo, will be sailed by the minimum crew. Apart from the obvious need to keep watches and navigate the ship between ports, the major task required of the crew is to raise, lower and to adjust the sails. Once the sails of the coasting gaffer exceeded the size which could be easily handled by a few men, the only solution was to reduce the sail area. However, so that the size of the sails could be reduced without loss of speed, it was necessary to maintain the total sail area by spreading more sails over a number of masts.

Any commercial vessel needs to carry the bulk of its cargo as near amidships as possible in order to keep the ends light. Avoiding stowing cargo or other weights at bow and stern improves sailing performance, apart from the obvious difficulty in overcoming bending strains placed on the hull. If the cargo is to be amidships, so must the hatchway, which therefore restricts the position of her masts. The ketch was one two-masted solution to this problem.

There are three variants of the two-masted configuration: the ketch, the schooner and the yawl. The schooner and ketch appear to be the two oldest rigs, but it is not possible to state which appeared first. John Leather in his definitive work on gaff rigs identifies the origin of both schooner and ketch as being during the seventeenth century, with the yawl taking to the water much later during the early nineteenth century.

There are a number of definitions which claim to explain the difference between the ketch and yawl. Traditionally it is said to be the position of the mizzen mast in relation to the sternpost or rudder head. The ketch has her mast stepped forward while the yawl's is stepped abaft the sternpost, but this immediately creates a problem. The Lowestoft Yawl illustrated by Dixon Kemp has her mizzen well forward of the rudder head and looks more like a ketch. The Falmouth Quay Punt on the other hand has her mizzen right aft and looks like a yawl but should not be anything other than a ketch because of her transom hung rudder.

I happen to believe that so far as the differences between ketch and yawl are concerned, the spirit of the definition is more important than a precise rule. Exceptions like the ones above should be ignored if the two rigs are to be readily identified. Comparing the size of the mizzen with the mainsail in conjunction with the position of the mizzen mast is, I suggest, a better guide.

Ketch

The ketch has a mainmast which is often just slightly shorter than the mizzen; the boom looks as though it has been shortened to such an extent that the sail's leach is nearly vertical. The additional deck space abaft the mizzen mast gives a greater base for the stays to support a taller mast, setting a mizzen sail which can be equal to (in area) half that of the mainsail.

Schooner

The schooner rig could be described as the opposite of the ketch, having the smaller fore mast forward and the large main aft. Schooners, provided they are all fore-and-aft rigged, can have two or more masts. Some versions are square rigged on the fore mast: the best known examples of this are probably the Sail Training Association's two topsail schooners *Sir Winston Churchill* and *Malcolm Miller*.

The rig has been closely associated with the North American east coast, but schooners were evident in Europe at a much earlier date. However, those on the European side of the Atlantic tended to be deep-drafted, unlike in America where quite small, shallow-drafted vessels can still be seen schooner rigged.

Yawl

The yawl closely resembles the conventional sloop or cutter with a full size mainsail but with a mizzen which is about one-sixth its area stepped over a counter stern or hard against the transom. The small sail can mean that the mast may be unstayed unless a mizzen staysail is to be carried. The mizzen aboard the yawl appears to be more of a steadying sail, although its value to windward should not be underrated.

A mast stepped right aft with its sail and boom extending over the stern presents a number of difficulties. When the mast is stepped on the centreline it will obstruct the tiller of a transom hung rudder, and there is nowhere to lead the sheet from. The bumkin was the answer to the sheeting problem, while the problem of how to steer was solved in a number of ways.

The crew of the working boat just moved the mast to one side or the other, but where symmetry was important, other solutions had to be found. Forming an ugly

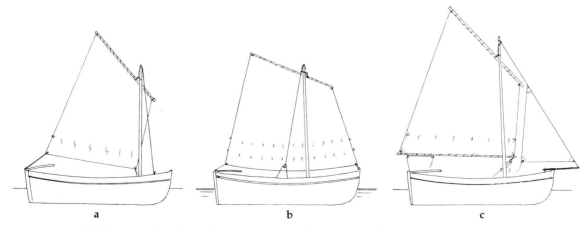

a   b   c

FIG 2 (a) The standing lug – the most common lug rig used frequently on small tenders and similar craft. The sail, once hoisted, can remain set and does not need to be reset when the boat is tacked. (b) The dipping lug can be found on larger craft; the sail must be lowered so as to be hoisted on the leeward side of the mast each time the craft tacks. (c) The balance or French lug is a fairly recent adaption of the rig, which makes it easier to handle.

bend in the iron tiller so that it fitted around the mast was one method, while the 27-foot Naval Whaler used a novel system employing the mast as a fulcrum.

Lugger

The origin of the lug sail has been lost in time. There are those who believe that it evolved from the lateen sail while others think that it was simply a result of efforts to make the square downwind sail more efficient to windward.

The lugger developed its two-masted rig in such a way that the maximum use could be made of its working deck space; as it was with two-masted gaff rigged vessels. The two-masted lugger is a sailing rarity, although the French have started building a number of replicas and even launched some three-masted Bisquines.

CHAPTER 2

A boat: defining the essentials

When choosing the type of boat you would like, various factors must be taken into account. The budget that is realistically available must be carefully considered; likewise the purpose for which the boat will be used: for example, it's pointless acquiring a fast racer if there are no locally organised events for your class. Local waters will determine the type of hull you choose; size and style of accommodation are equally important considerations. It is also vital to assess honestly how much time can be devoted to the new found hobby, not only on the water in summer but also on winter maintenance. Do try to be realistic about this: it is easy to underestimate the hours involved.

Cost

The budget that may be available to acquire a boat will naturally vary between individuals, so unless the resources are limitless a few points need to be considered. Firstly, whether the boat is to be new (either fully or partially completed), second-hand or a conversion. Do be realistic when looking at second-hand boats: not everyone can afford one of Nathaniel Herreshoff's fine yachts. Equally, don't take on more restoration work than you can handle yourself or afford to pay someone else to do for you. Remember too that not all the available money should be spent upon the purchase of the boat itself, as some will have to be spent on providing all the other equipment which is required to make a yacht seaworthy, safe and comfortable.

Surveys

The best advice for anyone with little experience of boats, no matter how they are built, is to commission a very thorough survey before buying. After your own initial inspection to see that it's basically what you want, a second-hand boat should be checked over thoroughly by a qualified surveyor. It is important that he is employed by you and he should submit his findings to you in writing. The report should obviously cover all aspects of the boat: its hull, machinery, sails, electrics, together with all the other fixtures and fittings.

All hulls will deteriorate with neglect: wood hulls suffer especially if they are left out of water for too long and allowed to dry out. Some GRP hulls, on the other hand, have been found to absorb water and can benefit from a period of drying out during the winter months. Therefore if a GRP boat has remained afloat for a number of years, make sure that the surveyor is made aware of this and checks the hull for water absorption, an early indicator of possible later problems from osmosis.

Type of sailing

A yacht will either be used for cruising, racing or a mixture of the two, and these will decide the course to be followed when selecting a boat. Unless your local club has a competitive One Design Class, racing a traditional boat will be done according to some form of handicap system, like that organised by the Old Gaffers Association.

A yacht's rig is dictated by the style and type of sailing for which she has been designed and the anticipated size of crew. Maximum sail area aboard an easily driven hull usually produces speed, and when coupled with upwind performance creates a craft more suited to racing. Reductions in sail areas and mast height together with increases in ballast ratios are usually desirable attributes to be found aboard cruising yachts. A number of small sails which are therefore more easily handled, frequently combined with a simple reefing system, make short or single-handed sailing much easier.

The area in which it is anticipated that the yacht will normally be used will also have a strong bearing upon her rig. This may result from restrictions in draft which affect the shape and size of her hull. Rivers with high or tree-shrouded banks, for example, may demand large amounts of sail set high on long gaffs, like the cruising yachts on the Norfolk Broads.

Hull shape

When looking for a yacht, don't rely solely upon the owner's description of her sailing qualities. Sellers of boats are notoriously reluctant to admit that their yacht might possess a few faults. They insist that she never takes a drop of water on deck in a gale, express horror at the slightest suggestion that she isn't quick in the lightest of winds or that she isn't ready and fully equipped for a round-the-world voyage!

Regardless of whether you are sailing with the family, single-handed or fully crewed, it is your local waters which must determine the type of hull you choose. If your mooring is up a narrow, drying creek leading off an estuary strewn with mud banks, a deep-drafted long-keeled 45-foot ketch will hardly ever allow you to go sailing. Therefore you must start your search by determining the most suitable rig and hull at the very beginning.

Whilst you are not looking for a second home, the age of the prospective owner and his crew is important, and as relevant to the accommodation as to the layout on deck. A narrow hull with a low freeboard, for example, may be quick and easily driven, but is likely to be lacking space below or on deck. A yacht without standing headroom and having narrow side decks is perhaps more likely to meet the long term needs of the young rather than the newly retired.

I enjoy travelling, so my inclination is towards cruising rather than racing round the cans, although occasional Old Gaffer events are always great fun. Sailing, whether with family or a few friends, needs to be varied. You may wish to make a quick beat across the bay to a pub for lunch or to a beach for a swim or sail a few miles down the coast to a quiet anchorage – this is my ideal for a relaxed weekend, especially if it involves a little pilotage into somewhere new. The ideal hull for this style of sailing should be full bodied with a length to beam ratio of around 3:1, and should have a deep, full length keel with plenty of ballast. However, if you will be sailing mainly along the East Coast with its beautiful creeks and estuaries, then a smack type hull which is shallower and broader is needed.

The bow should not be so fine that it lacks the buoyancy to ride the seas, but neither should it be so bluff that the boat comes to a halt each time it meets the oncoming waves rather than slicing through them. This would mean that a yacht of between 28 and 30 feet (8.5–9 metres) will have much more usable space below than many of her modern contemporaries.

I favour a plumb stem with little overhang at the stern so that overall and waterline length are almost the same. In this way little of the space below is wasted by inaccessible volume at bow and stern. Although the ketch or the yawl has much in its favour, the size of the sails make them more manageable and the options for increased light weather canvas are increased with two masts. I'd still prefer a cutter, mainly because unless you have a large craft in mind (40–45 ft [12–14 metres]), the second mast on the ketch can use up too much accommodation space, forcing fewer crew or cramped conditions in comparison to being on a cutter of the same length.

On a yacht of this size it is likely that, rather than having flush decks, a coach roof will be required to provide standing room below; nevertheless, the side decks must be wide enough (about 18 inches or 450 mm) for easy passage along them at sea. The gunwale must be substantial, stand at least 4 inches (100 mm) above the deck and have frequent scuppers draining over the side. The inclusion of stanchions and guard rails would very much depend upon the boat. Unless you have a very young crew, I tend to think that a safety harness and jackstay are just as good, provided they don't encourage over confidence.

The cockpit should be about 6½ feet (2 metres) long, with comfortable side benches or locker tops both at sea and in port, because, when the weather is fine, there is nothing nicer than sitting in the open air. Access into and out of the cockpit must be safe with an easy step up on to the side decks and grab handles which work well when stepping in and out.

I consider that a self-draining cockpit is essential even if the likelihood of open sea cruising in bad weather is remote. The odd wave can always break aboard even close inshore, while a heavy rain storm can pour a lot of water into the bilges in a very short time. I do not like relying upon automatic bilge pumps as they or the battery can easily fail.

Accommodation

Few yachts launched during the last century survive today, but the accommodation aboard those built before the 1930s was still influenced strongly by Victorian craftsmen. The use of space below was lavish: whereas a present day 30-footer will sleep 4 if not 6, a similar sized pre-war yacht may only accommodate 2.

The smaller, gentleman's yacht tended to be a rather basic affair, lacking much in the way of comfort, and even those that carried a single paid hand could hardly be considered luxurious. Often all that the cabin offered was a simple open-plan affair (and there can be few better descriptions than that given by Carruthers of *Dulcibella*'s cabin in Chapter 2 of Erskine Childers' *Riddle of the Sands*).

The comfortable forecabin is a comparatively new feature aboard smaller yachts. Formerly it served either to house the paid crew or acted as a vast locker for the sails, plus the many and varied smells which lingered aboard. Today we often forget how much we owe to technology for ridding us of some of the more loathsome commodities that had to be carried on board.

Accommodation should sleep 4 plus a quarter-berth for use at sea, so that three people can have a secure bunk no matter on what tack the yacht is heeled. A compact galley with a pressure paraffin, calor gas or diesel stove alongside a sink which pumps rather than drains over the side should face the chart table and navigation

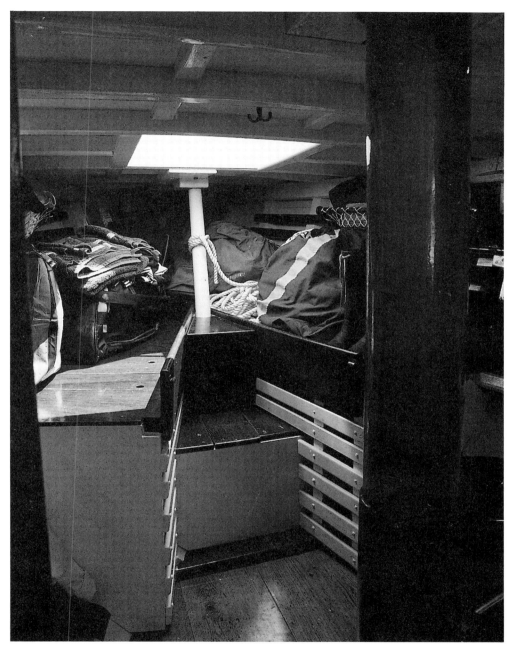

An Edwardian style forecabin used here for stowage of sails much as it would have been when first built, with battens across the locker fronts to improve air circulation through stowed ropes and sails. However there are two bunks with high solid wood leeboards and more battening over the frames again for ventilation and to keep the sleeping crew clear of the damp hull. The central pillar may well double as a spurling pipe feeding the anchor cable into a locker beneath the step locker between the bunks. *Photograph: Peter Chesworth*

area opposite, with a firm seat and backrest so that the navigator doesn't end up with a stiff back from wedging himself in place.

The cabin needs to be habitable at the beginning and end of the year as well as the summer months. Heating should come from a small diesel stove fitted in the cabin and, for fresh air, opening scuttles in the sides of the coach roof would supplement Dorade ventilators. The bulkheads should be painted white and complemented by

Traditional heads fitted in the open cabin rather than in a separate compartment. Much easier to clean and check the pipework than modern installations, although perhaps too open plan for today's crews. *Photograph: Peter Chesworth*

varnished edge trim to openings and lockers. All work surfaces including the chart table should be covered with a hard laminate for cleanliness and must be fitted with deep fiddles.

Rig and sails

To control the additional sails and spars on a traditional boat will obviously require more ropes to be pulled, all of which might seem a little daunting at first. However, some time spent looking around and working out just what each rope does should soon put the whole affair into perspective.

Extra ropes do not necessarily mean extra work: in fact less effort should be needed to control the craft when it comes down actually to sailing. The best performance of any boat, be she bermudian or gaffer, is achieved in much the same way. The sheets are used to adjust the sail's angle of attack to the wind and so drive the vessel through the water. The gaffer may have more sails but so long as the simple rules controlling their reaction to one another are followed logically, then there should be no difficulty.

The best rig to select on a first boat would be a gaff cutter with a long retractable bowsprit, fitted with a bobstay. The mast would have a spreader for the cap shrouds, also to take flag halyards and radar reflectors away from the mast itself. The standing rigging would be stainless steel, with all metal work on deck also stainless steel with a special finish which resembles galvanising.

Today we enjoy all the benefits of hardwearing modern materials, unlike our forebears who had natural fibre canvas and rope which required constant attention. The cordage and canvas always had to be stowed away dry, and considerable time had to be spent washing out the salt, and airing and drying the sails before stowing below.

After a weekend cruise during which it rained from beginning to end the gear went away wet; but it was a foolhardy owner who didn't make some provision either to visit the boat on the first dry day or get someone else to do so. Back in the days of the paid hand this was probably the only time that many of them earned their keep. Damp canvas would soon develop mould, rust spots around metal fittings, and finally rot out; any cordage also stowed away suffered a similar fate.

The problems of damp, faced by owners during the first half of this century, can best be illustrated by the large space on board which they almost exclusively devoted to stowage, unlike modern yachts where nearly all available internal volume is dedicated to berths and accommodation. Yachts built over fifty years ago frequently fitted out their forecastle with slatted racks and shelves which allowed maximum air circulation for drying out sails and ropes. The sheets in particular received special attention, but in reality all the ship's ropes would be coiled and hung up to air. However, as the only concession to comfort, it wasn't at all uncommon to find, amidst this mound of gear, the heads installed like a throne.

Synthetic sails are desirable and for them to be coloured does have advantages. For instance, tan masks stains and marks: it is, however, much more expensive to buy. Cordage should also be of man-made fibre, probably one of the hemp colour substitutes which are even available in braided versions as well as the three stranded laid rope. Ground tackle is about the only decision where I'd like at least one of everything – but more on that later.

A variety of sails spread over perhaps two masts allows a larger area for working in the centre of the boat, but without sacrificing seaworthiness upon the altar of convenience. The additional rigging resulting from two masts – not to mention the inconvenience they cause to the accommodation plan – does have its drawbacks. This means that some of the design criteria which were applicable to working craft soon lost their appeal when they were transferred to the smaller classes of yacht.

Where more than one mast can be stepped aboard the larger yachts, there are advantages to be had. The various permutations of sail which are available to suit almost any weather condition are as important as the reduction in their size and improvement in handling. Why use large, cumbersome canvas when small, compact sails will draw just as well?

Large sails do of course have their place; the Bristol Channel Pilot Cutter, Brixham Trawler or East Coast Smack are typical. Examples of all three have been either converted or used as the basic hull shape and sail plan for a larger yacht.

The gaff cutter, carrying her large mainsail and twin headsails, is probably the class of small yacht envisaged by most people new to traditional sail. It is the most common rig found on the thousands of older craft still sailing and this is probably the reason why it has been chosen by most of the replica builders in recent years.

Engine

The decision on whether an engine should be fitted will probably have already been made for you by a previous owner or the builders. Anyone planning extensive cruising, especially if it's to be mainly coastal, would be foolhardy to set sail without some form of auxiliary power. Open day sailers used only in bays and estuaries may simply employ an outboard or even rely upon the paddling ability of the crew to get them home if the wind fails. I know that not everyone will agree, but I think it takes many years' experience before an owner can be totally confident without an engine.

A craft designed to have an engine in the first place is unlikely to suffer any handling difficulties, but yachts originally built without an engine or sailing work boat conversions may be a different matter. Older yachts – especially those converted from or based upon working craft – were built for strength rather than performance. They may well have retained their huge, iron-bound rudders, which were strong enough to take the ground but not designed with water dynamics in mind.

During the period when working boats were first converted from sail to power, two engines were fitted because of their initial unreliability. The second, smaller engine was installed alongside the main power unit and became termed the wing engine. Once the boats' working life was over they were converted back into yachts: the large, main engine now took up too much space in what was to become the accommodation. So it was removed, leaving just the wing engine. This is one reason why there are still many older craft with a propeller shaft projecting through the hull to one side or the other of the sternpost. Other circumstances when a yacht may have an offset propeller are when the engine was installed after building, the owner preferring to face the disadvantages of a propeller to one side of the centreline rather than the laborious and expensive task of boring the sternpost.

CHAPTER 3

――――

The rigging

An owner would have to be very unlucky to be faced with rigging his boat for the first time totally unaided. Whether the boat is new from the builder or laid up in a yard, the chances are that there will normally be someone around to give advice and a helping hand.

Although individual differences in rigging each class and rig of traditional craft are much too diverse to discuss here, there are a few basic principles to be aware of and follow. Let me start by reassuring anyone unfamiliar with such traditional rigs as gaffers and luggers, cutters or sloops, ketches or yawls. Any working rig must be efficient, easy to handle in all weathers and perhaps, most of all, adaptable and kindly; these principles must also apply to a yacht. What then are the various items of gear with which the new owner must become familiar on board his new craft?

Standing rigging

Standing rigging has two functions. Its first is to support the mast; its second is to ensure that the sails set properly, the latter function perhaps not always so obvious. The loads that are imposed upon the mast and sails are a direct consequence of the rig and therefore dictate the quantity and type of standing rigging that a craft must carry. For example, comparing the mainsails of a bermudian and gaff rigged yacht with similar height masts will show that the sail areas are very different. A Hurley 22 sets 110 sq ft (10 sq m) while the 22 ft gaff rigged Oysterman can carry 190 sq ft (17.5 sq m).

The number of stays and shrouds needed will depend mainly on the height of the mast and how it is made. A heavy wooden pole mast may well support itself, whereas the thin, modern, heavily tensioned rig requires complex standing rigging. The change from gaff rig to bermudian called for taller masts and more elaborate and higher tension rigging.

A solid pole mast is an impractical means of achieving greater mast height, because of its weight. Body hoops had to be fitted around tall grown masts because of the difficulty in obtaining straight timber without shakes, and to strengthen scarph joints.

A separate topmast was one way of overcoming the height problem, although, as they were heavy, the sails had to be reefed or topmast struck during bad weather. As the move was made away from gaff rig towards bermudian, so hollow masts were introduced with high tensioned rigging to give support and keep them straight.

The traditional methods have much to commend them, not least their simplicity. The mainmast of a small lugger for example is often unstayed and will have no more

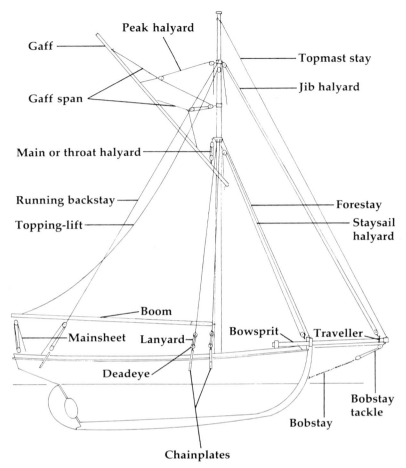

Gaff

Peak halyard

Topmast stay

Jib halyard

Gaff span

Main or throat halyard

Running backstay

Forestay

Topping-lift

Staysail halyard

Boom

Mainsheet   Lanyard

Bowsprit   Traveller

Deadeye

Bobstay tackle

Bobstay

Chainplates

FIG 3 The basic standing rigging on a gaff rigged cutter, together with the principal halyards. Sails and reefing lines, together with other optional rigging lines, have been omitted for clarity.

support than the halyard made fast to windward. The mast is short, stepped well forward, and relies solely upon its own strength to support the yard and set the sail. Even on larger craft the narrowness of the forepart meant that there was little space to spread the rigging on either side of the mast and so give the support needed. Those luggers which had shrouds did not set them up taut and used them more as preventers rather than for keeping the mast upright and straight. What little standing rigging a lugger did have was usually set up with deadeyes and lanyards that, while offering a simple solution, stretched and become slack immediately. This tendency towards comparatively slack rigging is also apparent with gaffers, for although the mast is stepped at the more beamy sections of the hull, it is shorter than a bermudian and does not need as much tension.

The ability of an unstayed mast to withstand over-canvasing is obviously limited, and the solution is either to further support the mast or to reef the sail. In order to retain simplicity and the maximum work space, some standing rigging was fitted to keep the boat seaworthy. However, as the early rigs evolved, complex reefing systems were neither suitable nor available and therefore a system of interchangeable sails came about.

This solution was particularly popular with two-masted luggers which carried a number of interchangeable sails which could be set on either mast or be reefed quickly. The roller reefing of today is a progression of this system, in that it provides an infinitely variable selection of sails, although less attractive.

Shrouds and stays

The first task for any new owner – assuming that the boat is either new or has been given a clean bill of health by the surveyor – is to become familiar with the rigging. Ideally the mast will already be stepped as it is easier to see where everything belongs; if it isn't, then hopefully the rigging is in place, lashed to the mast and labelled.

If not, unfortunately it means starting from scratch: the job will be less of a problem if metal hounds are fitted with each shroud shackled in place, as then it will be a fairly simple process to untangle everything and work out where it all goes. Even if the previous owner or yard is not available to help raise the mast, it is worth spending some time sorting out at least the principal standing rigging at this stage to avoid considerable frustration later. Imagine trying to learn the ropes with the mast hanging suspended from a crane, the cost of which is rising in direct proportion to the driver's temper. It would be a very good idea at the same time to make a rigging plan, not only showing where everything goes, together with the lengths and sizes of all the standing and running rigging, but also the numbers, types and sizes of shackles used aloft. This can save a great deal of time and effort climbing the mast to measure and replace gear.

The traditional method of securing standing rigging was to splice or seize an eye at one end of the shroud or stay which was passed over the masthead to rest upon a bolster. The more recent method is for the shrouds and stays to be shackled on to hounds, fitted around the mast. The lower end of the shroud was also formed into a eye, around either a deadeye for a lanyard or a thimble shackled to a bottle screw.

The older style of rigging is much more difficult to sort out, especially if the shrouds and stays are not already in place. The main problem for the unwary is that each of the shrouds is a different length. The reason is to ensure that the lower ends of each shroud are level with each other and the way this is achieved is simple once the principle is understood.

As each shroud eye is placed over the mast it rests upon the previous eye, so raising it up the mast by an amount equal to the total diameter of the previous shroud. The actual diameter of the wire may be increased quite significantly by the seizing and parcelling used to protect the shroud from corrosion and also the mast from being chaffed by the wire. The length of each shroud must therefore be increased by two diameters over the preceding shroud.

Traditionally, because odd numbers go to starboard and even to port, the order in which shroud eyes pass over the mast is fore-starboard first followed by fore-port, then alternating from side to side. The difference in length between consecutive shrouds would not be very noticeable but would be between adjacent shrouds along the ship's side.

Increasing the number of shrouds that are required will also dictate the way in which they are rigged. For example, if more than two are needed, then pairs can be formed from one length of wire by seizing an eye in the middle. There are a number of reasons for preferring a pair of shrouds to a single one: the former reduces the number of splices required, and the likelihood of damage due to crushing that will occur if too many eyes lie on top of each other. But the main weakness of the seized eye is that it demands careful inspection and maintenance of the seizing in particular. Failure of the seizing causes two shrouds rather than just one to become slack, probably resulting in a lost mast. The method should therefore not be adopted for masts with only a pair of shrouds per side.

Once the shrouds have been identified, they are passed over the masthead and slid down to rest on the bolsters. If the mast is fitted with a decorative 'acorn' this may have to be removed before the eyes are passed over the top. The baggywrinkle, which protects the mainsail when it lies against the after shrouds, should be checked and replaced before the mast is raised.

The forestay, which is usually fitted after the shrouds, counters their afterward pull. It is normally set up between the stemhead and the same mast band or bolster used by the shrouds. The method of supporting the mast from forward will depend on a number of factors, principally the length of bowsprit, the number of headsails, the height of the mast and whether a topmast is set.

A topmast – or even occasionally a high, single-pole mast – will have a topmast stay or outer forestay rigged from masthead to stem or bowsprit end. It is not uncommon aboard cutters for the luff wire in the jib to provide all the necessary support for the masthead. It is much more difficult to set and keep a topmast or fore preventer stay taut, so it is often run aft along the bowsprit to a small gun tackle. Except when a flying jib is set, the purpose of this stay is as much to counter the pressure exerted by the running backstays.

Although their name would seem to indicate the opposite, running backstays should be treated as standing rather than running rigging. They are usually rigged from the same band or cheeks as the topmast stay. Intended to counter the forward bending forces of a topsail, it is usually only the weather one which is set taut when broad reaching or running free.

A high pole mast and topmast will have to be similarly supported by shrouds, although one per side is normally sufficient. As the angle between topmast shroud and mast is acute, crosstrees are rigged to give the shrouds a greater spread.

The bowsprit

The bowsprit is the final principal spar which requires standing rigging (the other is the bumkin, set aft to sheet the mizzen, which is rigged in a similar fashion to the bowsprit). In all but the largest of Edwardian racing yachts the bowsprit is a single-section spar, regardless of its length, and therefore requires the minimum rigging.

Bowsprits can probably be divided into three categories, reflecting their construction and length. The traditional spar is long, can be reefed in to reduce sail in a seaway and also run right inboard as a convenience in port. The second type is shorter, commonly referred to as 'fixed'; and does not reef, although some variants can be brought inboard in port. Finally there is the plank bowsprit, which has come back across the Atlantic from the USA. This is very much part of the ship's structure and nowadays will often incorporate the pulpit.

The bowsprit enlarges the fore triangle, thus enabling more sail to be set, or the mast to be stepped further forward. The length of the bowsprit and the number of sails to be set will determine how much standing rigging is required. The greatest strain to be overcome is the 'lift' induced by the fore-topmast stay if rigged and the headsails when set taut and full of wind. It is essential that the luff of the jib is bar taut when sailing to windward and consequently this imposes considerable strain upon the end of the bowsprit and masthead.

Shrouds and backstays stop the mast from leaning forward, so it is essential that the bowsprit must be prevented from lifting and perhaps breaking under the strain. The solution is a bobstay which is rigged between the outer end of the bowsprit and

Right forward on the German yacht *Eliphant* showing an unusual use of deadeye and lanyard to tension the forestay. The lifting bowsprit is typical of the continental rig with only a single knighthead and, as a result, additional timber bracing to the port bulwark. The luff of both jib and staysail are laced permanently on to iron rings running on their respective stays. The jib, it should be noted, is set on a running topmast stay whch is reeved through the block on the bowsprit traveller and is all brought inboard when the sail is lowered.
Photograph: Martin Tregoning

the stem near the waterline. Because the strain tries to bend the bowsprit upwards, it is usual to induce a 'pre-bend' downwards so that any tendency to lift will reduce tension on the bowsprit.

The bobstay may be made of either wire or chain and can be rigged fixed or running depending upon use as much as fashion. The fixed bobstay is tensioned by a bottle screw between bowsprit end and stay, while this is replaced by a small purchase when rigged running. Although the reefing bowsprit is now comparatively rare, the running bobstay remains so that it can be slackened off and lifted clear while a vessel lies to her anchor.

Longer bowsprits mean that the angle between bobstay and spar is so narrow that it reduces the downward pull: to overcome this problem a dolphin striker is fitted. The striker projects below the bowsprit from its mid point, thereby widening the angle and so increasing downward tension.

The bobstay will overcome any tendency for the bowsprit to bend upwards but will not prevent deflection to one side or the other caused by sideways pressure of the wind. The only solution to this problem, which is most noticeable with longer bowsprits, is to rig side shrouds between the end of the bowsprit and the bulwarks at the beamiest part of the hull. In the same way that long bowsprits need dolphin

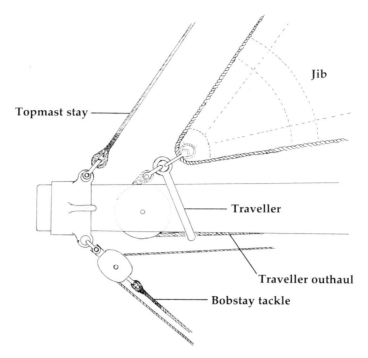

FIG 4 The topmast stay tension is adjusted in this example by the purchase between bobstay and bowsprit. The topmast stay is rigged standing, so the jib is hauled out on the metal traveller and the sail's luff set taut by hauling down on the halyard. When the jib is set and full of wind it is not unusual for the topmast stay to be slack.

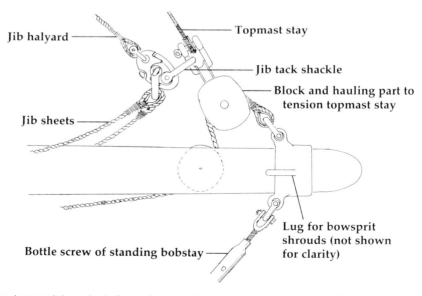

FIG 5 The bowsprit is typical of one rigged with a separate topmast and where the tension of the forestay is maintained by hauling through a lead block against the bobstay which is set standing. To set the sail, tension is eased on the forestay to enable the sheets and halyard to be brought inboard. The jib is hanked on to the stay while the head and tack are made fast to the halyard and tack shackle respectively. Once the jib has been hauled out and the stay retensioned the sail can be raised and set.

strikers to improve the effect of the bobstay in controlling lift, so they may also need whiskers to increase the efficiency of the side shrouds.

Deadeyes, lanyards and bottle screws

The standing rigging is secured at deck level in one of three ways: by deadeyes and lanyards, bottle screws, or just lanyards on their own (though this is only suitable for small craft). Whatever system is used to swift in the rigging it must not be done all at once, but a bit at a time, alternating from side to side.

Deadeyes are an efficient way of tightening the standing rigging consisting merely of a pair of round hardwood blocks with three holes bored in each one. A groove is cut all the way round the edge of the deadeye which holds the shroud eye splice in place and a metal band is secured to the chainplates. A rope lanyard – which should be at least seven times the distance between the deadeyes – is then rove through and, working like a tackle, is hauled taut, so tensioning the rigging. It is usual for one end to be whipped and the standing part to be finished with some form of stopper knot, such as a Wall or Matthew Walker knot, to prevent it being drawn through the hole. Instead of a stopper knot the standing part of the lanyard may be shackled to an eyebolt on the taff rail.

Starting inboard, the lanyard is always threaded through the deadeyes in the same way. Beginning with the forward hole in the upper deadeye, the lanyard then passes down and from outboard to inboard through the corresponding hole in the lower deadeye. The lanyard finishes inboard in the aftermost hole of the lower deadeye.

When setting up the shrouds, all the deadeyes and lanyards should have been laced hand taut before the task of tightening them up begins. A small handy billy is needed with a hook or eye at one end and a rope tail at the other. The tail block is

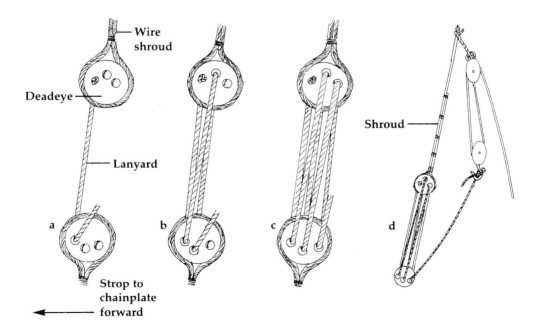

FIG 6 The deadeye here is on the port side and viewed from outboard. The method of passing the lanyard begins in the forward hole of the upper deadeye starting outboard (a). The lanyard then follows the sequence shown in b and c. After being tensioned with the tackle (d) the standing parts of the lanyard are seized together before the lanyard tail is made fast around the shroud.

secured to the shroud with a rolling hitch at a convenient height above the upper deadeye. The free end of the lanyard is made fast to the running block. You should tighten each lanyard a little at a time and stop it off before moving across the boat to the next pair of deadeyes, until you have tensioned all the shrouds evenly. The hauling part of the lanyard can be made fast in a number of ways depending upon local tradition, but it usually ends up being seized against one of the standing parts or the shroud.

Lacing the standing rigging of a smaller craft requires only lanyards threaded through a spliced eye in the shroud or stay and an eye on the chain plates. It is only necessary to pass a few turns when tightening up; too many will jam and stop the lanyard rendering through the eye.

Setting up shrouds or stays with bottle screws may appear simple because they are mechanical and therefore need little more than a spanner and marline spike to operate to tension. When fitting them make sure that the boat was intended to have bottle screws in the first place. They should not be secured to the broadeyed chainplate intended for lanyards as they may cause the metal to crack due to the high point-loading. Bottle screws should be tightened in a similar way to deadeyes, a little at a time on each shroud until they are all equally tensioned.

Running rigging

It is just as important to check that the running rigging is in good condition and rigged correctly as it is to check the standing rigging. Although failure of the running gear appears perhaps less serious than the risk of the mast falling about your ears, the consequences can be just as dramatic.

Start by checking all the running gear for any serious signs of wear or chafe, any frayed sections of rope or loose whippings at the ends. The obvious places to look are those areas where a rope passes through or round a lead which will cause repeated friction over a short length of the rope. Next look at all the splices: if this entails removing protective seizing or whipping, then do so, especially if they are rigged in an exposed position. If there is the slightest doubt about the condition, resplice or replace, for although this solution may be somewhat tedious or costly, neither is as bad as the sail coming crashing down on a dark and windy night.

Before the mast is raised, check all the blocks and make sure that all the swivels turn and sheaves run freely. Great care needs to be taken to ensure that none of the throat or peak halyard blocks or falls are twisted. Any that are can usually be corrected by dipping the running block through the parts of the tackle, but if that doesn't solve the problem, then unreeve the tackle and start again. Look for any signs of wear on the halyards; although rigging a new halyard isn't too difficult, it is a job to be avoided once the mast is up if at all possible.

The running rigging aboard a gaffer is probably what the owner, new to gaff rig, holds in greatest awe, presumably because there seems to be so much of it. One obvious reason for all the fathoms of extra cordage is that a rope passing through the blocks of a purchase is going to double its original length for each additional sheave through which it runs.

It's not usual for traditionally rigged craft to have the power advantage of small winches available to them for raising sail in the same way as the modern bermudian. Blocks and purchases used to the best advantage achieve just as much without the chores of maintenance and other problems of fixed winches. The winch lacks the flexibility of a purchase which can have its power increased or decreased or even be moved to another part of the craft to be used for a totally different task.

The running rigging may be divided into two basic categories: the halyards, which raise and lower the sails together with their associated spars, and the remainder, including the sheets which are used for controlling the sails. It is very important that the size and type of rope is not only the most suitable for the job but also that it is 'user friendly'.

Aboard bermudian rigged yachts there is a tendency for main halyards to be a combination of wire and fibre rope. The reason for the mixture is that fibre rope is easier to handle and it grips more effectively around the halyard winch, while the wire is stronger. Enough rope is spliced on to the wire so that when the sail is hard up there is just sufficient wire to wind round the winch barrel, leaving the crew with rope to hold.

It is less common for gaffers, or luggers for that matter, to use wire as part of their running rigging, and certainly not as hauling parts. Instead of using the mechanical advantage of a winch and wire rope to exert greater tension, blocks are used to increase purchase power. It is not at all uncommon for the jib of quite small craft to have two single blocks on the jib halyard to set the luff taut.

It is essential that the rope used for a halyard does not stretch: this will defeat the object as within a short time the sail will start sagging like an old coal sack! It is obvious that the rope selected must be strong enough for the intended task, but it is equally important that it should be easy to handle. As a result there will be occasions when thicker rope than is strictly necessary will be rigged, since there is nothing worse than trying to grip and heave on light line.

It would be impossible to give a table of sizes as this will vary from boat to boat. However, despite the great increases in breaking strains achieved in recent years, cordage of less than 8 mm diameter (the old 1 inch circumference) should be avoided. Rope this thin will tend to cut into the hands and should never be used when they have to be worked under load by hand, like halyards or sheets. The upper size limits will depend upon the task, so check the size of the block and don't try to force too large a rope through as it will only wear. (For further information on new measurements, see under *Blocks and tackles*.)

Single headsail sheets are a good example of where heavier rope might be used so that it is not too wearing on the hands. However, heavy sheets will drag the sails out of shape in light airs, so those owners who enjoy a certain amount of competitive sailing will invariably have a set of lightweight sheets for light air conditions. A 14 mm or 16 mm diameter rope, while totally unsuitable for light weather sheets, would be ideal for a storm trysail.

Blocks and tackles

The heaviest gear aboard a gaffer, with the possible exception of the mainsheet, is the throat and peak halyards for the gaff. These usually comprise a two- or three-fold purchase for the throat and either a double block or series of single blocks for the peak. The use of single blocks to hoist the peak is so that the load of a long gaff can be spared evenly along the yard as well as the upper sections of the mast, rather than high point-loadings.

Block sizes have usually been established by the builder or rigger; however, if you are introducing new rigging, look for existing blocks doing a similar task on board to get a rough guide. The traditional wood block is classified according to its size measured from crown to tail in inches, and is suitable for a rope whose circumference is one third that of the block: a 6 inch block therefore takes a 2 inch circumference rope.

The changeover in the way rope is measured now (by its diameter rather than its circumference and in millimetres instead of inches) will thoroughly confuse the owner who has to rely upon old documents when re-rigging his boat. To convert inches into millimetres multiply by 25.4, and to change the circumference into the diameter multiply the circumference by 0.31831. So the 6 inch block is now a 152.4 mm block and the rope should measure 16 mm in circumference. If modern blocks are used, however, this rule does not apply, so having established the rope size seek the chandler's advice on which block to purchase.

On larger craft, the mainsail halyards come down on opposite sides of the mast to give the hands enough room to haul on both at the same time. It's normal for the throat to come down the port side and the peak on the starboard. Aboard smaller yachts it is common practice for both to run down the same side so that one man can marry the two halyards together and hoist sail single-handed.

Purchases sometimes appear to be rigged at random around the running gear aboard some of the larger vessels, yet they all have a very specific function. The usual rule is that a tackle will be used whenever the wire or rope to which it is attached needs to be tensioned or slacked off frequently. Smaller sailing vessels will tend towards multi-purpose or watch tackle, which is light and easily shifted from one task to another.

Tackles may be rigged either to advantage or disadvantage, depending upon their task and how easy it is to haul on the moving block. When a tackle is rigged to advantage it means that the block with the most parts of rope passing through or attached to it will be the moving block, invariably the block from which the hauling part leads. When a tackle is rove to disadvantage then the hauling part leads from the block which is secured to a fixed point. A tack tackle is a good example of when it is more appropriate to rig to disadvantage due to the short length of the tackle rigged down close to the deck. In this case it is easier to haul upwards rather than trying to haul down a rope which is close to your ankles.

The larger the craft the greater the use made of tackles, especially on working vessels where manpower might be limited. Looking aloft aboard a French tunnyman I became almost cross-eyed trying to follow various parts of the running rigging, until I discovered that the main or throat halyard had two, rather than just a single hauling part, one on each side of the mast. On the starboard side, the fall was made up around a belaying pin while to port the halyard ended in a thimble shackled to a fourfold purchase. Hauling the single end hand-over-hand raises the sail quickly most of the way, before being made fast so that the sail can be set taut by hauling down upon what in effect is a luff tackle. This provides a simple yet very effective arrangement for setting up the sails aboard a larger craft, but is not necessary aboard a small, gaff rigged yacht where manpower is enough.

Setting up the mast

If the mast is to be raised and stepped first, start by clearing away all the lashings holding the rigging to the mast above head height when it is stepped. The last thing you want to do is either unstep the mast or have to climb up to free the rigging.

Masts stepped in a tabernacle may have been lowered with some of the standing and running rigging still made fast to their respective eyes, cleats and belaying pins. Check that the spider band around the mast plus the pin and fife rails are all clear, and that none of the halyards are made fast to them. Don't forget any electric wiring that may run up the mast. If the wiring breaks the whole lot will have to come down again, so make sure that this is unplugged or disconnected and will not catch.

The mainmast on board a Colin Archer, with the halyards secured on a wooden fife rail around the mast, and lesser running rigging made fast on the iron spider band. The apron can be clearly seen at the junction between mast and deck, all well painted to ensure a watertight seal.

The mainsail mast hoops and gaff parrel beads are clearly visible just above the spider band. In the background a jawed spar can be seen lashed to the port shrouds. This is a whisker pole for either the jib or staysail; the jaw fits around the mast and it's leathered to reduce wear.

The anchor winch is unusually mounted abaft the mainmast which is a more protected position from the sea than the foredeck, and the drum ends can be used for extra power to hoist sails or perhaps take in a reef. *Photograph: Martin Tregoning*

After the mast has been stepped, and starting with the standing rigging, it's worth checking that the mast is vertical athwartships before noting any rake along the fore-and-aft line. The rake may not be correct but you have to establish a starting point.

There is no hard and fast rule as to whether a sailing vessel needs mast rake or not; this is usually established either by trial and error or by the designer/builder. If starting from scratch without any information from previous owners, then a little investigation might yield a few clues. Firstly, check deck stepped masts to see if the protection of the tabernacle has left any weathered or darkened lines on the wood which might give some indication to the mast's possible rake. Next, once the mast is raised, see if the bottle screws can provide a clue to the shrouds' previous rigged length. This can be done by counting the number of threads that show signs of being exposed as against those protected within the body of the bottle screw. Finally, if lanyards have been used previously and are still secured to their respective stay or shroud, look for wear marks on the rope as another possible guide to their previous length. If there are no clues at all then raise the mast and set it vertical to the boat's waterline. It should never be raked forward.

Checking and recording mast rake

Once the mast has been set up either in an optimum position or based upon available information, the mast's fore and aft rake should be recorded for future reference. The easiest way to check and measure rake is with aid of a plumbline hanging down the mast so that it is just clear of the deck. The line should be secured either to the throat halyard crane or to the masthead. If the mast has a pronounced taper then the crane is probably better, as it holds the line well clear of the mast. The amount of rake can be found by measuring and recording the distance between plumbline and mast at the deck.

It is obviously best to do this when the boat is ashore on level ground, on legs, or in her cradle. Such luxuries aren't always available, so provided you always check this on the same incline (eg by allowing the boat to dry out with her legs on a sloping hard or slipway), you should achieve a consistent result.

If the worst comes to the worst, a rough check can be made afloat, but care must be taken that she is trimmed correctly and also that there is no wind and that there is little movement in the water. The principle is the same as with the boat dried out, but this will be a tedious process and necessitates climbing on and off the boat, as all the work has to be done from the tender or a pontoon so as not to affect the trim.

Adjusting rigging tension

The next task is to check the tension on all the shrouds. In particular it is important to ensure that the tension on one shroud is equal to the tension on its opposite number on the other side of the boat. Two adjacent shrouds do not necessarily have to be equally taut as they may tauten or slacken unequally under different points of sailing.

Bottle screws and stainless steel wire are now commonplace on all craft, frequently replacing deadeyes and lanyards, although smaller craft usually use lanyards as the means of tensioning their rigging. Compared with bermudian sloops, mast heights aboard gaffers are short; consequently shroud tension is not as critical and, even aboard large sailing ships, lanyards are still used as a very practical and economical method of setting up the rigging.

Once the mast has been set up, the standing rigging on the bowsprit should follow before either the forestays or headstays (topmast stay), as otherwise a lot of time can be wasted getting the adjustment right. The bobstay should be set very taut so that the bowsprit has a pronounced downward bow. Once the jib fills with wind, it tries to lift the bowsprit and will relieve pressure rather than exert it.

The bobstay may be rigged either standing and secured by a bottle screw, or running with its own tackle rigged to the outboard end of the sprit. I prefer the running bobstay, as not only can the tension be adjusted without climbing out to the end, but also you can prevent damage from the ground tackle or mooring. When lying at anchor or to a mooring, the whole bobstay can be slacked off and brought inboard to stop the anchor cable noisily fouling it or the mooring bridle wearing itself away.

The efficiency of the bobstay to counter lift decreases the longer the bowsprit becomes, which is why larger craft have martingales or dolphin strikers fitted to increase downward pressure.

A jib filled with wind will bend the bowsprit to leeward with the obvious risk of the spar breaking. The bend to leeward will not decrease the tension on the luff but the effect is almost the same, seriously curtailing the boat's ability to point well to windward. The solution is to rig side shrouds on the bowsprit which prevent any sagging off to leeward.

Like the shrouds, the forestays may also have a different tension from each other, especially if the mast is comparatively short. The head or topmast stay between the end of the bowsprit and the masthead, for example, may be left with less tension than the forestay. The reason for this is that the forestay is set against the tension in the shrouds, while the topmast stay is set against any running backstays. These are at various times slack or taut and consequently have a similar effect upon the topmast stay.

The inner forestay works in conjunction with the shrouds to maintain the mast's fore and aft rake, and as the shrouds are set taut so is the forestay. It should be set up before the topmast stay so that any adjustment on the latter will not alter the overall rake of the mast. To set the forestay up steadily, increase its tension on bottle screw or lanyard until it is as taut as the aft shrouds against which it works. Too much tension and the forward pair of shrouds might show signs of decreased tension, while if the forestay has too little tension it will feel slacker than the shrouds.

The support for the topmast when the jib is set is provided by the jib's luff wire rather than the topmast stay itself. In this way the topmast stay serves more as a preventer rather than providing direct mast support when beating to windward, although it does work downwind with the running backstays, as we will see later.

To set the topmast stay, first make sure that the running backstays are slack and then tighten the topmast stay until the topmast just begins to curve slightly forward. Now tighten up both running backstays equally and check the result upon the topmast. If the topmast returns to its original position in line with the mast then the adjustment is correct. If the stays curve forward, too much tension has been applied; if the backstays induce a curve towards the stern, there is too little tension in the stay. Don't try to make an adjustment against the power of the backstays; slacken them off before either increasing or decreasing the tension in the topmast stay.

Running backstays

Strictly speaking a running backstay cannot be standing rigging. However, as it is more concerned with the stability and safety of the mast rather than adjusting the trim of the sails, it is more appropriate to consider it under this heading.

Unlike the bermudian sloop where the backstays are a permanent fixture needing very little adjustment, those rigged on a gaffer must be movable. The reason is obvious when the sail plan is examined closely, because as the mainsail is four-sided, the straight line between masthead and stern cuts across the gaff. The leeward backstay must be slacked off to prevent it fouling the mainsail when the mainsheet is freed off. Consequently both backstays, rather than being tensioned by a bottle screw, are either set up on a tackle or Heighfield lever. It is therefore a simple matter as the boat tacks to tauten the new windward backstay and to free off the leeward one as the boom goes across from one side to the other.

The tension of all the shrouds and stays when not under load should not be so great that the wire sings like a plucked harp string; but neither should it be so slack that it looks like an old washing line. Judging the correct tension comes with experience, but always make any adjustments – especially to a boat with which you are unfamiliar – when the boat is at rest and all sails furled.

Do not follow the example set by one owner I know, who acquired his first wood gaffer after a number of years sailing bermudian sloops. The handover was halfway through the season and perilously close to the departure date of an annual cruise planned with some colleagues. The boat was delivered by road, accompanied by the previous owner who had agreed to help rig her. As soon as it had been craned off both men set about rigging the mast, working late into the night until all was finished.

Not unnaturally the new owner was impatient to try his new craft so, as the previous owner went home, he readied the boat for sea. He was thoroughly enjoying himself until he noticed that his lee rigging appeared to be much too slack. Assuming that in their tiredness they had both forgotten to tighten up the bottle screws, and as the mast seemed straight enough, he set about tightening his lee shrouds while he was sailing along, fearing what might happen if he had to tack suddenly.

On the next tack the other shrouds were also loose and received the same treatment; tacking once more he was dismayed to see that the first shrouds were now slack again. He then proceeded to tighten all his lee shrouds each time he tacked, until they were bar taut.

During the subsequent cruise the boat experienced some poor weather and,

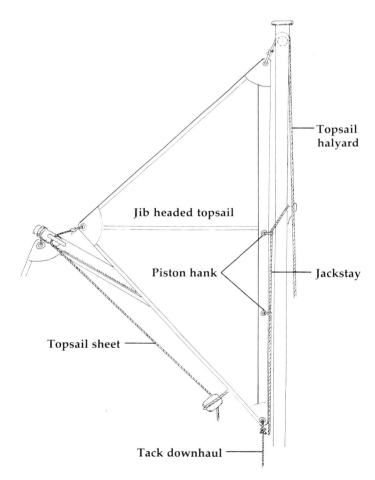

FIG 7 The basic jib headed topsail. To avoid complication, some of the detail of the gaff has been left out. The luff of the sail is set up on a jackstay which terminates at a point on the mast which is level with the clew and sheeting sheave on the gaff. By doing this the tendency for the sail to sag away from the mast under tension from the sheet is reduced to a minimum (see jackyard topsail in Chapter 4).

during one period when she was pitching very heavily, started to leak seriously. The situation got worse. The lifeboat was summoned but it was not until everything had been cleaned up in port that it was realised that excessive tension on the rigging had strained all the joints between garboard and keel.

Topsail rigging

Topsail rigging is not always carried but, when set, helps to improve the way in which the topsail sets against the mast. The jackstay should be rigged so that it lies as close as possible to the upper portion of the mast. It must then be made fast so that it terminates at a point slightly higher than the tip of the gaff, either on a hounds band or with an eye passed over the truck and resting on a cheek block. In this way the sail will be held close against the mast even when the sheet is bar taut because there is the shortest horizontal pull from the gaff to mast across the sail. The jackstay should be made either of wire or man-made fibre so that it doesn't stretch, and it must run clear of the peak and main halyard blocks and inside the boom topping lifts down to deck level. The jackstay is set up with either a bottle screw or lanyard so that it is as taut as possible, but do not tighten it to the extent that the topmast begins to bend.

The topsail halyard runs from the pin or fife rail either through a masthead sheave or through a block rigged on the topmast band. The simple topsail sheet is led from the peak of the gaff either direct to the foot of the mast or along the gaff and then to deck level, where both ends are made fast when not in use. On some very long gaffs a second intermediate sheet may be rigged for use with long jackyards but these are not often seen nowadays.

Mainsail vangs

Vangs fitted to larger mainsails are normally used when the vessel is rolling to stop the gaff crashing to and fro in light winds. The weather vang, however, can also be used to haul the gaff a little to windward so that it continues to fill and still drive the yacht. Sailing with the vangs set in this way requires great care: unless the vang is released when attempting to tack the yacht, she will end up either doing a Chinese gybe or 'in stays'.

Vangs are a common feature aboard ketches and yawls as the mizzen topmast provides a good lead from the end of the gaff and then down to the deck. Without the mizzen it is difficult to obtain such a good lead because of both the beam and proximity of the stern.

CHAPTER 4

▬▬▬

The sails

The selection of what sails will make up a standard suit will depend very much upon the owner's preference. An owner who cruises will probably choose more adaptable sails, perhaps roller-reefing, and will probably keep the sails for longer. The owner whose preference is racing, on the other hand, will probably renew his canvas more frequently and carry a fairly wide selection of sails for specific wind speeds.

The choice between cutter or sloop rig depends mainly upon the yacht's size. A small gaffer for example will perform better as a sloop than a cutter, as setting two headsails will probably result in a loss of performance unless the rig is so disproportionately large as to be suitable only for racing with a crew.

The standard suit of sails aboard a gaff cutter would normally comprise two working headsails, the main, and possibly a topsail of some sort. A well-equipped yacht might also carry a larger jib or staysail for light winds. The popular way of adding flexibility to the headsails for many years has been roller-furling – or, more recently, roller-reefing. Introduced during the period between the world wars, roller-furling was much improved, with Wykeham-Martin introducing the very popular gear still in use today.

The large variety of extra canvas, especially for use in light winds, requires some explanation. The evolutionary development of sails over the years has in some cases altered their shape and cut quite dramatically. The most obvious example is probably the spinnaker, which has altered almost beyond recognition from a full cut headsail into the free-flying, multi-coloured creation of today.

Most light weather sails come under the general name of balloon canvas, which encompasses not only headsails but also topsails as well. The balloon jib is perhaps the most common such sail still in use and is probably the largest, filling the whole of the fore triangle. Cut very full, unlike the modern genoa, it is set from the tip of the bowsprit to the masthead and has a foot that is almost parallel to the deck.

The balloon jib should not be confused with the often misquoted 'yankee', a name which has become very popular in recent times amongst those attempting to attribute false traditional qualities to a yacht. The yankee, although set between bowsprit and masthead, differs from the balloon jib by being not so large and having a clew cut much higher, so that the sheet is led well aft – perhaps even to the stern. The yankee is usually set over a large staysail and, unlike the staysail, the leach of the yankee does not overlap the mast.

A balloon or tow foresail, while still full-cut, was usually set hanked on to the forestay and extended further aft than the foot of the mast. In some respects the tow foresail is more versatile than either the balloon jib or yankee, because it can be used for windward work. However, its principal disadvantage is that the sheets are led

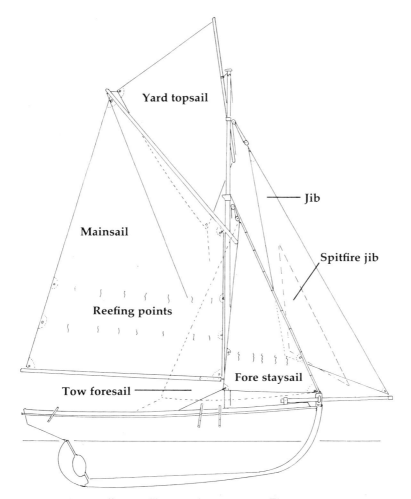

FIG 8 The sail plan of the gaff cutter illustrated on page 24. The more common selection of sail options has been shown, including the bad weather spitfire jib which may be carried with either a reefed foresail or simply a smaller foresail. The yard topsail has been shown to complete the illustration of the three basic topsail types: jib headed, yard topsail or the larger jackyard.

either inside the shrouds when on the wind or outside when reaching and running.

Topsails, whether you 'love 'em or hate 'em', depend in the main for their success on how they are rigged aboard your boat. If the halyard and sheeting arrangement is wrong, or at least not as good as it could be, then they can cause a considerable amount of grief! There are two varieties: the jib-headed; and those with additional yards to spread them beyond the existing masts and spars. Topsails are usually triangular, although in a few cases they look more like a lugsail with a portion of the sail extending forward of the mast.

The ketch and yawl have the advantage of being able to set canvas between the masts; the most common example of this is the mizzen staysail. This large sail can be used to great advantage when beam reaching especially, or when the wind is abaft the beam, if the sail has been boomed out.

The final group of fair weather sails are those miscellaneous ones which depend much upon the adaptive ability of the owner and crew. The water sails, drabblers and bonnets are the most frequently mentioned – and often misrepresented by today's sailors. Their strict definitions appear in the Glossary. The group can however be simply described as those temporary sails which are either lashed below a spar or laced on to another sail to increase sail area during light winds.

Checking the sails

The advantage that today's sailor has over his forefathers is that the sails don't have to be bent on to their spars every time he wants to go sailing. Thanks to modern materials, that task has to be faced only at the beginning and end of each season. So, assuming that it has still to be done in order to prepare the yacht for summer sailing, that's where we'll now start.

Because the gaff sail is irregular and four-sided, it is secured to the gaff, the mast and may be either laced or rigged loose-footed along the boom. The gaff mainsail, as its name implies, is the largest, and usually requires the greatest effort to rig, so a little time spent sorting out the main and checking all the other sails is never wasted.

In an ideal world the sail should have been stowed away properly, so now is probably the best point at which to mention sail stowage and general care. It helps if the wind isn't blowing a full gale and you have someone to lend a hand as you unpack your sails. Start by opening the sail up and laying it out flat. If the sail is too large to do this on deck, then select a smooth, clean, dry area ashore or on the pontoon, just so long as it doesn't have any sharp projections which could cut or tear the sail.

Inspect the sail thoroughly along all the bolt ropes for any sign of fraying. Check that there are no signs of damage to the sail cloth, looking carefully at the stitching along the tabling and around the cringles. Look for mould, stains or other signs of the effects of damp; if the sail has been stowed away properly, this will give a clear indication as to how your new boat and its gear have been looked after.

The sail should not be stowed into its bag like so much dirty washing. Instead it must be refolded by being flaked down or rolled up. On the main, start at the foot of the sail because this is longer than the head, and begin flaking the sail down in bands slightly less wide than the sail bag is long. The sail should lie in such a way that the luff, which has all the lacing holes, lies down on top of itself. Once the flaking has been completed then the sail can be rolled up loosely, starting with the clew or after end.

With the headsails it is best to coil the luff wire up and then fold this over into the rest of the sail before stowing it away into its bag.

To save the problem of not knowing which corner is which when removing a jib or staysail from its bag, the sailmaker always puts his mark by the tack cringle. Those staysails which are hanked on to their stays must have the piston hanks checked to make sure that they are securely fixed to the luff of the sail and that the pistons work smoothly. A jammed piston can be a problem when trying to change sails while working on a heaving foredeck. If the piston is seized or sticky then take care that whatever oil or agent is used to remedy the situation is not applied too freely and allowed to get on to the sail. Synthetic sails are made from oil based products and any oil soaking into the material will be almost impossible to remove.

Bending on the mainsail

When the gaff is bare without its canvas bent on, it will normally be stowed lashed on to the main boom. The first job is to make fast the main and peak halyards. Next raise the gaff horizontally to a convenient working height clear of the boom, so that the mainsail can first be bent on to it and, following that, on to the mast.

Bring the sail out on deck and lay it out beneath the boom with the luff closest to the mast and the head uppermost. Start by shackling or lashing the throat cringle to the gaff jaws; this may be either to an eye-bolt, a ring in the gaff or below the gaff saddle. Aboard older craft it was common for holes to be drilled through the gaff jaws and the lashing passed between them and the cringle.

I prefer to lash the peak cringle next rather than attempting to lace the head of the sail to the boom. The reason for this preference is that the head of the sail is stretched evenly along the gaff, making the lacing that much easier to do. By threading the lacing first you risk ending up with a series of creases and rucks along the sail. The peak cringle is lashed either to another eye on the underside of the gaff or passed through a hole drilled from side to side. The lashing must be drawn taut so that the sail lies flat along the underside of the gaff, without distorting or stretching the sail out of shape.

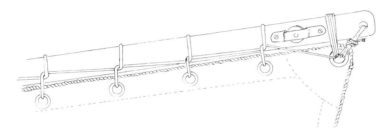

FIG 9 A typical method of lacing the head of any sail on to a gaff or a yard. The lacing is hitched to reduce movement of the sail against the yard, which will spoil its set and may also ultimately wear through the sail cloth at the head.

Once the head of the sail is lying against the gaff the lacing may be rove through, usually starting at the throat and working towards the peak. The method of lacing is very important; a simple spiral lacing is not good enough as it allows the sail to move to and fro along the gaff, alternately bunching up or stretching. This movement can significantly reduce the life of the sail by wearing through the sail cloth covering the bolt rope along the head of the sail.

The usual method of lacing is either by using a half or marlin hitch around the gaff, or using individual lashings for each eyelet along the head of the sail. The advantage of the separate tiers or robands is that in the event of one of them parting the whole sail will not come away from the gaff, but it does take longer to lace and it is harder to make the result look shipshape.

The move away from the use of natural fibre to synthetic in sails and cordage has resulted in a much easier task for the owner. Unless there is a need to be particularly traditional in appearance, a braided line can be chosen for the lacing. Not only does it resist kinking when being pulled through the eyelets but also grips well.

While it is important that the head of the sail does not move against its gaff, the luff on the other hand must run freely up and down the mast. Different methods of achieving this have been produced, such as mast hoops or a slack lacing, which is the more common method for yachts.

The mast hoops are more customarily used aboard larger craft, not least because the smaller diameter of yacht masts made the hoops much harder to produce. Formerly they were made from rope grommets and then from withies which were bent after being soaked in water. Later, oak and other woods were steamed before being bent into a circle and then riveted together. Aboard larger ships especially, other materials were tried, including galvanised iron and more recently modern materials including plastic.

Whichever method of lacing is used, it must be capable of maintaining the tension on the luff without binding and so making it difficult to raise and lower the sail. The advantage of mast hoops is that they are less prone to binding or jamming; but, even so, this can happen occasionally, with serious consequences if the sail is being lowered quickly in a squall.

One of the old methods adopted to reduce the risk of jamming was to rig a line stopping the hoops from sagging down or riding up when the sail was raised or lowered. The line ran from the gaff jaws down the foreside of the mast, keeping the hoops level: this could be used to haul on if they tended to jam up.

To lace the mainsail luff to the mast, raise the gaff jaws with the main halyard so that the first few feet are clear of the bunched sail. Next, haul on the peak halyard to hoist the gaff until it is set at the correct angle; then measure how far the throat cringle stands off from the mast. This is to make sure that the luff falls parallel to the mast: if the luff is too close to the mast then the lacing is too tight; if the luff is able to pull away then it is too slack.

As the lacing progresses down the length of the luff, it helps to raise the gaff in short stages a few feet at a time, provided of course that the wind allows! This will serve two purposes: making it easier to work without digging into folds of canvas, and ensuring that the lacing is not pulled too taut. You will probably find that when the sail is hoisted up the lacing is either too tight or too slack and will have to be adjusted. Provided that the mainsail luff is not too long then this adjustment can be made with the sail raised, although if this proves difficult, lower away and take up the slack or ease off the lacing and try again.

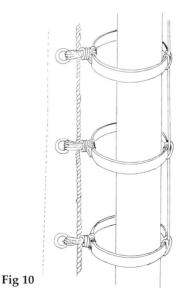

Fig 10

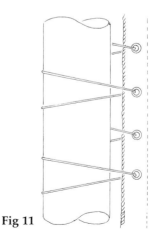

Fig 11

FIG 10 Mast hoops usually made from steamed withe (willow sapling) which are seized on to the sail's luff. Note the downhaul secured to the hoops on the fore side of the mast to prevent them jamming when the sail is being raised.

FIG 11 A good method of lacing the luff of the sail to the mast which reduces the friction of the lacing while the sail is being raised or lowered. Normal spiral lacing will bind against the mast and may even jam, so preventing it moving smoothly up or down the mast with potentially disastrous consequences.

A good guide to getting the tension right on a used boat are the shiny wear marks on the lacing where it has passed through the eyelets in the sail. The lacing should also be just long enough to make fast. Complete the lacing by securing the end to the last eyelet at the bottom of the luff with either a bowline or round turn and two half hitches which has its end seized back to the standing part. If there is any surplus from a well-used lacing don't cut it off as it may well be too tight and will have to be slacked off. If a new rope is being used for the lacing, then once you are satisfied that the sail sets properly, any surplus can be cut off because it is liable to stretch anyway.

Nowadays it's more common for a yacht to have her tack cringle lashed or shackled to an eye either fitted on the boom or fabricated as part of the gooseneck, although some loose-footed mainsails have the cringle hooked on to a luff tackle. Mainsails rigged in this way may have to be laced slightly more slackly to allow for the tack of the sail to be pulled to one side so as to clear the boom's gooseneck. Luff or tack tackles have generally fallen into disuse aboard yachts, although they are still relatively common on larger craft like the Bristol Channel Pilot Cutters.

Although it is common for gaff mainsails to be loose-footed, this is not always the case as some have the foot laced on to the boom or occasionally to a rail. The use of a rail fitted to the boom is well known in the USA but is less frequently used in European waters, although the Broads One Design is one class which has adopted this method of securing the foot of the mainsail. The system has two advantages; firstly that the lacing is clear of all the boom fittings when the tension in the foot is being adjusted; and secondly that the friction as the lacing is passed around the small diameter rail is considerably reduced.

The final task to be completed before the mainsail is bent on is to make the clew fast at the end of the boom. If the sail has been laced either to the boom or a rail running along its top then this lashing can be the same as the outer end of the gaff. However, when a loose-footed main is set, the clew must be able to move along the boom so that the foot lies flat and taut or curved and free. The simplest method of providing this adjustment is for an iron horse to be fitted on top of the boom and shackled to it. The shape of the sail's foot is then altered by an outhaul rove through a sheave at the end of the boom.

Rigging a gaff mizzen is essentially the same, although aboard a yawl it can present one or two extra problems because its boom is set out over the water. The lug mizzen common to Quay Punts and other working based rigs is an attractive compromise, as the gaff can be unhooked from the traveller and brought inboard, though care must be taken not to unreeve the outhaul on the bumkin.

Topsails

The only other sails which are normally laced on to a spar are the yard or jackyard gaff topsails with either a single or pair of spars respectively. The huge topsails commonly set by the larger classes of racing yacht like the 23 metre and, later, the J Class, have not continued to the present day. These vast sails had to be laced on to their yards each time before being used, and required a masthead man to lace the sail's luff to the topmast once it had been hoisted.

Although topsails are common in today's smaller gaffer, their proportional sail area has reduced quite significantly. It is now normal for these sails to remain laced to their spars throughout the season – and perhaps even longer if the truth be known!

The ordinary or jib-headed topsail provides a simple means of filling the space between mast and gaff, so gaining the maximum drive when sailing downwind

Two topsails; a traditional square topsail set on a single yard above the lugsail in the foreground, and a poorly set jackyard topsail on the Brixham trawler in the background. Note the large gap between the jackyard topsail and the mast. *Photograph: Peter Chesworth*

without resorting to extra spars. A good topsail will increase the effective mainsail luff length when beating to windward. The yard and jackyard topsails, however, use a yard to extend the sail higher than the masthead, and a jackyard to set it out beyond the end of the gaff's peak.

The length of the yard can vary greatly, so that it may be quite short; or, like the Falmouth working boats', on which it extends for the full length of the luff. The long yard makes for a very efficient sail when it is set, although the length of the spar can make it very unwieldy to handle and a problem to stow. The jackyard on the other hand is invariably shorter than the foot of the sail, seldom exceeding more than half that length.

The yard topsail is probably the more common of the two sparred topsails, particularly aboard those working craft carrying a high-peaked mainsail on a comparatively short mast. The addition of a jackyard is more common where the gaff is peaked much lower and there is consequently greater space to span between mast

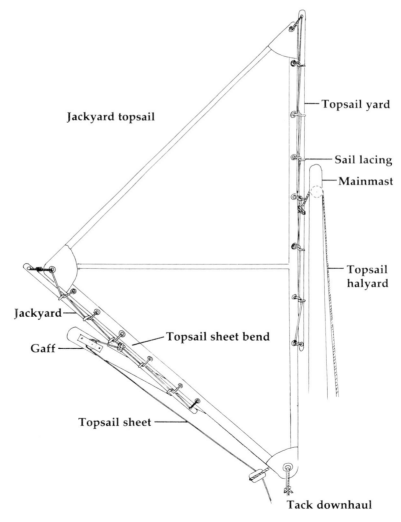

FIG 12 The jackyard topsail has a larger area than its jib headed sister, the yard and jackyard extending the luff and foot of the sail beyond the masthead and gaff respectively. The yard also ensures that the luff is straight, with little opportunity of sagging to leeward.

and gaff. The jackyard on its own is a very rare beast these days and may only be set aboard vessels which have a very high topmast or single pole mainmast.

The jackyard topsail is thought to have derived from the square headed topsail, set first above a lugsail and then over the early gaff mainsails. The horizontally rigged yard was gradually changed until it stood as near vertical as possible, lying almost parallel to the mast itself, and changing the sail's shape from four-sided to triangular.

Lacing the sail to either of the yards should follow the same procedure as for securing the main to its gaff, by passing lashings through eyes at each end of the spars. These sails are for light winds and are therefore made from lightweight cloth, so care must be taken not to overtighten the earings at either end of the yard as this will distort the shape of the sail. Once the earings have been made fast then the sail can be laced on to the spar in exactly the same way as the mainsail to the gaff.

Headsails

Unless a yacht is equipped with Wykeham-Martin roller-furling gear, the headsails will have to be made fast at the start of every passage. Although they don't require lacing on, care has to be taken until the job becomes second nature. The staysail is usually set hanked on to the forestay while the jib can be set flying which means that it relies solely upon the tension in the luff to keep it straight.

The straightness of the luff is all-important in determining the vessel's ability to point or sail close to the wind. Any tendency for the sail to sag off to leeward will mean a proportional loss in windward performance. This won't be very significant tacking back and forth across a river, but when hard on the wind, crossing the Channel, it can make all the difference between reaching the intended port or a landfall many miles downwind.

The method of tensioning the luff of the headsails may depend upon a number of factors, not least the size of the sail. The luff is usually strengthened with wire, which will withstand a considerable strain, and is not liable to slacken because of stretch. The halyard is frequently a purchase of perhaps two single blocks and, while more sheaves would increase the purchase's power, this has to be weighed against the considerable amount of additional rope once the sail is hoisted.

One answer to this problem is for the purchase to have two tails, both led down to the deck. One is the basic fall from the tackle, while the other is made fast to a second purchase used to apply the maximum tension once the sail has been hoisted by hand. This works very well on a fore staysail whose peak is not too far aloft since this does not therefore involve coiling large quantities of rope.

A jib or flying jib, on the other hand, which may be set from close to the masthead down to the bowsprit, may have to adopt another method. Aboard small yachts the tack of the jib is usually hooked on to the traveller before being run out to the end of the bowsprit. Instead of exerting the additional tensioning down the halyard, a short wire pendant is rove through a block on the traveller and led inboard to the foredeck. The jib's tack is made fast to the pendant's outboard end and a small luff tackle to the inboard end. Once the sail has been hoisted, the jib's luff can be set taut by heaving on the tackle before making fast.

Where running backstays are rigged, these should be set taut before the final tensioning of the jib's luff: this is to prevent bending the masthead too far forward, which could result in the mast breaking in a sudden gust. This method has the advantage of allowing a curve in the jib's luff when the backstays are slacked off, reaching or sailing downwind.

Many yachts – both ancient and modern – with traditional rigs have made good use of the Wykeham-Martin furling gear. The performance of the original system has been improved considerably by a matching improvement in the materials now used in sails, not least in the resistance to corrosion and twisting available from present day stainless steel wire.

Hoisting the main

It is best to make your first exploratory investigations of the rigging and sails while still on the mooring. So unless the boat is on a pontoon berth which happens to face dead into the wind, borrow a mooring or find a quiet anchorage. The move will of course mean leaving the convenience of an alongside berth, so the crew must make sure everything is aboard. It's so easy to forget that the chandlery is no longer a few paces away.

Under normal conditions the mainsail should be the first to be raised, so it would be best to follow that routine. The mainsail's large gaff may look intimidating but it should not be difficult to hoist and set. Unless aboard a large yacht, it is probably best for the new owner to raise and lower the mainsail on his own for the first few times, so that he becomes fully familiar with all the ropes.

The sail cover is removed first and stowed away; whenever doing any job aboard it is always good policy to stow the gear away as soon as it is no longer needed. Next remove most of the sail ties, leaving just one or two to keep the sail under control until ready for hoisting. Most yachts start with a full complement of ties at the beginning of each spring. Yet they escape at an alarming rate and only a small proportion are recaptured from the bowels of the boat at the end of the season.

Depending upon the details of the particular gaff rig or the preference of the previous owner, the mainsail cover may allow the peak halyard span blocks to remain secured on to the gaff. Alternatively the halyard may have to be released and made fast alongside the throat halyard or be overhauled so as to be laid flat along the gaff before the sail is covered.

Regardless of how the peak halyard has been secured, first check that its falls and those of the main or throat halyard will render freely and are not twisted or fouled with any of the other running rigging. If the gaff has a saddle covered with leather, then now is as good a time as any to give it a smear of saddle soap or tallow so that it runs easily up the mast.

The last jobs before you begin to raise the mainsail are to make sure that the topping lift is taut and will have the weight of the boom. Next free the mainsheet enough to allow the boom to lift once the sail is raised, and to allow you to remove the scissors or boom crutch. Once you are ready to start raising the sail, remove the remaining ties holding the sail, boom and gaff together.

Start raising the gaff by hauling on the peak halyard so that the peak is slightly higher than the throat. This is important: when the luff is set taut, if the throat rises higher than the peak it will be impossible to set the peak. Next, marry the main and peak halyards together and continue raising the gaff until the luff is nearly taut.

Now make fast the peak halyard so that the main can be sweated up until the luff is bar taut. If the sail starts to crease from the throat to the clew then the mainsheet is too tight and must be slacked off more. Now resecure the main halyard, release the peak halyard and continue raising the peak until the sail is slightly over peaked. It is easy to tell when this point has been reached as creases start to appear across the sail from the peak down to the tack.

It is essential that the sail is not over-peaked and the creases are not too bold,

Although both boats are sailing downwind in light airs and therefore making slow progress, the mainsails demonstrate the signs to look for when setting the mainsail. On the right the topsail has been set taking some of the weight of the main, but now with little wind to stretch the sail cloth the telltale creases running from peak to tack would normally be a sign of over peaking.

On the left the topping-lift seems to have been used to take some of the weight of the boom off the mainsail and allow it to develop more shape in the light winds. Had the sail just been hoisted the creasing in the sail, which this time is from throat to clew, would indicate a main which had not been fully hoisted. *Photograph: Peter Chesworth*

because they must disappear once the topping lift has been released and the sail filled with wind. The peak halyard will have to be eased back slightly if the creases persist.

Raising headsails

The use of furling headsails has contributed much to sail handling, making it easy to set or dowse canvas at very short notice and with perfect control. Long before an auxiliary engine was commonplace the only way to get under way from a mooring or anchorage was by sail. Obviously this required the sail to be set very quickly once the mooring had been slipped or anchor weighed.

The usual practice once the mainsail was set was to raise the headsails in stops, ready for instant release. This required each headsail to be doubled along the luff and then flaked down before being rolled up to the luff leaving the clew cringle exposed. Next it was tied at intervals with 'rotten cotton' which, as the name implies, is a weak yarn which will break relatively easily once strain is applied on the sheets.

When lying head-to-wind it does not matter which side of the forestay the jib is run out on the bowsprit traveller. In light winds the jib can be raised in the normal way and either allowed to flap gently or backed so that the yacht lies hove-to. In stronger winds the best method is to use stops in the same way as for the fore staysail. However, if the jib is not going to be set until the yacht is underway then it has to be led out on what would be the leeward side, where it will be clear of foredeck work. Hoisted with the sheets attached to the sail, it is ready for use, only needing the sheets to be hauled in, so parting the yarn and allowing the sail to fill.

It is usual for the fore staysail to be set in the same way as unless it is set in stops its flogging will hinder those on the foredeck preparing to cast off. This method can still be used today although rotten cotton is no longer readily available. Knitting wool will do just as well – for those brave enough, how about unpicking the Christmas jumper you were given the year before last!

Setting a topsail

The topsail is really no different from any other in that it requires a halyard, sheet and tack or downhaul to control and set the sail well. The set of the sail will be improved if its luff is held against the mast by a rope or wire jackstay. The sail can more easily be raised or lowered on the leeward side of the mainsail. Today it is unusual to have a halyard and jackstay on each side of the mast so, unless the wind is light, it's best to set it on the mooring or when on the favourite tack.

The easiest topsail to set is the jib-headed, as the luff is simply hanked on to a jackstay (though in some rare cases a mast track and slides are used). This method, which is still used aboard some of the more competitive small gaffers, was first attributed to Dyarchy and is still known as the Dyarchy system. It is suitable only for craft with a single-pole mast.

The best way to hoist and set any topsail is while lying head-to-wind, preferably on the moooring or at anchor. It should be done before the mainsail is finally set. So, beginning with a jib headed topsail, the halyard is made fast with a snap hook to the sail's peak cringle and the sheet tied to the clew with a small bowline.

The tack cringle will often have a rope pendant which will reach the deck once the sail is hoisted but make the end fast so that it does not blow out of reach in the wind. Once the sail is hanked on to the jackstay it is ready to be hoisted.

Start heaving on the halyard but keep the sheet under control: when hoisting the sail the sheet must not be allowed to fly as it can easily wrap itself around the end of the gaff – amid great embarrassment and frustration because the main will have to be lowered before it can be cleared. A topsail that takes charge does so with a mind of its own, and words can't describe the frustration of trying to bring it under control. Conversely, the sight of a topsail set and drawing well is reward in itself.

Once the peak of the sail is hard up the luff can be sweated down by hand (or bowsed with a small tackle if necessary), and then the sheet hauled taut along the gaff. The manner in which the luff of the sail is set taut once hoisted varies, but it is usual for a tackle to be hooked direct on to the tack cringle or to a pennant which reaches down to the gooseneck.

Cornish working boats refined the system by leading the tack downhaul of a yard topsail through a timinoggie or eye on the gaff to give very positive control of the lower end of the yard and keep it hard up to the mast. Gaffers setting very large jackyard topsails rigged additional sheets from both the inner and outer ends of the jackyard to give greater control.

Setting the topsail together with the main can be an advantage. This is done by setting the topsail over the main while it is still over-peaked during the initial setting. Once the topsail has been sheeted the mainsail peak halyard can be eased back until the creases girting the main vanish and both the sails set properly: this method is used mainly when the wind is fresh rather than in light airs.

The procedure for hoisting the yard and jackyard topsails is essentially the same, although the halyard is made fast to the yard through a strop or eye which is already fitted. When there is no eye the sail will have to be set by trial and error, hoisting it a number of times until with halyard, sheet and downhaul all set taut the sail sets uncreased. To set a jackyard you must follow the same techniques until the sail sets flat. Take great care when working either of the yard topsails that the spars do not catch under any of the running or standing rigging either going up or coming down.

The basic principles of setting and sheeting apply equally to topsails as to any other sail: when on the wind they must be sheeted in and while sailing free let off. So don't make the sheet fast once the sail has been set and forget all about it until it is time for the topsail to be lowered. The jackyard topsail requires more care and the sail should be sheeted just before the main sheet is hardened in. Due to the twist in the sail the jackyard may foul the end of the gaff as it becomes headed by the wind.

The mainsheet requires getting used to, because the gaff forces the top of the sail to twist more than a bermudian sail would as it sags off to leeward. When sailing close hauled with the main over-sheeted, the upper portion of the sail is into the wind, which spills out causing the sail to lose its drive.

CHAPTER 5

Manoeuvres under power

Whether leaving a marina or crowded moorings it is highly unlikely that on the first few occasions you will do so under sail. So your early manoeuvres with any new craft will be under power.

It can be argued with some justification that it is bad seamanship to sail routinely on to and off a mooring with a yacht which has a perfectly serviceable engine. Most mooring areas are becoming increasingly congested not only with moored boats but also large numbers of tenders and other small craft. Consequently the helmsman's visibility and room to manoeuvre are becoming very restricted and his options to avoid mishap therefore limited.

This being the case, it would be as well to learn a new boat's own individual peculiarities under power first rather than set off under sail for the maiden trip. I think it is always prudent to try out something new in an environment where as many as possible of the variable factors are under your control. This applies just as much to the novice aboard his own boat as to the experienced owner with a new craft. Even the most experienced ship's pilot when boarding any ship for the first time will ask questions about the propeller's direction of rotation, the ship's responsiveness ahead and astern and so on.

Hull, rudder and propeller

Before starting to handle any boat there are a number of basic principles and skills which must be mastered if everything is to go smoothly and safely. The effects of different hull shapes, rudders and propellers upon the behaviour of a boat when manoeuvring under power should be clearly understood. If not, the least we face is embarrassment and the worst, damage to our own or another boat.

Let's start with the hull, as its underwater shape, and to a certain extent its weight, will have the greatest bearing upon how the craft responds to helm orders. It is fair to say that in normal circumstances the heavier the yacht the greater its displacement or underwater volume. The larger the volume, the greater the friction, due to the underwater area or wetted surface, and therefore the greater the hull's resistance is as it is dragged or pushed through the water.

Despite being beamy and having a deep, narrow keel, the lightweight hull will float on the surface with minimal underwater volume and is consequently easily driven. The heavy displacement hull, on the other hand, will tend to have a well rounded and full body, a long keel and large wetted surface. Clearly, although she will be slower, the heavier hull will carry her way and be less vulnerable to being blown off course at slow speed. As the engine aboard any sailing yacht is intended to be the secondary means of propulsion, it is the owner of the tortoise who fares better than the hare in this comparison of fast and slow yachts.

It is not only the underwater shape which affects the behaviour of a hull through and over the water. The rudder and propeller also make a marked contribution to how well a boat will perform, even if they are not actually being used at the time. This applies especially of course to the prop.

The rudder relies upon the flow of water over and past its surfaces to give it the power to alter the direction in which a vessel is heading. The fast racing yacht with a minute engine needs to reduce its wetted surface by the absolute maximum. The motor sailor on the other hand is less interested in peak sailing performance but will want to maximise manoeuvrability under power. A large, flat rudder, which might even be counter-balanced to help reduce weather helm, will be fitted to enable the yacht to be precisely handled at slow speed.

The type of propeller, and its position, play as important a part in the control of a boat as the rudder itself. At first this may seem obvious aboard a modern GRP sloop, but it is also true of any number of older wooden yachts, especially those with wing engines.

A propeller mounted on the centreline will push the vessel ahead but where the thrust is to one side of the centre, then the boat will keep trying to turn towards the opposite side. The thrust from an offset propeller will not flow evenly past the rudder and may even miss it altogether, resulting in unequal opposite turning circles.

Normally the size of the propeller will be a compromise, determined by the power required from the engine on the one hand, set against the loss of sailing performance on the other. Also included in this equation must be the size and shape of the boat, as well as the number of revolutions produced from the gear box. The shape and construction of the after sections of a yacht's hull, together with the space available between sternpost and rudder, will have a very significant bearing upon how well the boat performs under power. The efficiency with which a propeller drives a yacht through the water is likely to be inversely proportional to the amount of streamlining incorporated to improve sailing performance. Transom stern yachts have a tendency towards broad rudders and so will normally be able to accommodate a much larger propeller than their raked stern sister with a deep, narrow rudder.

Transverse thrust: the paddle-wheel effect

The helmsman needs to know whether a propeller is right- or left-handed, which is the direction in which the propeller rotates when going ahead and viewed from aft. Going ahead, the right-handed prop rotates in a clockwise direction, and the left-handed counter-clockwise. The direction of rotation is especially important to slow speed manoeuvring, as in addition to creating thrust ahead or astern, there is also a sideways, paddle-wheel effect. This sideways movement is most noticeable when giving a short sharp burst of power to the propeller when the boat is stationary. The stern will try to move sideways in the direction of rotation before the thrust from the propeller's blades starts to drive the craft ahead or astern. The paddle-wheel effect experienced will vary from yacht to yacht, depending upon the hull, rudder and size of the propeller.

The fine lined, fast hull will want minimal drag to achieve the optimum sailing performance, and also needs less power to drive it through the water than the heavy displacement deep-keel yacht. Consequently the former will handle perfectly well with a small fixed or folding two-bladed propeller, while the latter needs a much larger prop: if this has three blades as well then so much the better; the loss of performance will be minimal. The owner with the two-bladed prop will be at a disadvantage, however, when he starts to manoeuvre at slow speed or to move astern. The narrow blade of the folding prop, or its fixed equivalent, will only build thrust slowly when going in either direction; the bladed version, on the other hand, provides substantial thrust quickly.

The combination of direct thrust ahead or astern with the advantages of the paddle-wheel effect will allow a yacht to be turned round in little more than its own length. Obviously the more use that can be made of the engine's power and the prop thrust the easier the yacht is to handle. However the yacht with the finer lines will be more responsive and, lacking the large underwater area, will turn quickly, perhaps almost spinning on herself. The heavy yacht will need to be turned round, making full use of engine power and rudder movements.

The way that a yacht, or any boat for that matter, handles under power is different when going ahead or astern. The rudder is located as far aft as possible to provide the maximum turning force when going ahead – which is, after all, the normal direction of travel! Tradition rather than practice prohibits installing a rudder at the bows, for when we want to go astern, so the manner in which the yacht responds to helm orders will naturally be different.

Anything that is free to turn or rotate does so about a central axis or pivot point and a yacht is no exception. When moving ahead the yacht's pivotal point lies along the centreline, usually beneath the foot of the mast. Start going astern and the position of this pivot point moves aft quite dramatically. The change is most obvious in the way that the yacht moves in response to helm movements, the stern swinging wide when going ahead while it is the bow which swings when going astern.

There will be many occasions when you will need to move astern in a controlled manner, sure of where you will end up. The rule is to be stopped in the water before beginning the manoeuvre, and not to try it while still moving ahead. So with the boat stopped and the rudder amidships, put the engine astern on tick over. It is essential to keep a firm grip on the tiller because if the water flow across its surface is unequal it will try to force the rudder hard over.

One owner I know of went full astern trying to leave his marina berth in style; the rudder went hard over, pinning him against the coaming on the opposite side from the engine controls. The speed increased and so did the pressure on the tiller. When he finally got free it was with a bent iron tiller and two cracked ribs.

Don't forget those parts of a traditional yacht which may make handling or manoeuvring more hazardous. The bowsprit is invaluable for increasing the sail area but it's a nuisance when trying to manoeuvre in a confined space; when looking down its length it is very difficult to judge distances. When using a forespring the pivot point (fairlead) may be as much as 15 feet (4.5 metres) aft of the bowsprit end!

Owners of yachts fitted with bumkins are liable to forget them, especially when trying to get alongside when there is only just enough room. You know the situation; the family on the yacht ahead are enjoying a midday drink and the owner's pallor and furtive eyes are the only sign that he's seen your bowsprit. Consequently the bowsprit gets all the attention while everything aft is out of sight and out of mind. A bumkin's shrouds can work like a hacksaw on the gelcoat of the yacht astern!

Although the basics that I have outlined above hold good for just about every monohull, it is when moving astern that differences show themselves. Knowing what to look for below the waterline will provide the first series of clues as to what might happen once afloat and under way.

A comparison of performance between the two extremes of the fine lined yacht with two-bladed prop and the heavy displacement craft will show that each is equally manoeuvrable but each achieves it differently. The former is more likely to be underpowered with a two-bladed prop when it comes to manoeuvring, will compensate for this by being lively and responsive, but will also be slow to react to sudden changes in engine speed or direction. The heavier displacement craft however will have plenty of thrust available from her prop but her bulk will make movements more ponderous and once under way she will require plenty of power to stop.

Getting under way from a buoy

Unless you have the dubious privilege of owning a yacht with a marina berth, the first movement will be away from a mooring buoy. When getting under way initially the yacht will be moving very slowly and will be at her most vulnerable to the effects of wind and tide. It must always be remembered that the traditional yacht tends to fall into the heavier displacement category of yachts, so whilst engine power is available, sudden acceleration or changes in direction are not advisable.

The advantage of lying to a mooring buoy is that the effects of wind and tide will be reduced to a minimum because the yacht will be lying head to whichever of the two has the greatest effect. It may appear that all that needs to be done is to let go and get under way. The helmsman however has a number of decisions to make before slipping a mooring and getting under way; not least is the way out to open water.

The variety of craft to be found in any harbour will be illustrated by the way that they lie, either when the tide turns or when the power of the wind equals that of the tide. On such occasions boats will be seen lying pointing all over the compass. At one extreme the traditional long-keeled hull will lie to the tide, while the modern, ultra light displacement yacht will be wind-rode, with all the rest pointing somewhere in between. Unfortunately this could mean adjacent craft lying in opposite directions or, worse still, at 90 degrees to each other, leaving little room through which to manoeuvre.

The soundest advice is to pick the route which requires the smallest alteration to your boat's existing heading. After all, while moored the yacht is presenting the least resistance to the various forces acting upon her, and once broadside to the greater force she will become less manageable. One other important factor is which side of the bow the mooring comes aboard, as trying to manoeuvre against the pull of a mooring bridle under the bobstay makes things rather difficult.

It is highly unlikely that the safest way off the mooring will be anything other than straight ahead between the lines of moored yachts, but this does not mean that the mooring bridle should just be let go and the throttle pushed full ahead. The least risk in this method would be running over your own pickup buoy and fouling the prop, while a collision with your neighbour ahead couldn't be worse.

The traditional yacht is more prone to be tide-rode, which means that water is flowing equally across both faces of the rudder: this can be used to full effect. Try putting the tiller over so as to turn in the direction in which you want to leave. In ideal conditions this will be the opposite direction to the side on which the mooring comes aboard. If this is successful, the bow should start to swing that way.

Next prepare the foredeck so that letting go is a simple matter of slipping the mooring and not undoing shackles or climbing down to release hooks from the bobstay eye. The bowsprit and bobstay do of course pose an additional hazard, as usually at the worst possible moment the stay is liable to catch and foul on the mooring buoy.

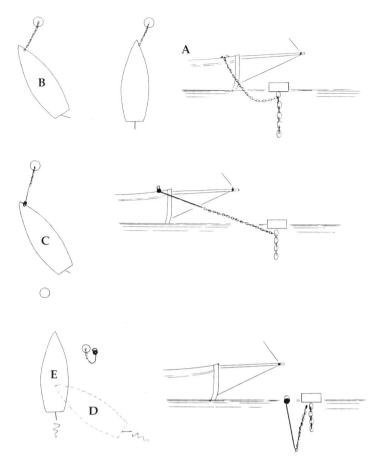

FIG 13 Slipping a mooring under power. (A) Lying to the mooring, determine which side of the mooring bridle leads and then see if the rudder will sheer the bow in the opposite direction (B) with the flow of the tide. Once the boat is ready to get under way and the tiller is back amidships, release the bridle and slack off on the pick up buoy rope until its end is reached. Put the tiller over again (C) to sheer the bow away from the mooring buoy before letting go. Making sure that buoy is clear of the bow go ahead around the mooring (D) into clear water (E).

One answer, provided there is enough room astern, is to slip the main mooring bridle and just lie to the longer rope on the pickup buoy or, if this is not practical, a slip rope. Doing this serves two purposes. Firstly it gives more room to manoeuvre; and secondly, because the pickup rope should be weighted, it will draw away and lie next to the main mooring buoy.

Finally, try putting the engine in gear to see exactly how much throttle is needed just to overcome the combined effects of wind and tide and keep the boat stationary.

We are now ready to get under way. So, with the engine ticking over and out of gear, cant the bow in the desired direction. Once it is far enough over, engage gear and increase speed just sufficient to slacken the buoy rope and then let go while briefly bringing the tiller amidships so that stern runs clear of the buoy. The important thing is to do everything possible to keep the buoy in view until well clear of it.

Although the principle is the same, a slightly different approach is needed when the effects of wind and tide are strong with craft close astern. Instead of dropping back you will have to stay on a short bridle, cant the bow in whatever direction is needed, then go ahead, slacking off before letting go the mooring once under control.

In the very unlikely event that both the yachts ahead are lying to the wind while you are tide-rode, then you will need to decide which side offers the clearest exit. Remember that if your manoeuvre is likely to force the mooring buoy under the bobstay, it would be better to rig a slip rope from the other bow and then let go the bridle.

Buoys fore-and-aft

The problem of getting under way smoothly is a little more difficult when lying moored fore-and-aft, whether between buoys or pilings. This system is usual in rivers where there is a strong prevailing wind. There will be occasions when a strong wind on the beam or fast-flowing tide present problems. In these circumstances when all is not in your favour, special care is needed.

Whatever the element causing the problem, it is always a good idea to try to use the yacht's power to advantage if at all possible; and it is always prudent to have a fender or two ready when moving into or out of a berth.

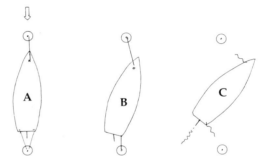

FIG 14 Getting under way from between two mooring buoys or piles against the tide. There is usually insufficient space to drop astern (A) although the method of getting under way is similar to Fig 13. Let go the bridle which is on the opposite quarter to the direction in which you intend to proceed (B) and put the tiller over to start a sheer, slacking off the second quarter rope if required. As soon as there is room to move clear, engage gear while slipping moorings fore and aft (C).

Lying to buoys fore-and-aft but with clear space on either side is probably the least difficult situation, but will still depend upon the mooring system. It is fairly common for such systems to have a single pickup buoy linked to both mooring buoys which lies down the side deck once the moorings are made fast. The danger with this method is that if the connecting line is not weighted, it is all too easy to foul the propeller, and you are limited to leaving the same way as you came in to avoid going over the line.

One way to overcome the problem of the line linking the forward and after mooring is to fit a brass Inglefield clip or stainless steel snap hook midway so that the line can be parted and reconnected on the opposite side. Passing the line round the bow will need care on the first few attempts to avoid fouling or passing it through the bowsprit's rigging. Provided the problems of the linking line are overcome, this mooring system has one redeeming feature. When the wind is blowing other than from forward or aft, the mooring at one end can be released so allowing the vessel to lie to the wind.

Moorings situated between pilings in fast-flowing rivers pose a problem of their own, though following the basic rules should overcome the difficulty even if there is a beam wind. Let's take the simpler of the two cases, when the boat is stemming the flow which is strong enough for her to respond to the rudder.

Provided that the pilings are not double-banked the first job is to sort out the mooring ropes. Replace any permanent bridles with ropes on the bight, with a head rope on the opposite side of the bow to the way you intend to leave. Next let go the stern line and allow the boat to lie to the single offset head rope, which should cant the bow in the direction you wish to go. Increase this angle with the tiller, put the engine ahead, and as the head rope becomes slack let go and recover quickly.

If for some reason it's not possible to use the tide alone to give the sheer, due to wind on the bow, then use the engine to counter the strength of the stream. As the boat sheers across the stream so the boat's resistance to the flow increases and it will be set down against a piling, so build up the revs to clear the berth.

Leaving the berth with a strong stream running under the stern is much more tricky, and owners with this type of permanent mooring had best practise before trying the manoeuvre on a full spring. Leaving bow-first is probably the safest option, even if your boat is fitted with a powerful engine; and craft with plenty of engine power astern will not have too much trouble if the helmsman is experienced.

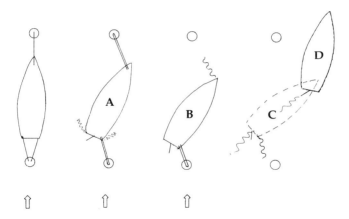

FIG 15 When the tide is flowing under the stern slipping is more difficult. Start by changing the fore-and-aft mooring bridles for doubled warps that can be easily slipped (A). Using tiller and engine induce the bow to sheer before slipping the forward mooring to allow the bow to swing further (B). Then let go aft, swing clear of both moorings (C) and then proceed down between the lines of moorings (D).

Inducing and controlling the sheer will be a delicate operation which is probably going to need plenty of engine power, and a stern line led from one quarter so that the boat lies askew. Rig mooring lines forward and aft on the bight before letting go the permanent bridles.

Ease out the head line while using the engine to stem the stream, and shorten the stern line to get as close as possible to the after piling. Use the engine and rudder to sheer the bow out into the stream but take great care that the sheer does not get out of hand. Once the bow is clear of the piling, let go forward and aft, increase revs, and turn quickly downstream so that the stern clears the piling.

Probably the worst situation is when, having berthed between two pilings, you discover next morning that you have a crewless neighbour secured alongside between the same pilings. Just to make the situation worse the tide's under your stern and there is a steady wind blowing you against your new-found friend.

The solution is not without its problems, including the fact that you are almost inevitably going to touch the yacht next door. That being the case, the risk of damage will be minimised if you start off touching cushioned by a fender, as then there will be no sudden knocks. I suggest that the simplest way out of the dilemma is to spring out holding the bow between the two pilings, rather than use your neighbour. The objective is to hold the bow between the two pilings with a forespring and stern line which are both very tight. Start by slacking off the head rope slightly and taking up as much slack as possible on the stern line so that the transom is as close as possible to the piling. Double a forespring so that it can be slipped between the after piling and the inside bow and then haul as taut as you can. Now slacken the stern line a little and go ahead on the spring while taking in the head rope slack.

The combined effort of engine and manpower should hold the bow firmly between the pilings with the stern projecting out into the stream against the pressure of the wind. Let go the stern line and, either using the engine or the force of the tide, allow the stern to swing further out until clear.

The crew forward and aft must be warned to let go together and the forespring recovered very quickly to keep it clear of the prop. When ready, let go and come astern until both bow and stern are clear and then go ahead between the line of moorings.

Returning to the buoy

When it is time to return to the mooring, again look at adjacent craft so as to determine the line of approach. It is important that the buoy is approached as close as possible to the heading which she will be lying in when brought up. The way that other craft are lying may prevent the yacht from approaching the buoy on the correct heading until the very last moment, so plan carefully.

Explain carefully to the crew what you are going to do and what is expected of them: the distance between cockpit and bow isn't great but engine noise can drown out speech. It is a fundamental rule of sailing that orders shouted from the cockpit which are inaudible to the foredeck crew can be heard by other yachts at least a quarter of a mile away.

The objective is to bring the mooring buoy close under the bow on the side on which it must be recovered and for the yacht to have stopped in the water. Stopping too short is easily corrected by a little extra power, however the antics of a crew trying to grasp and hold a buoy flashing past at 6 knots can be memorable to all involved. The helmsman should approach, keeping the buoy just to one side of the bow so that he can see it until the last possible moment. Hold the boat steady on the mooring if necessary by giving small engine bursts ahead or astern, but take care not to surge in either direction.

The position of engine controls may prevent the helmsman from standing up, so he must either use another member of the crew to work them or rely upon directions from the foredeck. When this is the case, always remind the crew forward to turn and face the cockpit, as it helps if the helmsman can read their lips as well as trying to hear! Hand signals from the foredeck crew are also helpful.

Mooring fore-and-aft

Returning to a berth between a pair of buoys or piles is obviously easiest when wind and tide are together but if they are opposed then make your approach against whichever is the stronger. The problems increase for the helmsman when the approach heading has to be made with a strong wind across the tide.

The piles will almost invariably lie along the line of tidal stream or river flow so the final approach must be made with the wind on the beam. The problem is that now the boat will be least manoeuvrable because the wind will be having its greatest effect. The approach will almost invariably involve stemming the tide to gain some advantage from the flow across the rudder to give some manoeuvrability even when almost stopped.

It has been suggested that the stern mooring should be picked up in passing from the bow and then the warp quickly walked aft as the boat manoeuvres on to the forward mooring. This manoeuvre requires considerable skill and no small measure of luck, because the stern mooring is downtide and there are long lengths of mooring warp involved. Any hesitation in taking the warp aft or a momentary lapse could see the boat with her prop fouled by the warp or becoming entangled with the craft moored astern. The safer technique would be to decide first whether the wind is so strong that it will prove impossible to manoeuvre to pick up the stern mooring. If this is the case, prepare the tender so that it can be used to run the stern line aboard as soon as the bow is made fast. However if the wind will allow you to retain control, decide whether the tide will swing you round to the stern mooring or whether you will have to use the engine. If stern power has to be used make sure that the crew appreciate whether you want the forward mooring slack or tight, but don't forget that if it's too tight your bowsprit will sweep across the forward boat's after deck.

Make your approach against the tide and on the leeward side of the craft moored in the same trot, along a line as near parallel to the other moorings as possible. At the last moment round up towards the mooring so as to clear the yacht ahead with your bowsprit. Stem up to the forward mooring and pick it up before using rudder to sheer the stern towards the after mooring. If the wind prevents you from doing this even with the engine, send one of the crew in the tender to make fast before hauling the stern into position. Reverse this technique when the wind is on the quarter and is strong enough to overpower the tide.

Marina and quayside berths

There is a fundamental difference between the pontoon and quay which is not always obvious until it's too late. Most harbour structures and certainly those used for berthing small craft tend to be of solid construction. Consequently while a river or tidal current will run under a pontoon, the water alongside a quay wall – no matter which direction the water is flowing in – will invariably run parallel to the face of the wall. The traditional displacement yacht may be subject to unexpected surges as the tide or river current runs under marina pontoons.

Quayside and pontoon berths are not usually as exposed to the elements as the open mooring, although of course subject to tidal streams. They do however present their own problems, not least the minuscule amount of space that some of the modern marina companies allow.

One of the unfortunate trends which has come about as a result of the marina pontoon is the universal lack of suitable warps aboard today's yachts. So many owners have warps fixed on their pontoon berth, with the addition of a couple of short ends retained aboard for when they first come alongside. Cruising from marina to marina has led them into a false sense of security which does not include the possibility of being on the outside of a six-boat tier.

Cowes Week is probably the worst illustration of this attitude, as vast numbers of yachts form themselves into articulated snakes. The end result resembles a giant legless centipede, trapped in a vast spider's web of mooring rope. Used to berthing in marinas they lack basic mooring warps, a line at bow and stern accompanied by a spring to the next yacht are deemed to be enough. So lacking a rope long enough to reach the shore, the very last arrival may even secure their boat to the tier ahead, adding to the chaos.

The situation I like least is when I'm approaching a berth with at least one eager helper ashore, just waiting to grab my warp and make fast. The result is a juddering halt as the bow is snubbed hard in and the bowsprit executes a leg-sweeping arc across the deck of the pontoon. Try and avoid this problem by having your own crew ready to leap ashore from the shrouds. This is the safest place for them to jump from and also keeps them clear of the helmsman's line of vision. Hopefully the approach will place the shrouds much closer to the berth.

The extensive use of short mooring lines has meant that practice in warping craft in and out of tight corners is rapidly being lost. The lightness of the modern crop of yachts may also be a contributory factor, due perhaps to the fact they are that much easier to stop by hand.

The heavy-displacement wooden hull is altogether another matter, as it can carry its way with potentially disastrous consequences. I remember towing an elderly 50-foot Colin Archer design, formerly a Norwegian customs cutter, into port after she had suffered disabling damage to rig and engine. We stopped towing as we entered through the pier heads and because she carried her own way, her single-handed owner was able to steer her for well over a quarter-mile to the berth and we still had to put a tow rope on her stern to stop her.

A close examination of marina berths doesn't seem to suggest a pattern of berth allocation, although there is a very good case for planning berths according to a vessel's ability to manoeuvre. Twin-engined motor boats for example can moor either side of a finger pontoon while right-hand turning single-screw craft are best moored port-side-to. Depending upon the proportion of each type of craft, this could leave half the marina empty which is perhaps why some of them don't attempt logical allocations.

It's a lucky owner therefore who can berth on his boat's favoured side. Having said this, much will also depend upon the direction of turn needed while going astern in order to face open water. The advantage of berthing port-side-to can be lost if the exit from the marina is on your port side and therefore demands that the stern goes to starboard when you leave.

I can remember being taken very safely broadside down the full length of a marina under power, due to a strong wind preventing a yacht turning as she came stern-first out of her berth. My skipper on this occasion was not only very familiar with the yacht but also the marina; some, unfamiliar with the boat, would probably have been less fortunate. Remember 'if the boat will not do it your way then do it hers'.

The scope for manoeuvring in a marina is usually limited – more especially if you've just been squeezed into the berth for the night. Always assume that the adjacent exposed berth will be occupied, hence leaving you minimum space in which to turn.

Letting go

Let's start with departure, port-side-to. As with all the following examples, the yacht is assumed to have a right-handed propeller. If yours is left-handed then the opposite applies. The way out is to starboard which requires that the stern must fall

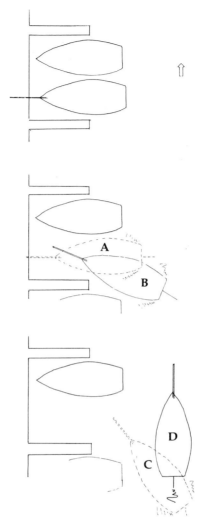

FIG 16 Moored in a marina port side to with wind or tide to port as well. Single up the moorings to a single line fore-and-aft with a crew member tending each (A). Move slowly astern picking up the stern line (and crew!) once the stern is under control. The transverse thrust will start a slow swing to port (B), so use the forward line to stop the bowsprit becoming too fond of your neighbour's guardrails. Recover the forward line and crew while still moving slowly astern into clear water (C). Finally, go ahead between the pontoons (D).

away to port once we are clear of the berth. The only real problem is to stop the bow swinging too quickly and so clouting the yacht to starboard.

First replace any warps fixed to the pontoon with normal ones and have them ready to slip. In addition to any fenders already in place, have a spare one available for use on either side and a member of the crew ready to use the boathook if necessary. The crew on the bow, if nimble enough, will walk along the pontoon to stop the bow swinging to starboard, while the crew aft tends the spare fender and makes sure that none of the other fenders catch, so bringing everything to a splintering halt.

Let go the stern line and, with the rudder amidships, go astern at low revs until about halfway out of the berth with the end of the pontoon amidships. The foredeck crew can now leap aboard, at which point the bow should be clear enough for the rudder to be moved gently to port, so that the bow starts to move to starboard. The rate of turn can be made tighter by a sudden brief increase in revs to induce more paddle-wheel effect, but care must be taken not to increase speed at the same time.

Once the bow is clear, put the tiller over the opposite way and give a short burst ahead on the engine. This serves two purposes, one to stop the progress sternwards and secondly to kick the bow round further to starboard. Lined up between the pontoons it is now just a matter of motoring slowly out of the marina.

Left to her own devices without sails set, a single-masted yacht will tend to head downwind because the bulk of mast and rigging are forward of midships. The ketch, yawl or schooner, on the other hand, may take up a position slightly across the wind depending upon just how much windage the after mast carries. In this case a small jib set on the bowsprit or a few turns slacked off the roller-reefing will keep the yacht lying stern into the wind.

This tendency to lie to the wind can be used to advantage when manoeuvring stern-first with the wind on the starboard side and wanting the stern to turn to port. The inclination for the stern to work to port when going astern is opposite to our requirements so we need to have the stern as far to starboard as possible. The best way to achieve this is with a forespring led well aft on the pontoon and doubled so that it can be slipped. After singling up, move the yacht astern by hand if necessary so that the midpoint is level with the outer end of the finger pontoon.

Once everyone is ready, and with fenders on both sides, go ahead against the forespring with the rudder to port so that the bow lies along the pontoon and the stern swings out to starboard. Once the stern has lifted off as far as possible, come astern with the rudder amidships or near enough to keep in a straight line. When the bow is clear of the pontoon end, either increase the turn to starboard or, if there is insufficient room, turn hard to port and kick ahead to bring the bow round.

Probably the most difficult departure from a pontoon is when the wind is pressing you against the berth and also trying to turn you in the opposite direction to the way you wish to go. Imagine a yacht with a typical auxiliary engine, right-handed propeller, berthed starboard-side-to, and needing to swing the stern to starboard to reach open water.

The paddle-wheel effect wants to take the stern to port, and the wind is trying to blow the bow to starboard; so, for a start, you have forces working against you. The wind might catch the stern when it first pokes clear of the other craft, but the prop and – later – the wind on the mast and rigging will counter what little effect this has. It's fairly common to use a forespring; the backspring as an aid to manoeuvring is more commonly associated with large ships, although it still has a place on board a yacht in these circumstances in particular.

The object is to use a backspring to counter the effects of propeller and wind by forcing the stern to starboard as the boat comes astern. The spring, which must be about twice the yacht's length, will be doubled through a cleat and must have a whipped end so there is no risk of it snagging. The same precautions are made as with the earlier manoeuvres and the most experienced member of the crew should man the backspring.

Move the yacht astern by hand as far as possible, then start to move astern under power. The spring must be allowed to pass round the cleat on board, retaining just enough friction to keep the boat straight until it is clear to swing. The engine revs astern can now be increased slightly while the spring is snubbed gently which starts the starboard swing. If too much friction is applied then the bow will crash into the yacht on the port side. As soon as the bow is clear then the spring must be let go and quickly recovered so as not to foul the propeller.

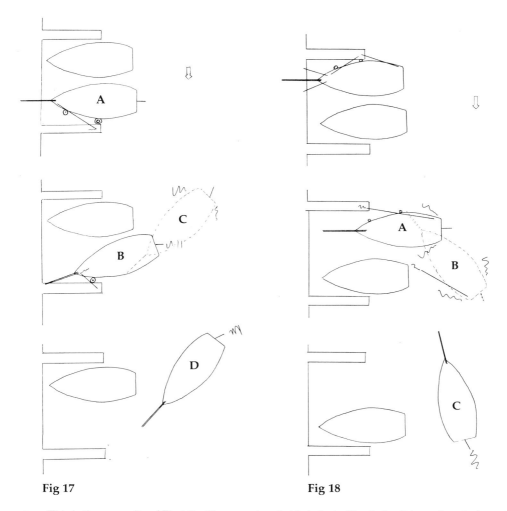

Fig 17   Fig 18

FIG 17 This is the opposite of Fig 16, still moored port side to but with wind or tide on the starboard side. Single up to a doubled fore spring plus fenders with crew to tend them (A). Go ahead against the spring with the rudder to port (B) to lift the stern off to starboard. Keep checking the bowsprit and starboard quarter. Now go astern putting the rudder over to starboard (C) and let go forward. Checking that neither bowsprit nor stern foul adjacent craft, move into clear water (D) before moving the rudder back to port and going ahead.

FIG 18 Berthed starboard side to with the wind or tide on the same side poses a more difficult problem. Going astern the stern will try to swing to port, so a back spring must be retained to keep the stern up (A). Once the bow is clear to swing then the spring can be cast off, but have a fender on the port quarter just in case she swings too quickly (B). Finally, once clear of the berth, steady up and move ahead towards open water (C).

Quayside berths

Berthing alongside a quay wall requires more attention to detail, not least because it is much more solid than a pontoon which will give slightly when hit hard! Streams and currents flow through marinas and may set a yacht on to or off a berth; this is not the case in a harbour. A stream will flow along the walls either increasing or slowing your approach speed, so before attempting to come alongside check which way it's running.

The rise and fall of the tide means that mooring lines have to be tended and precautions taken if there is any risk of taking the ground. Fendering against a granite wall can play havoc with paintwork or the gel coat, so rig some form of protection because the fenders pick up small particles of grit and dirt. A canvas apron hung over the side for the fenders to work against is one method or, if the quay face is uneven, a plank rigged between fenders and the wall.

A weight or sentinel rigged to the head and stern lines will keep them taut regardless of the tide's rise and fall. The owner of a yacht which has to be moved by the harbour staff will not be very popular if the weight is too heavy! The sentinels used to increase the anchor's holding power will do the job.

When returning to a pontoon or quayside berth always make sure that you do so against the tide, so that even at the slowest speed there is as much water as possible flowing across the face of the rudder. Make the approach slowly with the crew forward and aft ready to leap ashore with the lines. Unless the situation is desperate, discourage throwing a line ashore to an unknown volunteer – for that courts disaster. The willing hand ashore may be the berthing master but if it is not the chances are that as soon as the warp reaches his hand it will be made fast. The usual result is a bow secured snub hard against the quay wall before an engine going full astern can take the way off.

The craft should be brought alongside if at all possible by manoeuvring with the engine and not by the efforts of the crew heaving on the lines. When this is not possible because of a tight approach and limited space, then use a spring and fenders to come alongside. The helmsman must manoeuvre close alongside and when both he and the crew are ready give the order to jump ashore – don't forget that looking along its length foreshortens the bowsprit, so do not approach bow on. The crew who can jump 12 feet from a standing start is rare – don't waste a valuable asset.

CHAPTER 6

Getting under way

The ability to navigate safely or deal with an emergency situation is desirable, some would say essential, from the moment that a yachtsman leaves his mooring or berth for the first time. Like everything that we need to know, these skills can and should be studied in theory before even venturing on the water. However, they can't be perfected without practical experience, so with a sensible approach in selecting the conditions and perhaps the crew, there should be no need to put the emergency drills into practice on the maiden outing!

The first manoeuvres to be learnt under sail can be divided into three categories. Firstly those needed in order to get under way; secondly manoeuvres in order to navigate safely; and finally the correct response to emergencies of one sort or another. How and where you start will depend very much on where your yacht is normally moored, just as with getting under way with the engine. It may not be unusual to see an owner sailing his yacht on to a marina berth in France, but it's certainly not a common sight in the UK. Neither is it a first lesson upon which the novice should embark!

Selecting the sails

One important aspect of setting sail is just how much canvas to hoist in the first place. Detailed aspects of reefing for heavy weather are discussed in Chapter 11, but the sensible use of your sail wardrobe for everyday cruising is just as important.

The decision to take a reef because you are in doubt about the weather conditions or the yacht's capabilities is not a display of weakness. The sun may be warm and shining but it's much easier to shake a reef out than to tuck it in on a heaving, slippery deck. We have all seen those hardy souls who seem intent upon thrashing along with the lee rail submerged, being blown almost flat by every other gust. A careful look around will probably show another yacht nearby carrying much less sail area, standing upright and going just as fast, if not faster.

There is nothing wrong with listening to other people's advice, especially when you have yet to gain your own experience; so if the opportunity is there, seek and take advice. Sailing a class or rig of which there are many similar examples in the area at least gives you the opportunity to see just what the consequences of the others' choice of sail can be.

When looking around take account of the less obvious aspects; two yachts which appear to be the same size can weigh differently and will therefore behave totally differently. The heavy displacement yacht with a fixed keel will carry more canvas for less heel than a shallow-drafted craft fitted with a centre plate. A yacht's balance must also be taken into consideration. Some older yachts start to carry more weather helm the greater their heeled angle, consequently – if for no other reason than for the comfort of the helmsman – they may be sailed upright. The more weather helm that a yacht carries the harder she is to handle and also the slower she will go.

Some years ago when I first owned *Melloney*, I took part in events with some other Cornish Crabbers during Falmouth week, in marginal conditions so far as that fleet was concerned. In the organised way of such things I arrived at the start line behind the other boats, carrying two reefs in the main to their one, and they soon pulled away. I became rapidly convinced that all was lost and was just about to shake out a reef when those ahead suffered the first of a series of quite dramatic broaches as they moved out into less sheltered water. By the time we had reached the first mark I had passed all bar one; we passed her soon after and were never to be overtaken – so far as I was concerned that was a good lesson learned. Make a decision and don't dither, even if at first it appears that you are being too cautious.

So let's start by having a fairly clear idea of what sails to set for the first few excursions under good weather conditions. Choose a day with a steady breeze, neither too strong nor too light, because nothing will really be learned if the whole day is spent with sails slatting on an oily sea. Ideally the forecast should be for winds to remain around force 3–4, with no indication of any expected increase. The mainsail can be set full, the normal working headsails hoisted and it should be possible to include a topsail if one is carried. A jib headed topsail will be more suitable for winds towards the top end of force 4 while a yard or jackyard can be set in force 3 and lower 4.

Having decided what canvas to set, it is time to look at the problems that must be overcome before clearing the mooring and beginning to sail.

Harbour congestion

The owner who keeps his boat on a swinging mooring must bear in mind the two golden rules for getting under way or returning to a mooring under sail alone. Firstly to make sure that there is a clear water all round and secondly to have the engine going just in case.

Many owners I am sure would consider this latter advice insulting. True, there will be many occasions when it's simplicity itself to hoist the sails, let go the buoy and sail off under full control. The honest owner will also admit to the odd situation when the totally unexpected or unforeseen happened and either the engine came in very handy or there were a few moments when the adrenalin flowed uncomfortably fast!

Good seamanship dictates that we take all reasonable precautions to ensure that we navigate safely, not only for our own sake but also for the sake of those around us. There could easily be circumstances when for one reason or another we may have to get under way without the benefit of an engine, which is why it's wise to become familiar with the manoeuvre; but that is no reason to take unnecessary risks.

Before looking more closely at the various methods of getting under way, remember that at some point you will have to return to your mooring. Although it is important to be able to pick up the mooring again, it is probably better to spend some time getting used to the way that the yacht handles instead of returning immediately to the mooring or anchorage.

It is much easier to leave a mooring under sail than to 'sail out' the anchor, the technique for which we will examine later; the basics of getting under way are however the same. Leaving a mooring is not without its own difficulties, which are in the main dependent upon whether the craft is moored in a river or harbour. If the former, the boat will usually be lying to the effects of the river current, with the wind as a secondary consideration. The yacht with a harbour mooring, on the other hand, is most likely to be wind-rode, with the tidal stream having a lesser effect in all but the lightest airs.

The need for space in which to manoeuvre is essential, but just how much varies from yacht to yacht. Traditional yachts being that much heavier require more room because time is needed in which to build up momentum and enough water flow across the rudder to give positive steering. The problems arise when neither wind nor tide has supremacy and consequently the heavy, deep-keeled yachts will lie to the tide, the very light ones to the wind, with a whole range of craft somewhere in between.

Provided, of course, that all the boats are lying in roughly the same direction, a yacht will still have gaps through which to leave on either bow and each quarter. Unfortunately neither of these options is likely to amount to much because of the space constraints imposed by modern harbours.

Ahead the gap will probably be too close to the wind for the sails to fill and there may be insufficient space on either side to allow a full 180-degree turn in order to make use of the gap astern. The situation is not impossible, but let's assume that on the first few occasions that you have left your own mooring under power and picked up one on the outside of the mooring area with clear water around.

Preparing to get under way

Start by deciding whether the tender will be left on the mooring, towed astern or brought on board. If it is to be left on the mooring then it must be brought along the windward side and made fast to the mooring. When the tender is being towed then it must be kept close astern, again on a very short painter. If the pickup buoy is allowed to trail aft prior to letting go then the tender's painter can become tangled with it or, worse still, could foul the propeller. Nothing could be more embarrassing than to creep slowly away from the mooring, just luffing across the bow of an adjacent yacht, only to find yourself and your tender hitched up on opposite sides of it!

It used to be the practice to stream the mooring pickup buoy over the side before letting go. Probably because ropes were made of natural fibre and spent most of their life in the water so the strength could not be relied upon. Modern materials have changed all this so that now it is much more usual to let go the mooring chain and lie to the pickup buoy. An advantage of adopting this approach is that the boat can lie to a longer scope, allowing greater freedom of movement. The length of the buoy rope which is let out can be adjusted to allow the boat to fall astern or be held up tight to her mooring buoy.

The yacht should now be readied for sea before even contemplating leaving the mooring, otherwise you risk being caught out once under way, because the wind and sea prevent you from leaving the helm. Begin by clearing away all the lashings and protective covers used while the boat is on its mooring. Don't forget the light lines which are used to stop the halyards beating against the mast and wearing away the varnish, not to mention annoying the crews of yachts in adjacent berths. Open the sea cocks, switch on the batteries and make sure that the engine is warmed through even if it's not planned to use it.

Remove the sail covers; when you bend on the headsails either keep the bulk of the sail in the sail bag or lash them down so that they are not free to flog in the wind. Run the headsail sheets aft and don't forget to uncoil the mainsheet; nothing is worse than slipping the mooring before finding that the mainsheet is still in its neat coil and hanging jammed into the block! If you are only going a short distance before anchoring, for example, then make sure that anchor and cable can be let go with the minimum of preparation.

While working around the decks, take notice of how the yacht is moving around. Is the wind gusting and causing her to sheer from one side to the other as first wind overcomes current, then the reverse? All this sort of information will help decide which is the best direction from which to leave the mooring.

We are assuming that the first attempt at slipping a mooring under sail will be clear of other moored yachts, with ample sea room, and under favourable conditions with wind and tide setting the yacht in the same quadrant; the preparation in these circumstances is simple and forms the basis for setting sail when at anchor as well.

The wind will be forward of the beam so the mainsail can be set first, followed by a topsail if the wind is light. It's much easier to set topsails when lying head-to-wind rather than trying to do the job under way, particularly on the first few occasions. Once the main is set, its sheet uncoiled and the topping lifts slacked off, it's time to move forward and look at the headsails.

The use of roller headsail furling or Wykeham-Martin gear is fairly common but, as these are so simple to set, let's consider ordinary headsails, which have to be bent and hoisted each time. Unless the bobstay is fixed, the bobstay purchase will have been released to keep it clear of the mooring bridle. Before setting the jib the bobstay must be first sweated hard in so that the outboard end of the bowsprit is bowsed down.

The foredeck must be kept as clear as possible until after the mooring has been slipped, so hopefully the jib should be sufficient to get under way and clear of the moorings. Provided that the wind is not too excessive, the jib can now be hoisted, with the sheets slack so that it flaps until the mooring is released. The sail should not be allowed to flog in a breeze, as it might be damaged; and to be hit in the ear by the clew cringle can be a little distracting.

Leaving a clear mooring

A final check round the decks should ensure that everything is ready, and that the mooring is ready to be slipped and not jammed tight on the samson post or bitts. Let's assume that it's intended to leave the mooring on the port tack, which means that the jib must first be backed to starboard so as to cast the yacht's head to port.

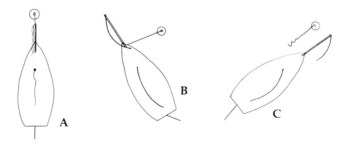

FIG 19 Getting under way from a single mooring under sail with the wind the only factor to be considered is fairly simple. Set the main and enough headsail to give full control (A); ideally only the jib on a cutter to give room to work on the foredeck. Sheet in the main and back the jib to sheer the bow away from the intended direction of departure (B) until the limit of the mooring bridle is reached. The tiller must be put over to tack the boat quickly, and once she has gathered way slip the mooring (C) before it starts to check the bow round again.

Ease the mainsheet just enough to allow it to fill and as soon as she gathers a little way put the tiller over and tack while backing the jib again, this time to port.

When the yacht's head has paid off to starboard, let the mooring go smartly before it becomes taut and snubs the bow round; make sure too that the buoy doesn't foul either the bowsprit shrouds or bobstay as it goes over the side. Once the bow has come round far enough, tack and sheet the jib, adjusting jib and mainsheets to lay a course that is not too close to the wind until you are clear of the moorings.

Once in clear water you can give some thought to setting your second headsail. Whether single-handed or crewed, this is more easily achieved when heading to windward. When sailing alone, this is probably the first opportunity you will have of heaving to, and it will provide ample proof that this is not a tactic for use only in storms. To heave-to, round up towards the wind, sheeting in both jib and main before putting the helm down and tacking, but without letting go the jib sheet as the bows pass through the wind. The immediate response will be that the boat will lose her way through the water. The jib is now sheeted to windward and is unable to fill, so the bow continues to pay off, probably until the wind is close to the beam.

Provided that the tiller is lashed slightly to windward the boat will ride quietly, making slight headway while steadily drifting to leeward. There is no risk of the unexpected happening so it is quite safe to leave the tiller and go forward to hoist the staysail. Once the sail is set then the windward sheet of the jib can be released and sheeted to leeward, allowing the boat to gather way before tacking again to resume the original course.

However, if the power of the main is too great and the jib comes over, the bow will come back up into the wind, so it will be necessary to de-power the mainsail. Start

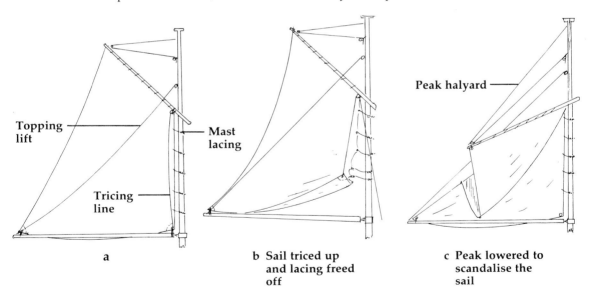

FIG 20 As a means of decreasing the power of the mainsail the tack can be either triced up or the peak lowered or scandalised. (a) Only loose footed sails can be triced and they need to have either parrel balls or mast hoops instead of lacing along the luff. (b) The weight of the boom is taken on the topping-lift before the tack of the sail is raised up the mast by the tricing line. (c) A sail which is truly scandalised has the tack triced up and the gaff lowered. However, nowadays lowering the gaff is often considered sufficient to justify the name. Again the weight must be taken on the topping-lift before lowering the gaff peak. Gaffs with a single peak halyard and span should not lower the gaff past the horizontal as the gaff may well prove impossible to raise again without also lowering the throat.

first by easing off the mainsheet to see if this will achieve the desired result; if this doesn't work then the main will have to be scandalised.

A simple definition of scandalising is to 'trice up the tack and settle the peak of the mainsail', but as most gaffers nowadays lack a tricing line for the tack of the main this action must be modified somewhat. The quickest action will be to raise the boom on the topping-lift so that the sail loses shape and spills out much of its wind. If this is not enough then, provided a topsail is not set, lower the peak of the gaff as well which will further reduce the effectiveness of the sail.

Leaving a crowded mooring

Now that you have successfully sailed off a mooring which has ample clear water around it, let's examine the technique for attempting to leave your usual mooring under sail. The same factors have to be considered when choosing which tack to leave on: the direction of open water, the proximity of adjacent craft and the way they are lying. If Murphy ever went sailing no doubt his law would explain that open water is dead upwind and a fleet of dinghies are circling under your stern.

The choice isn't usually too difficult because, no matter in what direction the open water, it is the space required to get under way initially that is most important. It is essential to be as close as possible to those moored craft or other obstructions which lie to windward before tacking and letting go. The problem is how to get there without attempting to run warps and heave your boat bodily across.

The answer lies in the way that the jib is used to cast the bow off to one side when first getting under way. This should not be attempted without at least one crew member until you are confident that the cockpit can be quickly regained after letting go.

Once the mainsail has been set, use the jib to sail the yacht across the mooring from one side to the other as before. This time start by heading in the direction you intend to leave with the jib backed, then allow the jib and the main to fill and draw until the bow is snubbed round. This automatically backs the jib again as the bow passes through the wind and the boat heads off on the opposite tack with increased momentum. Repeat the same procedure as before but this time as soon as the bow has been snubbed round slip the mooring immediately; the jib may need to be briefly backed before being sheeted to leeward.

This manoeuvre has given the boat speed and more room in which to steer around adjacent moored craft passing either up- or downwind depending on space. The slingshot effect of snubbing the bow round helps the heavier, long-keeled craft build up their momentum and so achieve steerage way more quickly. The length of the buoy rope before starting not only affects the space used but also the position from which the track through the moorings is started.

Wind against tide

When the wind is abaft the beam, because the current or tidal stream is having a greater effect than the wind upon the moored yacht, different tactics have to be adopted. The general preparations are the same although the main isn't set first, largely due to the risk of the boat yawing back and forth across its mooring, alternately under the influence first of wind and then of tide. This increases the risk of collision when moored amongst other craft, as the boat changes from being tide-rode to wind-rode.

Once everything is ready, with most of the ties off the main and the jib and staysail hoisted in stops, you are ready to get under way. Now slip the mooring and break the headsails from their stops and sail clear before raising the main. Do not attempt this manoeuvre when single-handed, unless you are moored well clear of any other yachts; use the engine instead until you have had the chance to practise in clearer water.

When there is only minimal sea room ahead it means that the boat must be turned sharply, setting a course to windward. Provided that there is sufficient space on either side the main must be hoisted immediately before the mooring is slipped, the helm put down and sail sheeted in. This will swing the bow up towards the wind so that minimum ground is lost to leeward while the headsails are broken out of stops and set.

Wind abeam

At first glance the simplest situation might appear to be when the wind is on the beam, especially if the wind is light or at least not as strong as the effect of the tide. A closer look at the circumstances will show that neither of the two methods discussed already will work. Setting up the jib will tend to push the bow round, causing the boat to sail across her mooring buoy, and hoisting the main could have the same result.

It is no good hoisting the main in the hope that, by freeing it off, it will spill all its wind. The lee shrouds will stop the sail from being freed right off, and in this position it can still catch some of the wind, forcing the bow up into the wind as well as catching the mooring buoy.

The answer, so long as the wind is light, is to hoist a jib, set in stops, and scandalise the mainsail. A gaff sail is scandalised by sweating up on the main halyard until the luff is bar taut, but only allowing the gaff to rise just above the horizontal. The main, almost set, still fails to draw any wind and so will not overcome the force of the tide, but will only take a moment to set.

Once the mooring is released the jib is quickly broken out of stops and the boat reached clear before the main is finally set, although the crew could raise the peak enough to give some additional drive.

There is one further method of leaving a mooring when the wind is ahead, there is insufficient space to turn on either side, and the only clear way out lies astern. The tactic does however require at least a full boat's length astern to avoid risk of collision although, with experience, this safety margin could be reduced. Prepare as for leaving under headsails and then run a slip rope from the mooring buoy to the stern. The painter should be passed through the eye on the buoy and used on the bight. It must be led down on the side opposite to which it is intended to turn and be made fast with a hitch which will not jam and can be slipped easily.

The principle of the method is for the jib to be hoisted and backed well out so that not only does the bow pay off but also the boat starts to gather some stern-way. Once this happens the mooring is slipped, although the jib must not be allowed to fill but instead drive the bow round so that boat's stern spins on the slip rope; the rudder should be used to encourage this movement.

Once the boat is beam-on to the wind the jib sheet should be trimmed to give steerage way and the stern rope should be slipped. The boat can then be reached clear of the moorings under her jib before raising the main and staysail.

Sailing out the anchor

The problem of getting under way from a mooring in a variety of different conditions usually means that the only real difficulties are those posed by the close proximity of other craft. Sailing out an anchor, on the other hand, adds another dimension which is the retrieval of the anchor and its cable while still retaining control.

When anchored in the isolation of a quiet bay there is little difference between getting under way and slipping a mooring. The main is raised and the jib hoisted in stops, before the anchor and cable are brought aboard. The yacht may gather stern-way so that the rudder may have to be put over as well as backing the jib before starting to forge ahead.

Faced by the shore or other craft close to one side, the yacht can still be got under way without too much difficulty. Start by bringing in most of the cable but stop before there is a risk of breaking the anchor out of the bottom. CQR and similar anchors require more scope of cable to be left lying along the bottom to counter this tendency than the Bruce or traditional Fisherman's anchor because it will be much heavier. The cable should be shortened before hoisting any of the sails; there seems little point in making that job any harder than it needs to be by increasing the windage.

Let's assume that the moored craft are to port so departure must be made on the port tack. Unless the anchorage has only been a temporary one it will help to shorten the cable to an easily manageable length. Lash the tiller so that there is a little starboard helm before hoisting the main, leaving the sheet belayed but with some slack.

Hoist the jib and then back it to starboard until the bow pays off, at which point the sail can be sheeted to leeward. The boat now gathers way, straight towards the other anchored yachts – one good reason why the cable should have been shortened. Wait until the bow is snubbed round and then heave in the slack cable as the boat, now effectively hove-to, sails slowly towards and across her anchor. This is a second reason for shortening cable, because if it is not shortened it is hard work hauling in hand-over-hand while sailing towards the anchor.

As soon as the cable is nearly up-and-down, catch a turn on the bitts or samson post and the boat will break her anchor out of the ground, so that it can be brought on deck and stowed. The yacht will continue slowly making her way to starboard until the foredeck has been cleared, then the windward jib sheet can be released and the sail trimmed to leeward.

Getting under way when the wind is aft and the yacht tide-rode shouldn't present any difficulties in a clear anchorage with plenty of sea room astern, as it is merely a question of raising the anchor before setting sail. The strength of the current being stronger than the wind means that, as the yacht gathers way astern, she is not under full control until some sails are set. The seamanlike approach is either for her jib to have been hoisted prior to the anchor breaking free if the course lies ahead, or for the main to be raised as soon as the anchor is aweigh. The wind on the main will quickly luff her up and the minimum ground will have been lost to leeward.

Years ago an owner might have tried 'dredging', which entails dragging an anchor along the bottom and relying upon the flow of water across the rudder to give steerage. The haphazard congestion of modern anchorages and moorings dictates that the probable consequences would be a fouled anchor, not to mention the likelihood of breaking out your neighbour's anchor and towing him along with you!

If the yachts moored nearby are too close for comfort, then one way of clearing the anchorage is to use a variation of the method used on a mooring. After deciding the tack on which to leave, pass a rope down the opposite side outside the shrouds,

An Irish hooker sailing out the anchor under just mainsail and jib to give the foredeck crew space in which to work. The boat has just tacked with the jib backed as she reaches the end of the cable, and the crew are hauling in the slack on the cable as the boat gathers way on the new tack. *Photograph: Peter Chesworth*

between the anchor cable and the stern. Getting the lead right is all-important, as one mistake will be potentially damaging to your hull and your pride.

The easiest lead for the warp is down the same side as the bow roller over which it passes; otherwise the warp must be dipped under the bowsprit and bobstay. The sight of the crew gingerly balancing their way out along the bowsprit with a coil of rope between the teeth, can be the stuff on which reputations are made and wagers are won!

There is no need to rig a slip rope as any line thick enough to heave upon will tend to jam in a link, so either use a rolling hitch or a prussik knot formed in the bight of the line around the cable. After the line has been led aft, make it fast to a cleat and then slack off the anchor cable so that the yacht now rides by the stern to the slip rope.

The jib should be hoisted in stops and everything readied for getting under way before the anchor is heaved home over the stern. Once the anchor is aweigh the jib must be broken out and the yacht sailed clear before the remaining sails are set; all the cable must also be cleared from the cockpit and restored up forward.

The lee shore with strong onshore wind can be a difficult enough situation without finding yourself anchored off it. The careful seaman who has studied the forecasts should have little difficulty as he will get under way long before the strength of the wind is significant. The yacht will probably be riding to a fairly long scope of cable and, with a strong wind blowing, it will be difficult if not impossible to shorten cable by hand. This is an advantage because several tacks will have to be made so as to get all the cable aboard, which will provide a clear and important indication as to whether you will be making headway once the anchor is out.

Set the sails according to the weather conditions, well reefed if necessary, and with one person left on the tiller go forward and sail the anchor out. If the worst should happen and the anchor fouls an obstruction on the bottom, then be prepared to slip the cable with your own anchor buoy securely attached for later recovery. Don't forget to keep the anchor ready for letting go once it's back on deck, just in case your efforts to get under way don't succeed.

CHAPTER 7

Manoeuvres under sail

Once clear of the moorings and under full sail, it is time to take a quick stock of the boat generally. If the tender is under tow then the painter can be eased away until she is riding smoothly astern and not creating too much drag. Check that everything is stowed safely away (this should have been done before getting under way). With all secure below, take a look aloft to check that all the sails are trimmed and that nothing was only half done in the haste of departure.

The basic sheeting rule to remember is that the stronger the wind the flatter the sails, so in light breezes the sheets should be eased to allow some shape. If the mainsail has an outhaul it can also be eased to further induce a curve along the foot of the sail.

When sailing to windward the creases across the main between peak and tack should have vanished once the sail has filled. If they are still there don't rush to the halyard until you've checked that the topping-lift is all slack. The topsail should be sheeted as flat as possible but if sailing very close to the wind it may not be drawing well although it must not be allowed to flutter too much. Check up forward that the luff of the jib especially is bar taut. If it isn't then the boat will not point as well as it should.

Trimming the sails

Although it is a good idea to see what sails other yachts are setting before you feel fully confident about selecting your own sails unaided, once it comes to trimming your sails, other yachts are the last things you should use when judging how well your own boat is performing. In particular, never use yachts close by as a guide to how close you are pointing: the other boat will always seem to be sailing much closer to the wind and the reason is that you do not notice her leeway. This is why it is so easy to make a mistake in trying to copy her; instead you will end up trying to pinch too close to the wind and as a consequence lose speed, increase your leeway, and see your selected example disappear into the distance.

Unless involved in some particular tactical duel during a race, when it's essential to out-point the yacht alongside, there is no real substitute for allowing your boat to romp along. The sheets need to be eased slightly and the sails allowed to fill; only time and practice will tell what is best for your yacht. Just because the craft ahead has her boom sheeted hard in over her transom doesn't mean that you can do the same.

The difficulties of relying upon the activities of those around you are easy to see amongst a gaff racing fleet in light winds. All of the boats start in the same direction, but as the wind becomes more unpredictable you might even see two boats sail to within a few boats' lengths of each other, both running before the wind. The moral is: use your eyes as a guide in light winds but don't always believe what you see!

There are a number of telltales or dog vanes which can be used as a guide to the wind direction, but unless sophisticated electronics are available they will always indicate the apparent wind – which is the combined effect of the true wind and your own speed. The burgee fluttering at the masthead is one guide, although once a yard topsail is set it is useless.

Yarn tied to the shrouds is an alternative method and a good one, so long as your trust in it is built up over a period as you become used to actual wind angle which relates to the indicated one. Some people like to sail from the lee side because there is a better view of the headsails and they can sail watching the luff of the jib. Don't be deceived into thinking they are sailing by burgee or shroud telltale. They can't see the first, and the latter only shows the direction of the wind flowing between the staysail and the lee side of the main!

Sailing by the jib luff takes some practice but at least it is consistent and does not depend upon whether the burgee is caked in salt or has just been washed in the latest fabric softener. The sails are the logical source of performance information as, after all, it is they that are driving the yacht through the water, and the jib is the closest sail to the wind.

Out at the end of the bowsprit the jib is not subject to anything other than the true wind affecting the boat, plus of course the speed through the water. Even if that wind is foul and coming off another yacht's sails, it is at least the wind by which you are trying to sail.

The theory of sailing by the jib is based upon the reaction of the sail when pointing into the wind or close by – it flutters or shakes. The reason for this is that the wind is blowing down both sides of the sail and the sail is trying to stream out like a flag. Don't forget that it is when the wind is nearly in line with the sail that it shivers, so unless the jib is sheeted hard in, this will not indicate that the boat is sailing as close as possible to the wind.

When the jib starts to shiver slowly turn away from the wind. This will cause the shivering movement in the sail to decrease slowly until it ceases and the sail fills with wind. The reverse of this reaction is to turn gently into the wind until the sail starts to show signs that some wind is getting on the opposite, or lee side, of the sail and causing it to move.

All the sails will react like this as the wind starts to flow along both sides, so the objective of trimming the sails is to get the jib to start lifting or fluttering before the main. A cutter has of course to fit another sail in between the main and jib, so the trimming will need a little more attention.

Aboard a well-rigged yacht the mainsail can be laid flat in a breeze, and sheet leads for both headsails should allow them to be sheeted hard in without affecting the flow. It is important that the wind of the staysail doesn't back-wind the main and that the jib doesn't do the same thing to the staysail. Starting with the main, the fore, and then the jib, each should have slightly more shape than the preceding sail and in effect it is closer to the wind, yet the jib must still not start lifting.

Some yachts always seem to have the jib a-flutter and no matter how the owner trims the sails it simply will not stop. The reason is often that the sail has been imported from another yacht and so the cut is unsuitable, perhaps being too low-cut along the foot, so that it cannot set without affecting the staysail which in turn spoils the main. The large, low-cut jib similar to the genoa can be improved by getting the sailmaker to cut it higher so that it more closely resembles a yankee jib, and then by moving the sheet leads further aft.

Sudden wind changes

Provided that the course isn't changed or the wind shifts, you will continue sailing steadily, but as nothing ever stays the same it's as well to be prepared. Let's look first at those changes which can't always be anticipated, like a sudden gust of wind.

The dinghy sailor spends much of his time looking over the shoulder anticipating the sudden wall of wind which might descend and tip him into the water. The tactic used by the small boat sailor in this case is to reduce the wind pressure on the sails by easing the sheets or even turning up into the wind. Anyone with any dinghy experience will employ the same tactic when taking the tiller of a larger displacement yacht, but it's not actually necessary.

A yacht has a ballast keel which provides the righting moment to keep her upright while a dinghy only has the weight of the crew who aren't fixed. In all but the most exceptional sea conditions a yacht doesn't turn over; and, even if she did, the weight of the ballast keel makes her self-righting. So when the wind heels a yacht the area of sail presented to the wind decreases and the wind spills out, allowing the yacht to start righting herself.

Most yachts have been designed and rigged to carry a certain amount of weather helm, which means that the boat has a tendency to point up into the wind if the tiller is released. When a yacht heels over in the wind this weather helm is increased; so, provided the rudder angle remains the same, she will start turning into the wind. The consequence of both these reactions is that the yacht herself eases the wind pressure upon her and comes closer to the upright.

A 'steady' wind is never steady, although the slight fluctuations will hardly be noticeable and it is only when the wind becomes gusty that any difference in how the yacht responds becomes apparent. The stronger the breeze the closer the yacht can sail to the wind, and this can be used to advantage. When attempting to reach a destination upwind from the point of departure, losing ground because of leeway is frustrating; therefore any ground that can be stolen back is a bonus.

When the yacht heels to each gust the pressure increases slightly on the tiller as the weather helm increases. Instead of countering this, ease the tiller slightly and the boat will continue sailing at the same speed but point closer to the wind, so making ground to windward. Making up ground which would otherwise have been lost in this way is called 'luffing'. The tiller will ease as the gust decreases and the original course should be resumed.

The long-keeled heavy displacement craft is at a disadvantage in short-lived gusts because it takes time to alter course and build up speed from the increased wind speed. These craft do, however, gain when the gusts are lengthier because their weight enables them to build up momentum. This can carry them from the end of one gust to the beginning of the next; something which a light yacht cannot do.

Tacking

A yacht cannot sail directly into the wind. In order to reach a windward destination, therefore, the yacht must approach by a series of zigzags across the wind. The gaffer isn't able to sail as close to the wind as a bermudian rigged yacht, so trying to sail too close to the wind is counter-productive. The gaffer should be sailed free, slightly off the wind. This means that she will sail a longer distance because she doesn't make as much progress upwind with each tack, but she will make a good time because she sails faster that little bit more off the wind.

Putting about or tacking a yacht is not a difficult manoeuvre, but there can be differences between a large, heavy gaff cutter and her smaller sister which may mean that they cannot be tacked in the same way. To tack any boat effortlessly it is important that the bow of the boat passes through the wind and fills her sails smoothly on the new tack as soon as possible. In this way not only is the direction changed as quickly as possible but also there is a miminal loss of speed.

A small light gaffer can be spun round just by pushing the rudder hard over and letting the headsails fly. However these actions court disaster if tried on board a heavy displacement gaffer. Firstly because the large rudder blade will act as a brake and slow (if not stop) the boat's forward progress. The boat may spin round quickly if it has enough way on, but the loss of speed will have to be made up on the next tack. Secondly, letting the headsails fly too soon may result in the boat not even tacking at all, merely coming up towards the wind before falling away again. The yacht must instead be sailed round on to the other tack with slight rudder movements, using the power of sail until it is of no further use.

One of the principles of sailing is to use the elements to do the work so, where possible, the wind should be used to help take the sails across. The size of the headsails will, of course, affect the speed with which they can be tacked from one side to the other.

Hauling one or both of the sails across too early as the bows approach the eye of the wind could result in them being back-filled and the bows blown back on to the original course. Leaving them until the bows have passed through the wind risks both sails becoming backed, with the bow being blown past the new course before the sails can be resheeted. Added to this there will be the possible damage to the sails as, filled with wind, they are dragged across the stays.

The compromise is to use one sail to help bring the bow round while the other is allowed to tack across with help on the sheets. The smallest headsail should be the one backed as it is the easiest to control and will be least liable to damage from fouling on the standing rigging. A backed sail will belly against any obstruction such as the forestay; so, once it is let go, the belly may have to be heaved from one side to the other.

When the helmsman has made his decision to tack, he should make sure that the crew know and understand what the new point of sailing will be. In other words, is he intending to sail close hauled, or is he going to lay a next course which will permit the sails to be set freer? When the boat is sailing hard on the wind it would be as well for the helmsman to free slightly to gain speed before tacking.

Do not try to tack quickly when sailing off the wind without trimming the sails because, as she comes on to the wind, the sails will lose their wind, start to flog, all way will be lost and the boat fail to tack. So when sailing off the wind the yacht should be brought closer to the wind and the sails must be trimmed to keep her sailing up until she tacks.

Whether used as an order or a warning, 'Lee Oh' tells everyone that the tiller is being put to leeward. Unless it is urgent, the tiller should be put gently to leeward so that the bow comes up into and through the wind. As the jib first lifts and then flogs it should be sheeted flatter if at all possible so that it becomes back-filled quickly and helps to bring the bow round. Once the boat has started to come up into the wind and so the pressure of wind is reduced, then the weather running backstay should be eased off prior to taking up on the other backstay once the boom has crossed over.

The staysail sheet can be cast off, the sail brought round and even pre-sheeted on the new leeward side. The main will initially take care of itself, although if it is proposed to sail free on the new tack then the mainsheet will have to be eased away.

Once the bow is well round, the jib's weather sheet can be released and the sail sheeted to leeward.

In the explanation I have assumed that the boat will handle better with the jib backed, but the procedure will be just as valid if the staysail is used instead. But, as explained earlier, it is best if the smaller sail is backed.

When sailing very close hauled in a light wind, in order to make the maximum ground to windward, a yacht may have to be freed off so as to build up speed before tacking. The same tactic can be used when a short, steep sea is crashing against the bow as the boat comes up into the wind, preventing the bow from coming round on to the new tack. Over-caution by the helmsman, or the effects of a rough sea, may prevent the yacht from tacking and she will stop with her head into wind and the sails a-shiver. When this happens and the yacht refuses to tack or pay off again she is said to be 'in irons'. There is only one way to correct the problem, which is by going forward, backing the headsails and even using the rudder to swing her stern to one side or the other if she starts to gather stern-way.

So to summarise: the tack commences with the tiller being put down to bring the bow steadily up towards the wind while the sheets are adjusted to maintain speed. Once the headsails start to lose wind the staysail sheet is released, the jib hardened in while the weather running backstay is released. Once the mainsail boom starts to move across, the staysail is sheeted and the new weather running backstay hauled in. Finally, as main and staysail start to fill, the jib sheet is freed so that the sail can be sheeted on the new tack.

Tacking problems

What should you do if for one reason or another the yacht will not tack, or if you must manoeuvre to avoid a close-quarters situation with another yacht? The solution is to 'wear round', which means taking the yacht from close hauled on one tack all the way to the other but by passing the wind across the stern. The great disadvantage with wearing is that you may lose a lot of hard-won ground to windward.

There are a number of reasons why a boat may not tack. One is that the sails are set too free, consequently they stop drawing before the bow nears the wind. Adjusting the sail trim will solve this problem. In light breezes a short sharp sea slapping against the weather bow can also stop the boat rounding up, and the only way to overcome the problem is to wear the boat round. First the tiller is brought to windward, and then the sheets freed off slightly to build up speed until the boat is reaching along.

Continue altering course until, with the wind and sea approaching the stern, the boat is gybed. However, once the wind is on the new weather side the sails must not be eased too much, so that she comes hard round close hauled on the new tack.

Sailing downwind

Sailing in any direction, be it close hauled or reaching, requires that the sails are trimmed and sheeted properly; going dead downwind is no exception. When the wind is well aft, the burgee will give a clear indication of the true wind (although not its strength) and is an invaluable aid to the helmsman.

Sailing off wind the headsails should be eased until they just start to lift, and then taken back in a little. If running backstays are rigged these too must be eased as they induce tension in the luffs of the headsails and, when slacked off, the jib and staysail can fill better. The backstays will foul the main and even prevent it from being eased

The cutter in the foreground is sailing downwind and has both main and topsail setting well. She could be about to gybe and is freeing off the headsails – or if she intends maintaining her course with the wind almost astern she might do better to boom out her staysail on the opposite side. *Photograph: Peter Chesworth*

off fully if they haven't been completely slacked off. In strong winds the boom can be snapped or the backstay part, both with disastrous consequences.

The main needs just as much attention. Not only must the mainsheet be freed well off but also the clew outhaul along the boom eased so that the sail bellies. If the wind is right astern you will find that the mainsail will shadow the headsails when they are all set on the same side. The staysail can be set boomed out on the opposite side to the main, and in this way all three sails will draw successfully. The wind will spill off the main on to the staysail which in turns spills on to the jib.

The main should be set on whichever side is least likely to be by-the-lee on the particular course, or the side which will be the lee side on the next tack. If the yacht is going to be on the same course for a long time, a preventer should be rigged which will stop the main from being back-winded and crashing across should a moment's distraction cause her to be caught by-the-lee. The size of the yacht will naturally dictate the strength of the preventer and whether it should be a purpose-made pennant and purchase or just comprise a handy lashing. A pennant stowed on the underside of the boom, the inboard end of which can be easily reached when the gaff is freed right off, is a sensible precaution.

Once the boat has settled upon her downwind course, the pennant is led as far forward as practicable and secured so that it can be released quickly. The pennant could be made fast with a short tail lashing or, aboard a large craft, hooked on to a light tackle so as to set it taut against the mainsheet.

In light winds and a swell the motion of the yacht will cause the boom and gaff to slat back and forth, spilling what little wind there is from the sails. The preventer working against the mainsheets will stop the boom moving, while a single vang led forward from the peak of the gaff will help steady the upper portion of the sail. In very light winds with a heavy swell, two-masted craft have the advantage, in that the gaff can be held firm by rigging a second vang or temporary preventer from the mizzen mast to hold the gaff steady or even haul it slightly to windward to improve the set of the sail.

Performance downwind can be a little frustrating when winds are light and you are not making much headway with a suit of sails which lacks the more exotic canvas like balloon jibs and so on. Even with the topsail and tow foresail it seems that you are only drifting along at perhaps a knot or so. Now is time to set some extra canvas.

The water sails, drabblers and bonnets are names given to a variety of sails which were originally cut to add area to existing sails but are now used to refer to this extra canvas. In the main this means lashing smaller sails, including perhaps storm jibs or trysails, on to the boom or a whisker pole to fill in the area between the spar and the water. The sails do not need to be light canvas; in fact the reverse is preferable because they are not cut for the purpose nor do they have proper sheeting arrangements so they rely upon the stiffness of the material to hang straight and catch the wind.

The watersail on *Ark Royal* will catch just a little extra wind once it arrives, although the helmsman is faced with the task of peering through a narrow slot. The staysail could perhaps be set boomed out on the port side in preference to the jib, as it will catch more wind, and a second water sail could be set beneath it, which would not be possible with the high cut jib boomed out. *Photograph: Peter Chesworth*

The photograph of *Ark Royal* (page 81) illustrates the technique clearly. Note that the sheet is no more than a light line just to prevent the sail billowing forward should the wind increase slightly. Another similar sail could be set beneath a whisker pole booming out the staysail on the other side. This will, however, restrict the helmsman's vision forward, as it can be seen it is almost like looking through a slit trench already!

Yachts frequently make use of this type of additional sail area when taking part in Old Gaffer Races, or on a long passage when the peace and tranquillity are too enjoyable to shatter by starting the engine. In such cases the sail under the main can be lashed on to the boom and rolled up when not in use or sailing to windward. The same can be done to a sail which will set under the whisker pole; just make sure that the lashing holding them in place is easily slipped while the boom or pole is right out and that the sheet doesn't fall into the water out of reach!

Gybing

Whenever sailing downwind with the preventers set, the helmsman has to take great care not to start sailing by-the-lee. If the sails become back-winded in a squall, the job of trying to release both vang and preventer under pressure would be very difficult and even dangerous. The alternative is not to rig them and then risk the damage, breakage or even dismasting were the boom allowed to crash across. Much depends upon the experience of the helmsman but if there is any doubt it would be better to steer a course with the wind more on the quarter rather than risk damage.

The risks of being caught by-the-lee when sailing downwind are the same as those faced when gybing, although that is a deliberate manoeuvre which should be executed fully under control. Many actions which involve an element of risk are viewed by those who have yet to experience them with unnecessary trepidation. The perceived risk in this case is that the boom will scythe across the cockpit, at least breaking gear if not decapitating the crew. It is true that if the yacht is gybed accidentally or without the helmsman appreciating the danger, then the worst could happen. The gybe does therefore require more attention than tacking, but it should not be feared or avoided; on the contrary, it is an essential manoeuvre which needs to be mastered early and if properly executed it need not be dangerous.

The objective is to alter course so that the wind is brought from one quarter to the other, which means that the boom must be brought from one beam to the other. The outboard end of the boom may pass through an arc of perhaps 160 degrees and, if allowed to do so out of control, will build up considerable momentum by the time it has completed its swing.

The strength of the wind combined with the boat's movement will necessitate the greatest attention; a roll in the wrong direction can add a lot of weight to the boom! The headsails, on the other hand, present few problems, unless they have been set boomed out, in which case the order to bring the booms inboard must be made soon enough for the crew to stow them safely. In light winds the two sails may collapse once the booms are removed but will then need minimal attention.

Once the yacht and crew are ready, the helm should be put gently to leeward to bring the stern towards the wind; at the same time the mainsheet must be hauled inboard. When the end of the boom is far enough inboard so that it is just over the quarter, pause a moment to set the running backstays; the new weather runner should be hauled taut while the lee runner is cast off and the blocks over-hauled if necessary. Then it's back to the mainsheet and tiller to continue moving the stern towards the wind. The headsail sheets should now be released if you are to continue downwind or sheeted if reaching or close hauled on the new tack.

It is the work on the mainsheet which is the most important. The ideal is that the boom should be over the rudder stock at the same moment as the wind passes from one side of the stern to the other. Provided the boom is well sheeted over the quarter, there is little risk of problems or of the boom taking control when it swings on to the new lee side. The mainsheet should then be eased away around a cleat or pin unless the wind is light, so that there is no risk of the boom taking charge until it is just clear of the lee rigging.

When the main starts to fill it must be freed off very quickly if you plan to continue sailing downwind; otherwise it will try to bring the yacht's head up towards the wind. This tendency is actually a great help if the new course is to be a reach or close hauled. The headsails, which will have been flogging, should now be tacked if it is intended to continue sailing downwind, or if you are going to boom them out again.

When the winds are light and the helmsman very confident, it's not unusual to see him leave the mainsheet made fast and just haul the whole tackle across. A warning, though; only try that when you are completely confident about the manoeuvre. The gybe should not be seen as a last-resort manoeuvre, but instead as just one of a number of tactics to be used.

To summarise: for a gybe the boat needs to be sailing steadily down with the wind on the opposite quarter to that on which the main is set. Slowly bring the wind round until it is right astern while at the same time hauling in the mainsheet so that boom and wind are on the fore and aft line at the same time. The running backstays must be changed at this point and if there is time the headsail sheets can be changed. Once the wind has passed round the stern the mainsheet must be eased away rapidly if you are going to continue downwind. Depending on how close the wind will be to the quarter the headsails can be sheeted on the lee side or boomed out on the weather bow.

CHAPTER 8

Helmsmanship

Helmsmanship is by definition more than just the competent steering or helming of a boat in differing weather conditions. It requires a higher level of skill than mere proficiency. Just about anyone can steer a boat given a few hours' practice – and can even make quite a good job of it – but that doesn't make them a helmsman. It's one thing to steer from one port to the next, but quite another to helm the boat while gaining maximum advantage from wind and weather.

So are helmsmen born or merely made? Certainly someone who is gifted with a natural feel for the boat and ability to be at one with it has a very distinct advantage. There would probably be many more good helmsmen if being gifted was the only answer but, like any skill, helmsmanship also requires a lot of practice to become really proficient.

The person who just steers probably uses only their eyes to see what's happening and responds accordingly, but the good helmsman makes use of all the senses, recalling what has gone before to anticipate what will happen next. He will have noted how the boat has risen and passed over the last few waves and so, when a slight difference is detected, will use more or less helm than previously.

It may sound obvious, but it is essential that the helmsman sits comfortably – not jammed into an awkward position – so he can give his full attention to steering. The tiller or wheel must be close by. The tiller is usually at arm's reach, the sway of the body moving it rather than muscles in the arm. The helmsman needs a clear view of the sails and also of the horizon because he will also have to keep a lookout for other craft.

The tiller should never be gripped hard unless in extreme fright! Instead, rest the hand lightly with the fingers hooked over; it is a far more comfortable way to sail than with white knuckles and is also less tiring on the arm. The same rule applies equally to heavy weather as to light airs, although a slightly firmer grip will be needed in strong winds and the extra effort on a cold, windy night helps keep you warm.

Tiller movements should be kept to the minimum. Never use more rudder angle than is necessary, as such action achieves nothing other than a faster and more violent reaction. Too much rudder angle will slow the yacht down in the same way that excessive weather helm does. When the wind is light, take your time whenever possible, even if a large alteration is required, making a wide, gentle sweep on to the new course rather than trying to spin on the spot.

As with learning to ride a bicycle, in the beginning the learner wobbles all over the place, legs and arms going every which way trying to maintain balance. It isn't very long before we stop correcting what our eyes tell us is going wrong and trust entirely

The comfortable cockpit of the yacht on page 123. All the sheets are kept on the side decks, providing a clear uncluttered working space for the crew free from any coiled cordage. The long elegant tiller is held in place with the tiller rope. The compass could be subject to magnetic error as it is mounted very close to the engine beneath the cockpit sole.
Photograph: Peter Chesworth

to our sense of balance. So with good helmsmanship, anticipation is the key: it should not be the task of the helmsman to correct what has already occurred but – so far as possible – to prevent it happening.

A yacht should be well-balanced in all but the worst conditions. This does not mean that the tiller can be left unattended but that only minimum effort is required to keep a steady course. Bad weather will of course place a greater strain upon the boat, her steering gear and the helmsman, but with sails balanced she should ride steadily.

A tendency to turn into the wind is common to most sailing craft and is a consequence of the combined reaction of hull shape and sail plan to the pressure of the wind as the boat heels. To keep the yacht sailing in a straight line and to counter this effect, the tiller is put towards the wind or 'to weather', and it is from this that we get the term 'weather helm'.

Craft which gripe or come up to windward despite weather helm are termed 'ardent': it is an undesirable characteristic to encounter in a yacht. The opposite is a yacht which falls off, an equally disagreeable feature, as it makes holding a steady course much harder as well as making it restricted in its ability to luff up in a squall. The strength of the wind and balance of the sails will determine just how much weather helm is required. It is also a matter of personal preference: what one owner finds totally acceptable another may spend weeks and vast sums of money trying to eliminate. Its existence is however a desirable safety feature in a cruising yacht and is usually included at the design stage.

Steering gear

The ease with which a yacht can be steered will not only depend upon her balance and inherent weather helm. The steering gear is just as important and should, like all efficient machines, convert minimal input into maximum effect. This depends not only on a smooth transfer of the instruction from tiller or wheel to the rudder but also the manner in which the rudder is designed and hung on the hull itself.

Friction in the bearings, gears and pintles must be minimal, while the shape of the rudder blade must encourage the free flow of water across its surface. It is very important that the steering gear should communicate both ways between rudder and tiller or wheel, moving the rudder in accordance with the helmsman's instructions and feeding back a sense of the forces acting on the rudder blade.

The need for the steering gear to be both sensitive and powerful imposes a number of constraints upon its design. Ideally, whenever the wheel or tiller is moved one way or the other the rudder will stay at that angle, but it is important that this is not achieved through friction or stiffness in the system.

Designs common to older yachts raked the sternpost, but often this raking causes the tiller to flop to one side or the other. One method of correcting this fault is to fix small vanes to the rudder which disrupt the flow of water across it and try to balance the rudder amidships. Another method which has been used is to place balance weights on the after edge of the rudder, although I suspect that this includes elements of the first solution.

Walk along the pontoons of any marina and you will find that an increasing number of craft are now equipped with wheel rather than tiller steering. A wheel has obvious advantages, especially as the size of the yacht increases, and it is also well suited to racing when small, precise amounts of rudder can be applied. Anyone seriously starting to sail, though, should learn the basics with a tiller before transferring to a wheel. The reasons may not always be apparent to the beginner but

An iron tiller held firmly in place on board a classic yawl by brass pins in a tidy tiller rack; useful in port to stop the rudder and steering gear slamming back and forth, at sea when the sails are well balanced and there is no autohelm, or when just lying hove-to.

The mizzen mast apron is obviously new and the cover plate can be clearly seen screwed over the canvas into the afterdeck. The mizzen sheet is fed through the block on the bumkin to a jammer on the left of the picture. *Photograph: Peter Chesworth*

probably the most important is that the wheel lacks feel or response. The gearing reduces the effort needed to maintain course, and a wheel can also hide the fact that the yacht is 'hard-mouthed'.

I sailed one yacht upon which the owner had lavished much care and a very substantial amount of money. It sailed well but had one of the worst wheel-steering systems that I have ever come across, lacking any feel or sensitivity. I have steered ships which were more responsive; it was impossible to tell whether the wheel was hard over or amidships. The result was a very disappointing sail and an owner whose helmsmanship could easily deteriorate instead of improving.

The combination of the modern naval architect with his computer and his forebears with their experience should have eliminated the risk of unpleasant steering characteristics. Why then are there still problems?

One reason is that some older yachts have had their rig altered or modified by a succession of owners, not always successfully. One owner I know built a large sloop from a set of plans, but found she wouldn't sail until he added a couple of extra tons to the keel. Indeed some craft don't have any plans in the true sense of the word, being just an idea in their builder's head!

The late Eric Hiscock, who is probably better known than any other cruising yachtsman, had a yacht designed for him which was very difficult to steer. Considerable inconvenience and not inconsiderable sums of money later, another designer reshaped the sternpost and rudder as the only way to improve the situation.

It is important to recognise the symptoms before you accept the financial responsibility for putting things right. A wheel can be used to disguise poor steering, so question why wheel steering has been fitted if it was not part of the original equipment. And beware answers that indicate that it was to eliminate a lot of effort. Wheels should not be avoided like the plague, but a poor tiller is much easier to replace than a bad wheel steering system.

Whatever is used to steer the yacht it should be viewed as an extra sense, telling the helmsman much of what he needs to know about the way the boat is performing. Usually there will be a little weather helm so that the tiller can be pulled rather than pushed when sitting to weather.

The effects of ballast

When a yacht is well balanced for sailing, the centre of effort of hull and sails lies in line, one above the other. This centre of effort is offset to one side of the hull when the yacht heels, which then causes the yacht to turn into wind, because the forward motion from the sails is slowed by the resistance of the hull through the water.

If the boat is trimmed either by the bow or the stern, these centres of effort get out of line. A yacht which is down by the bow will tend to round up into the wind; if she is trimmed by the stern she may be difficult to tack. I experienced an extreme example of this when sailing under fully reefed main, plus jib and staysail, in some local racing. The conditions were lively and, to get the most from the boat, the crew decided that they were going to increase our performance by sitting on the weather rail to keep her as upright as possible. Not the sort of behaviour to be expected aboard a gaffer, but they enjoyed themselves to start with!

Despite the reduced sail, we still managed to fill the cockpit on a number of occasions but it soon drained away without too much fuss. The wind increased as the race progressed, forcing the crew to leave the rail to keep clear of the thrashing sails each time we tacked. They returned to the cockpit and helped with the sheets.

Each time we tacked it was becoming increasingly difficult to do so, taking several attempts to get the bows through the wind. The urgency increased as we were heading towards a very hard shoreline which tended to focus the mind almost to the point of giving up and starting the engine, but we managed finally and headed to the finish. Afterwards I discovered that there was water in the engine compartment, the two cockpit lockers and down below under one of the bunks! It didn't take too long to pump out and confirm that it had got below when the cockpit filled. No wonder it drained away so quickly – only a little was going over the side.

Weight was the cause of our tacking problem: not only was the water trimming the boat quite significantly by the stern, but so also was the large crew by coming aft. The result was that I had very severe lee helm which had been disguised by the strong wind. This illustrates the effect that weight can have upon the way a yacht handles and gives a clue on how any undesirable characteristics might be eliminated or reduced.

Ballast and trim

The helmsman has to balance the craft in the prevailing conditions, so the more that he can do beforehand to self-balance the forces acting on his craft, the easier she will be to handle. Where to start is almost a chicken-and-egg problem, so in the first instance it is probably best to assume that the sail plan is correct. Trimming the hull will therefore come first because once done it should not need to be repeated. The best advice is to trim the hull and balance the helm with all the sails drawing well so that at least all the factors under your control are constant. Once the hull seems to balance then work on the sails. It may be necessary to repeat the cycle a number of times before everything is satisfactory.

A boat will normally be trimmed by the builder when she is first launched and all that an owner will be required to do is to make minor adjustments to the internal ballast to compensate for extra or particularly heavy gear. Many owners retain a record of the internal ballast, numbering each pig and listing its position in the bilges as the ballast should be removed every time the boat spends the winter ashore.

Modern yachts encapsulate the ballast within the keel, but the older designs often have it bolted on to the foot of the keel and movable ballast inside the hull. The position of this ballast can make a considerable difference to the yacht's performance even though the vessel may be floating on her marks. To take an extreme, all the ballast could be in two large piles at the bow and stern, or alternatively in a single large heap in the mid-sections. The fast racing yacht usually performs better with light ends and all the ballast amidships, but aboard the cruiser it is not so crucial.

A new owner who takes over his boat at the beginning of the season may have no way of knowing whether the ballast was stowed correctly until he takes to the water. However, never move internal ballast until you are certain of what you are trying to achieve and what the likely effect will be. The decision to shift ballast should be made only after an assessment of the boat's performance with all the normal gear stowed on board, together with full fuel and water tanks. Nothing could be more frustrating than shifting several hundredweight of dirty ballast only to find that the addition of 30 fathoms of chain and a large anchor forward has destroyed all your calculations. So first take her for a sail in a variety of wind strengths to see how she sails and don't forget when evaluating the possible effect of ballast movements that changes in crew position and gear will also have an effect. In a strong breeze it's a common sight to see the crew shivering along the weather rail when beating to windward, as is a cluster of bodies aft when sailing downwind. A light breeze should see the crew in the lee shrouds, trimming the yacht slightly by the bow and to leeward.

Once you have sailed her a few times and are satisfied that the sails have been trimmed properly yet she still does not feel quite right, then there is a basic rule to follow in deciding whether to relocate lumps of pig-iron. The yacht which is hard-mouthed and requires large amounts of weather helm to prevent her flying up into the wind needs to be trimmed more by the stern. This may mean that ballast must be moved from forward to midships or from midships to aft. The reverse of this rule applies to yachts which carry lee helm and are reluctant to tack and pay off readily.

Moving only small quantities of ballast can produce quite significant changes in weather helm and even overall performance so the rule is to move a little at a time. Repeat the procedure until she feels right.

Trimming the sails

Ignoring for a moment the effect of waves upon a yacht, and that the wind is never a steady, constant force, a yacht will sail in a straight line once the right amount of weather helm has been applied. If the task of steering a steady course is to be accomplished successfully, then the helmsman has to learn to anticipate what is going to happen, and will make the necessary corrective movements of the tiller by instinct.

It should soon become apparent that a yacht develops a rhythmic movement as she sails in a seaway, and the good helmsman must become part of that rhythm. Once the synchronisation is lost then instead of gliding over each wave the yacht will lose her fluency and start crashing into each oncoming wave or tumbling over its crest.

Once the hull balance has been refined as much as possible it's time to practise trimming the sails. The yacht should by this time respond quickly to helm orders, coming up towards the wind as soon as the tiller is put down to leeward or paying off when the tiller is moved to weather. Balancing the sails can be a much harder task, once the optimum hull balance has been achieved. One moment everything is going well and next the yacht is sailing like a leaky barrel. There can be few hard and fast rules for trimming the sails as, rather than being separate, they all inter-react; therefore the first problem is to discover which one is not performing efficiently.

When trimming sail it is essential that adjustments to the sheets are done slowly, so that there is time to evaluate their success or otherwise. Unless the yacht is quite small, crew members will tend the sheets and relay information to the helmsman. Until the whole crew is well practised they must never adjust the sheets without telling the helm what they are doing. It is important too that crew relay information to the helmsman about what they can see, especially when he is unsighted. In the early stages the visual information available to the helmsman will take preference over anything else, but as his skills develop other factors are included.

The first task is to make sure that there is plenty of sea room in which to carry out the adjustments. It is annoying to keep having to tack due to lack of space or because a fleet of optimists are out on a training sail. Next lay a course to windward to check visually that all the sails are drawing and filling, before seeing how well the yacht responds to her helm.

Once settled on the course, see if the boat starts to round up as she should and that it takes only a slight pull on the tiller to weather to keep her steady. If so, then the weather helm is acceptable. Flying up towards the wind indicates two things: either that the main is set too flat or that the headsails – the jib in particular – aren't working enough. Start by freeing the mainsheet slightly to see if this eases the helm without spoiling the set of the main. Then, if this is not enough or doesn't cure the problem, sheet in the jib making sure that it does not back-wind the staysail. Don't flatten the jib too much as it will lose its drive. Continue making one small adjustment at a time and give yourself plenty of time to evaluate each; continuous tweaking will have disastrous results.

Steering

The demands of helming to windward are very different from those of running downwind, especially if there is also a sea running. A heavy sea can be hard work, as the rudder will require constant attention if a safe and comfortable passage is to be completed. Running downwind in a seaway requires the greatest effort, with the helmsman's arm sawing back and forth across the cockpit. The movement of the tiller early enough, almost before the yacht has started to sheer one way or the other, will achieve as much if not more than substantial angles of rudder applied too late, and all at less physical cost to the helmsman.

The beat against the wind is likely to be cold and uncomfortable, with spray or even bucketfuls of salt water across the deck. As the yacht forges her way through each sea, there will be occasions when the pressure upon the rudder is such that just for a brief moment the tiller will take charge if allowed to do so. The tendency will be for it to fly to leeward, returning amidships or even coming up to windward before settling again. The experienced helmsman will quickly recognise this tendency and won't try to counter or check the movement. Instead, the boat should be allowed to have its head, and to find its own way over the seas – with a reduction in wear on both steering gear and helmsman!

The modern Autohelm has its own important part to play, although it must be remembered that heavier wooden boats may require greater power from their pilot than equivalent sized GRP craft. My 28 footer, for example, uses the largest tiller pilot supplied by Autohelm, the ST4000, which works very well. It is responsive, working efficiently and quickly even when going downwind which has always been the biggest problem for automatic pilots. The only problem with the pilot is that its very versatility means that it can be used in almost any situation, consequently starving people of steering practice. Steering is, after all, a skill which once learnt should never be allowed to fall into disuse. You may be able to teach a crew member how to steer, but his only chance to become a helmsman will be after plenty of practice.

The person on the helm has a very important part to play in the navigation of the yacht, especially during a long passage or when positions are difficult to acquire. The navigator will lay a course, and from then on it's up to everyone steering to keep as close to that course as possible. The task of holding a course is not one of rigidly keeping the bow fixed on one compass heading; that is not possible for more than a few moments at a time. It is to ensure that, so far as possible, the bow oscillates equally either side of the course.

So how closely can the helmsman follow the course that has been set him? There are two principal factors; neither is under his control, but one is constant and the other variable. The constant is the configuration of the hull and the yacht's perfor- mance under sail: it must be assumed that the boat is being sailed competently even if not to its theoretical maximum.

If there is any tendency for a yacht to turn from her course it should be to windward rather than to leeward, so that weather helm is experienced. A yacht which carries a large amount of weather helm will sail more slowly than one which has none or only a little weather helm because the large rudder angle has a braking effect as the hull moves through the water. Quite considerable physical demands can be made upon the helmsman due to the effort needed to hold the tiller over against the pressure of water passing across the rudder blade. The practised helmsman will use the pull on the tiller caused by weather helm to help him maintain his course, increasing or decreasing to counter the sudden movements of the boat fed back through the rudder.

If all things were equal then a yacht's track over the ground would be slightly to windward of the course line because the bow would point up due to weather helm. In practice the story is different, and the resulting track is in the opposite direction due to the sideways movement or leeway of the vessel. I have heard it suggested that a good helmsman will compensate for leeway; for example if the yacht wanders off course to port he will correct by the same amount to starboard.

Without debating the slight increases and decreases in speed due to sailing free or harder on the wind, it is asking too much of anyone steering to be able to judge divergencies that will last no more than a short while. The effects of leeway are always important; but it is, after all, on long offshore passages lacking external references that it becomes really significant. As no two people steer alike, never mind compensate for off-course errors, it is far better to leave the navigator to do his job and just concentrate on steering the course asked for.

To start with, even staring at the compass can produce all sorts of problems, especially at night, when the binnacle light has an almost hypnotic effect. So to steer well requires all the senses. The first, of course, is sight, but this must be used in close conjunction with balance.

How best then to steer, especially aboard a long-keeled classic yacht which can feel much heavier on the helm than it perhaps should be? Balance the boat as best you can by adjusting, where possible, ballast and stowage of the heavier items of equipment. Always make sure that the sails are trimmed to full advantage. Try not to fight the tiller, especially when there is plenty of motion. However, if the only solution is to modify the rig, the cut of the sails, or to make even more radical changes to the ballast distribution, then these might not be possible in the short term. One answer to heavy steering is the tiller rope.

The tiller rope

There can be times when your arms need help of some sort when working the tiller. The trading craft which plied the European coast – schooner, ketch, barge or trawler – all used a relieving tackle on the tiller. Our present-day yachts may not need the power of blocks, but a length of soft line slightly longer than the cockpit's width can be invaluable. The softness is to minimise any scoring of the tiller by the rope, while the diameter of line will be down to personal preference depending upon what is most comfortable in the helmsman's hand: a braid line of 6 mm–8 mm should be about right. Apart from the obvious use in lashing the tiller in port, the tiller rope can relieve the helmsman in two ways.

Firstly it can be used to lash the tiller when under way and when there is little or no sea to push the bow off course while the yacht is sailing in a steady breeze. In light weather the ends of the tiller rope should be secured as though in port, except that one or two turns are taken around the tiller. Provided that there is some slackness this will allow a slight see-sawing of the tiller whenever the yacht is under way: the friction of the rope turns will prevent the tiller moving too far. By resting his hand on the turns the helmsman can roll or twist the rope around the tiller so that any alterations or corrections can be made.

The tiller rope can also be used as a simple purchase to work the tiller, relieving the arm muscles of some of the strain. The combined effects of wind and sea during poor conditions often cause an increase in weather helm which can be quite pronounced. Under these circumstances the tiller rope can be used to reduce the strain on the forearm. One end is made fast on the same side as the helmsman while the other end is kept in hand with the weight of the tiller taken on the rope rather than the arm. A simple purchase is made, so reducing the effort needed to hold the tiller steady or haul it to weather.

The long-keeled yacht tends to maintain her directional stability far better than her modern fin-keeled sisters, but when an alteration in course is needed don't expect her to spin on sixpence. The strength of the wind will determine how much effort the helmsman needs to steer. Light winds require a very delicate touch on the tiller so that speed is not lost by excessive use of the rudder. Consequently alterations to course must be made smoothly with the tiller eased gently across, so that you are almost coaxing the yacht round on to the new course.

There are three things to remember when steering a yacht. Have a gentle touch, make as few rudder movements as possible, and use the minimum effort when you do have to move the tiller.

CHAPTER 9

━━━━━━

Mooring

Before looking at the best ways to return to a mooring – or coming to anchor for that matter – it is worth spending a little time examining the type of gear required. Starting with the mooring, this may be either your own property or provided and laid by the harbour authority or yacht harbour.

Making use of the harbour authority mooring releases the owner from the tiresome and dirty task of checking the gear at the beginning of each season. Against this must be set the annual cost of harbour dues which may be much higher; and the likely restrictions imposed by the terms and conditions of the licence or lease. One example is that local authorities frequently prohibit owners from reassigning their mooring when selling the boat. Consequently, owning the ground tackle usually means greater freedom and a lower licence fee, but periodic high replacement costs if the gear is to be maintained in peak condition.

The mooring can be of two types: either the boat is made fast to a bridle secured to a support buoy, or to a chain which lies on the harbour bottom until recovered by a pickup buoy. The former is suitable for almost any size of craft since the buoy takes the weight of the mooring chain. The latter is suitable only for smaller boats since it is limited by the weight – due either to the size of chain or depth of water – which has to be lifted from the bed each time.

The mooring

The simple buoyed mooring has five constituent parts: anchor or sinker, riser chain, buoy, bridle and pickup buoy. The choice between anchor or sinker is dictated by the consistency of the bottom and the conditions in general. The anchor may be one of a variety of differing types – purpose-made or modified – while the sinker will depend upon bottom density and materials available. Large granite or concrete blocks are common where, even at low water springs, there is no danger of the yacht grounding on them.

The riser chain may be in three sections, depending upon the nature of the bottom, the tidal range, and the size of boat. The portion of the riser which spends all its time lying along the bottom should be much heavier; old ship's cable is ideal because it can withstand the considerable abrasion. This section is called the thrasher because of the way in which it is dragged across the bottom in bad weather. The remainder of the riser should be heavy galvanised chain with a large swivel fitted at a point which will never touch bottom. This prevents the mooring becoming weakened by twisting and it may be a means of linking different cable sizes, with the lower, heavier one touching bottom at low water springs. When there is only little tidal rise the thresher can be longer and the swivel fitted below the buoy.

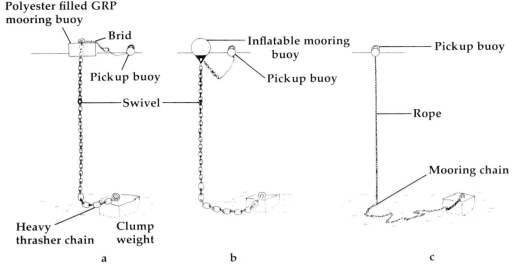

FIG 21 Three types of mooring: (a) and (b) are heavy deep water moorings with the mooring chain supported from a buoy, while c is a common method of providing visitors' moorings for lighter weight craft. In (a) and (b) the mooring is secured to a heavy clump weight buried in the harbour bed by a short length of very heavy chain to take the wear across the bed. The riser chain is often split by a swivel, which will still be clear of the bottom at low water springs. The support buoy can be either a Hippo type solid buoy or one of the inflatable type. The Hippo has the advantage that chain passes through its centre and so will not sink if vandalised or punctured. In (c) the chain remains on the bottom until the buoy is picked up, which cuts down the daily wear from tidal movement. The buoy and rope are brought on deck and the chain is made fast around the sampson post. The only problem with this system is the large quantity of weed, mud and small creatures which invariably come aboard with the gear.

The mooring buoy should be designed for the job, and not a couple of plastic cans lashed together; use either the inflatable buff or polystyrene, encased in fibreglass. I prefer the unsinkable GRP/polystyrene buoy in place of the buff which will leak and sink due to age or damage. The Hippo style buoy only supports, and its own strength is not an integral link in the mooring, because the boat is secured to the riser chain which passes up through the centre of the buoy.

Due to its exposed position the bridle is the most vulnerable part of the mooring and regardless of which material is chosen they each have their drawbacks. Rope must be leaded or weighted; if left floating it will foul passing propellers, while chain will corrode quickly because it is constantly in and out of the water.

The manner in which the yacht is secured to the buoy depends upon how the bridle is made up and made fast. The inflatable buoy usually has the riser and bridle hanging down below, so needs a pickup buoy to be recovered. Some of the inflatable buoys have a steel bar up through the centre with a large ring on top; the boat's painter is passed through this ring and back aboard.

The GRP/polystyrene buoy should have the bridle lying across its upper surface which may not need a pickup buoy, although it is prudent to have one. Finally the bridle has to be made fast on board, usually through the bow fairleads or roller on to the sampson post or cleats. Alternatively chain bridle can be hooked on to the bottom eye of the bobstay, which reduces wear and stops the bridle noisily fouling the bobstay as the boat swings to and fro.

The rope from the pickup buoy should be a heavy nylon or braided polyester and used as a back-up for the main bridle. It is not usually subject to wear since it never takes any of the weight (unless the bridle parts) and therefore should be in good

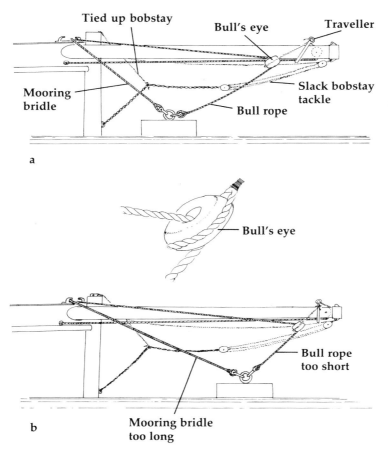

FIG 22 A typical mooring arrangement (a) for a cutter with long bowsprit where the bobstay is liable to foul the mooring buoy. The craft is moored in the normal way with the addition of a second lighter warp lead through a hardwood bull's eye hauled out to the end of the bowsprit on the traveller. As the boat will always lie to the greatest pressure the weight will always be on the mooring bridle. There is one exception (b). If the bridle is left too long and the bull rope too short, the full weight of the mooring will hang off the end of the bowsprit end when the end lifts if the boat should pitch in a swell. So be warned.

condition. The pickup buoy needs to be a bright colour, kept clean so that it is easily visible, and have a large eye on top so that it is easy to recover with a boat hook.

Some situations or harbour authorities require very large mooring buoys, which will foul under the bobstay. One answer is of course to release the bobstay but this isn't always possible; neither can the boat be allowed to ride to an extra long bridle. The answer is to rig a bull rope between the buoy and end of the bowsprit in addition to the bridle. This gets its name from the bull's eye which is probably the best method of reeving the rope.

A bull rope is an additional rope mooring bridle which is rigged from the fore deck through a bull's eye secured at the end of the bowsprit and then made fast to the mooring buoy. Its task is to keep the mooring buoy clear of the bow at all times and prevent the bobstay becoming entangled. If there isn't sufficient room to keep the bull rope rigged all the time the bull's eye can be run out along the bowsprit on the jib traveller. The bowsprit is not subject to excessive strain as the yacht will always lie downstream or downwind of the buoy so the bull rope only stops the tendency to surge forward rather than take the full weight of the boat.

Drying moorings

Drying moorings are encountered in many harbours. Craft may be on either single-point swinging moorings or moored fore-and-aft, but what is often forgotten is the additional load imposed on such moorings. Now the catenary principle (see page 105) is accepted by most small craft sailors, they think that the same rule can be applied to a drying mooring. However, like all such things there is an exception to the rule, because a yacht which regularly goes aground when lying either to its anchor or mooring is at far greater risk of parting her mooring cable. The recommended size of mooring chain used by most owners does not take account of the additional loads imposed when the yacht is rising and falling as she takes the ground or is just coming afloat.

The size of chain selected for a mooring should be more substantial than that chosen for the ground tackle which is inadequate. The reason is that it is solely the holding power of the mooring system and strength of chain which keeps the boat safe. The catenary of a yacht which is aground either at anchor or on her mooring is the smallest possible. It is during the short period when the boat is taking the ground or is coming off that she is at greatest risk. The cable lies stretched out ahead of the boat which starts to lift and bounce off the bottom, moving slightly astern and bringing the cable up until it is bar-taut. A trough in the sand which is deeper than the surrounding bed or the keel landing on a high spot will be enough to cause the boat to topple slightly, so that her full weight will act on the cable. Something is almost bound to break; if it is not, the chain itself then one of the shackles or even the deck cleat are likely weak points.

The rule for calculating the breaking strain for chain is to square the number of 16ths in the diameter and then divide them by 10. A typical modern 30 footer will weigh much more than the 2.5 ton breaking strain of her 5/16 in (8 mm) chain anchor cable. The wooden classic yacht built 50 or more years ago will be even heavier than her modern counterpart; her cable may be even more likely to snap like a carrot given the chance. For example my Heard 28 has a displacement of around 8 tons and would therefore require a minimum mooring chain of 9/16 in (14 mm) to give a breaking strain of 8.1 tons – ¾ in (19 mm) would be a much safer choice at 14.4 tons.

Returning to the mooring

It's comparatively simple getting under way from a mooring or anchorage under sail or, if the area is congested, under engine. Returning to the mooring or anchorage can be a totally different matter, particularly if for whatever reason the engine is out of action and the manoeuvre has to be done under sail.

Anticipating the worst, there is every reason to practise the methods before being forced into trying to moor with everything conspiring against you. It's the same elements which cause problems leaving as when arriving – with one major difference. When departing it's essential to gain speed so as to manoeuvre; when arriving, on the other hand, it's stopping in the desired location that's the biggest problem.

When tacking, a boat continues to move forward after the sails have ceased to drive her, but the boat will slow and finally stop altogether if she is kept pointing into the wind. These two phenomena can be used to advantage when approaching the mooring buoy or point in which it is intended to drop anchor.

With a mooring you do at least have something to aim for, but anchoring demands two objectives neither of which is visible! The first is the desired position in which

Just returned to a mooring with plenty of room around to make the approach under sail. The headsails have been let fly and the main scandalised on the topping lift. If you have an engine running take care in case the jib sheet trails over the side as in the photograph; it could easily foul the prop.

The singlehanded helmsman has just recovered the mooring and still has the boat hook under his arm; he is fortunate to have a sampson post sited well forward around which to catch a turn. *Photograph: Peter Chesworth*

the boat is to lie, and the second is where to drop the anchor to achieve this. Preparation is the clue to success whether picking up a buoy or dropping the anchor.

I believe that picking up a mooring is the easier operation, although anchoring is probably the most forgiving of the two manoeuvres; although if you drop your anchor aboard a neighbouring tender, or end up with the hook in deep water while your stern is on the mud you will not convince anybody that it was your intended course of action!

Few owners have to resort to keeping the yacht on an anchor throughout the season, so it's more common for a mooring to be picked up at the end of a day's sailing. The problem in recovering a mooring is that, unless an isolated buoy can be found on which to practise, the first efforts could be rather public.

Anyone can pick up a mooring buoy provided they sail close enough, but keeping hold of it can be a very different matter. Sailing at speed towards the buoy in the hope of a spectacular arrival will probably end in the equally dramatic departure of he who grabs the buoy!

In the same way that the wind and tide in particular can be used to help get under way, so they can help the final close approach to the buoy. Ideally the approach speed should be just enough to maintain steerage way without the risk of losing control, before finally stopping with the mooring buoy just under the bow. Anticipation is the key to a successful conclusion, not only in terms of handling your boat but also in observing the activity and influence of the elements around the mooring. To know the directions of wind and tide are obvious, but so too is knowing the way in which adjacent craft are lying, as this will have a direct bearing on the direction in which the buoy should be approached.

The halyards must all be readied for a quick lowering, and the slack on the main topping-lift taken up just enough so that it doesn't girt the sail. Reducing the total sail area may be the best way of keeping speed down to manageable proportions, and the number of sails controllable; certainly the topsail should be lowered. Where practical it is best that any sails that are not required should be lowered in advance to save trying to do it at the last moment.

It might be thought that approaching a mooring in harbour would be easier than doing so in a river or creek, but both present their own problems. The harbour is congested and liable to have six or more parallel trots all full of boats which may make a direct approach difficult. The river on the other hand is probably narrow and manoeuvring space is limited to up- or downstream, although it may only have two or three trots either side of the main channel.

I will assume that the moorings that have to be picked up are lying in a river or similar tidal stream although the rules apply equally to a harbour. The harbour-based owner will have more scope to choose a favourable direction of approach even though he might have to thread a passage through many moorings.

Beating – wind against tide

This is probably the simplest approach provided that neither wind nor tide is too strong and being deep-drafted the boat will be tide-rode on the mooring. Beat up with the tide until just past the mooring when the mainsail should be lowered as the boat is brought round to run before the wind towards the mooring. She will be stemming the tide and this will help to slow her progress; free the sheets of one or both headsails if she is still too fast. When the buoy is just ahead and you are sure that she will carry her way up to the buoy then quickly furl or lower the sails while the mooring is picked up. Then stow both headsails quickly so that they don't flog.

If the wind is very light and you are unable to stem the tide then the main need not be lowered until you pick up the mooring when it should be scandalised. If the main has already been lowered and you realise she won't reach her mooring, raise the mainsail peak gradually until it provides just enough drive.

Beating – wind and tide together

Picking up a mooring under these conditions has much in its favour as all the sails remain set because you will be lying to wind and tide. The yacht is tacked towards the mooring so that when she is luffed up head-to-wind she will lose her way next to the buoy. The distance off when the boat is luffed will depend upon her speed through the water, and this will only be deduced from a good deal of practice. It is probably better to be going slightly too fast rather than too slow, because a modest speed gives control: by losing way control could be lost and not regained before a collision occurs. If sailing too fast to pick up the mooring then you have the option of going round and making a second approach. Once secured the sails can be lowered and stowed.

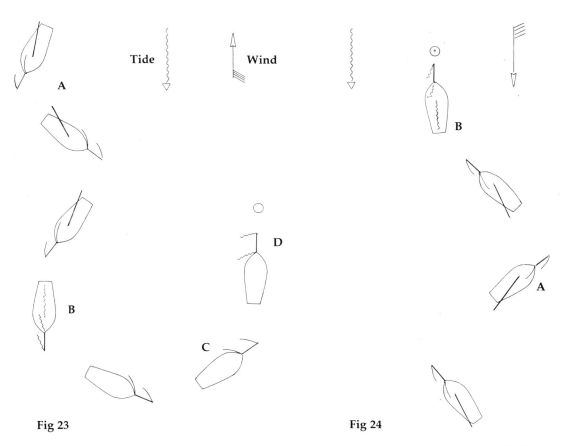

Fig 23

Fig 24

FIG 23 Picking up a mooring with wind and against tide. Tack towards the mooring (A) until it is just past the beam, when the mainsail should be lowered (B), before turning to run under headsail alone (C) towards the mooring. As the buoy is approached, free or even lower the headsails to reduce speed against the tide next to the buoy.

FIG 24 Approaching the mooring against wind and tide requires only that the boat is tacked up towards the buoy (A) before luffing up just downwind and carrying way to the mooring (B).

Running with wind and tide

When running downwind with the tide under you, you will be making a good speed and may need to reduce sail area so long as when finally rounding up to the buoy you carry enough way to reach it. Sail downwind: the yacht should pass the mooring to leeward before beginning to round up luffing and so approach the mooring.

This approach requires more practice than either of the previous ones as the manoeuvre to round quickly up into the wind and on to the buoy leaves you committed to picking up the buoy or bearing away to regain control if the buoy is either passed or cannot be reached.

Wind across the tide

Before making the approach the helmsman must decide whether his boat is going to lie wind- or tide-rode to the buoy once it is secure. If wrongly executed, the boat will swing as soon as the buoy is picked up with possible serious consequences to itself and adjacent craft.

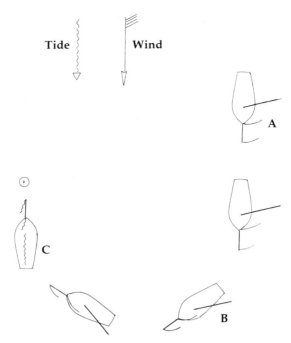

FIG 25 When wind and tide are together and the approach has to be downwind, sail downwind (A) until the mooring is past the beam before hauling in and sailing close hauled up towards the buoy (B). As the buoy is approached, luff up to take the way off and pick up the buoy (C).

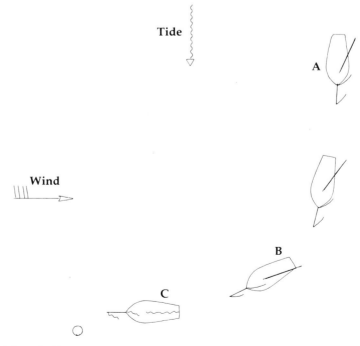

FIG 26 Should the wind be across the tide and the boat is to be wind-rode, approach with tide under you and reach across the wind to leeward of the mooring until the buoy can just be reached closed hauled (A). Alter course and point just up tide of the buoy, keeping it on the lee side (B). As soon as it is close under the lee bow luff up (C) to allow the tide to carry you down towards the buoy.

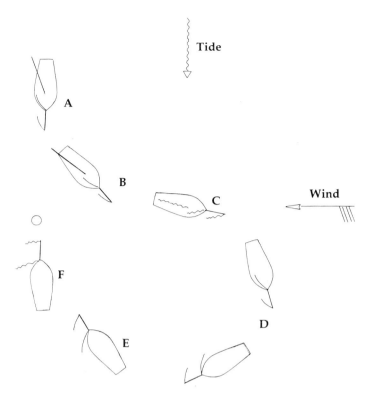

FIG 27 When the yacht is to be tide-rode the approach can either be made by reaching slowly up against the tide or downtide. Sail downtide towards the buoy (A) until just before reaching the buoy, then luff up (B) and lower the main (C). Now bear away and run down to gybe the headsails and reach against the tide towards the buoy, freeing the sheets to slow down as the buoy is approached.

A boat that is to be wind-rode may have to make her approach either with or against the tide to do so. Stemming the tide is obviously preferable as full control can be retained at a much slower speed. Start to leeward of the buoy and beam reach steadily towards a point two or three boat-lengths to leeward of it, then luff up to the buoy while freeing the sheets. Take care to adjust the speed so that you do not reach the buoy going too fast for the fore deck crew to hold on to the buoy.

When the boat is to be tide-rode then the approach can also be made with or against the tide. When the boat can stem the tide under headsails then she should reach against the tide; release the sheets as soon as she will carry her way to the buoy. The sails must be lowered or stowed immediately to stop her trying to sail round the mooring.

When the only way to reach the mooring is downtide, start under full sail until just before the mooring is reached, when the boat must be luffed up and the mainsail dropped. Quickly bear away again to gybe the headsail while rounding up on to the buoy. This method requires room and experience, not least to douse the mainsail quickly.

CHAPTER 10

Anchoring

The choice of which anchor and cable to use is probably the subject of more heated discussion than any other item of sailing equipment. A small yacht floating trimmed by the head with her marks covered is a sure sign of an owner who has yet to make up his mind and has one of each type of anchor on board!

Unless unlimited space is available the choice of anchor is often dictated by its size and intended stowage as much as by personal preference. Larger traditional craft may well have a cathead on either bow from which to hang the anchor, so for them stowage is not difficult, but for a yacht it can be a problem.

It is stowage which has led to the current practice of having a small, lightweight anchor for brief midday stops often referred to as a 'lunch pick', which aptly describes its intended use. Unfortunately in many cases it has now found its way on to the fore deck in place of the proper heavy-duty ground tackle because it is easier to recover. The anchor may be a means of keeping the boat in one piece while the crew enjoy a light lunch but this is not its prime function. The ground tackle has to serve as a portable mooring, suitable for almost all weathers, and when all else fails it must become a brake, so it must be ready for release at a moment's notice. Your principal anchor ought not therefore be kept stowed in a cockpit locker or, worse, down below.

Anchors can be divided into three groups: fixed anchors, like the Delta or Bruce types; CQR and other ploughs; and those which collapse or stow flat, of which the Fisherman's and Danforth (or cruising anchor) are two examples. During the early part of this century the universal anchor was the Admiralty pattern and its variants. Heavy and very difficult to stow on deck because the stock seemed designed to catch the jib and staysail sheets, it does however have good holding qualities. The problems which were due in the main to the fixed stock were only partly cured by the collapsible Fisherman's anchor.

During the late 1930s Taylor's revolutionary CQR, with its swivelled plough blade, dispensed with a stock and claimed better holding power for less weight. It was soon a success. Like its more recent competitor the Bruce, and similar one-piece cast anchors, it could be self-stowed on large bow rollers, though these are not always compatible with a rigged bowsprit. The American-inspired plank bowsprit overcomes this problem, allowing even the more extreme of modern anchor designs to be self-stowing and out of the way of sheets and canvas.

Different types of anchor claim various advantages over their competitors, but the heavy traditional yacht often lacks the space to stow some of the more modern designs. The decision about what type of anchor to use will therefore tend to be governed by the available stowage, the expected holding ground and whether the type of cable will be chain or rope.

It is prudent to carry two anchors, a principal or bower anchor and a secondary or kedge. Ideally they should be different types so that most eventualities can be dealt with. The bower anchor should be heavier and suitable for anchoring in the usual cruising area, while the kedge must cope with other bottom conditions.

The CQR provides good all-round holding in seabeds that are clear, be they sand, mud or even rock. They do suffer from rapidly becoming fouled by weed when first trying to dig in and therefore failing to bury in and grip. A rule of thumb based upon the standard CQR sizes suggests that the bower anchor should be 1 lb for every 1 ft of length and the kedge weighing 75% of the bower.

The Fisherman's anchor is probably the most versatile of the anchors, ideal for rock, penetrating through thick weed or kelp, and even holding well in hard sand and mud. It is not so good, however, in loose sand, shingle or ooze, where it lacks palm size for holding power. The suggested size rule for the Fisherman's anchor is 1½ lbs for every foot of length.

The Danforth or Meon are commonly referred to as sand anchors, although they hold equally well in mud and because of the stock have good burying properties. Sizes should be governed by the same rule as for the CQR.

It is often claimed that the Bruce or Delta types can be significantly lighter than their equivalents; the Bruce is also said to retain high holding power on a comparatively short scope. It does seem to work well in most seabed conditions including rock. The manufacturers produce detailed tables giving advice on what size to choose but so far as heavy traditional craft are concerned I would tend to go at least one size over that suggested.

The type of cable is just as important a part of the ground tackle as is the anchor. It is not enough simply to load the chain down into a locker and forget about it until needed or leave a long coil of rope in the bottom of a locker. The chain locker needs to be self-draining and easy to clean because if mud, sand, weed and crystalline salt are allowed to build up and are then gently mixed with sea water the resulting brew will play havoc with the chain. If rope is chosen it must not be allowed to lie damp, muddy and uncared for underneath fenders, spare cans of fuel, etc but be dried out and ready for immediate use.

Rope or chain?

It is probably better to decide on which type of cable to use before selecting the type and size of anchor. A chain will have more than enough weight to induce a catenary; on the other hand nylon or multi-plat rope compensate for lack of weight by using their elasticity and a greater length.

As the size and weight of the boat increases, so the freedom of choice decreases: certainly for any craft over 25 feet planning to spend nights at anchor rather than in a marina the chain is the only sure answer. As the weight of the chain is a significant factor in the ground tackle's holding power then short link should be used in preference to long link chain as it is around 25% heavier for any given length.

Chain cable should always be galvanised rather than self-coloured to increase its working life as well as improving its handling qualities. The mud that comes on board is bad enough without adding rust to the mixture.

When you do have to use rope anchor cable then current advice is that laid nylon or anchor plat is preferable to polyester cordage because nylon can have up to 20% stretch whereas polyester is designed to have the minimal give. The best performance will be obtained from rope if a length of chain is used between the anchor and

A simple stowage for a Fisherman's anchor in port or in sheltered waters, where it is ready to let go. Left like this at sea, however, it could easily damage the hull. Note that the bobstay appears to have no tensioning tackle and looks slack. *Photograph: Peter Chesworth*

the rope to keep the pull on the anchor as near horizontal as possible. The 2 or 3 m (6–10 ft) often fitted is inadequate; 5 or 10 m (16–32 ft) is much better.

To achieve similar breaking strains rope needs to be thicker than the equivalent chain for a given size of yacht. The accompanying table provides some comparisons but as a general rule rope should be about 50% thicker; so, for example, instead of 8 mm chain, 12 mm rope should be employed.

The end of a chain must be made fast in the locker, but not with a shackle which will easily seize up. A strong, light line spliced into the last link, which can quickly be cut, is a good solution. Ideally it needs to be long enough to come on deck without the splice jamming in the spurling pipe. It is also a good idea to mark the cable so that the amount paid out is quickly identified. White paint does the job very well but quickly becomes dirty and then chips off the links. A combination of paint and those plastic electric cable ties fastened to successive links is probably as good as anything. The ties should be cut but not too short so that they stand proud and are easy to see. I usually mark my cable every two fathoms because by the time one mark is sliding below the surface of the water the next is just coming on deck.

One good reason for marking the cable for touch as well as sight is so that at night it will soon be clear either how much has been paid out or has to be recovered. I can remember one fraught occasion when, amidst a packed anchorage, we started to plough the seabed towards the beach. The only answer was to bring the anchor aboard and get under way. The foredeck hand heaved away in the darkness, until the cable came up tight and would not move. The engine had been taking the strain so more power was used in an attempt to break the anchor out, with no obvious effect. Eventually we realised that all the cable had been pulled up from the locker rather than over the side. A simple system of touch marking would have saved a lot of wasted effort.

So before deciding what to equip your yacht with, let's take a closer look at the various factors which have to be considered.

Catenary – how ground tackle works

It is not simply a question of a larger anchor or strong cable; both must work in unison. Merely hooking a high holding power anchor into the seabed is not in itself enough to hold the boat, as a wave lifting the boat could pull the anchor out. The gear must counter the steady or sudden shock loads of wind, wave and current, which could easily exceed the breaking strain of an anchor cable.

Reducing these loads to manageable proportions is achieved in two ways: first make sure that the anchor will hold in the bottom and then to cushion the loads imposed upon it. Holding power is given by the anchor's designer but effective cushioning is down to you. It is the weight of chain or length of warp as it curves down to the seabed which acts as a shock absorber either by trying to lift all the chain off the bottom, or stretching the rope to its fullest extent before the full tension comes on to the anchor itself. This curve is called the catenary and for it to be effective the anchor must have enough holding power to remain in one place and prevent the cable being dragged across the seabed.

To gain holding power an anchor must dig into the seabed. This requires weight, but it is impractical to expect the anchor to bury itself by weight alone. Therefore the anchor must be dragged across the bottom horizontally, as any tendency for the strain to be upwards reduces its holding power or may even prevent it digging in in the first place. The weight of the cable lying on the seabed ensures that the pull on the anchor is always along or parallel to the bottom, so keeping the anchor firmly dug in. The easiest way to achieve this horizontal pull is by keeping the cable on or very close to the bottom which is where the weight of the chain or length of rope become important. Here we are back to the catenary again and the final factor in the equation: scope.

Scope and depth of water

Scope is the term used to define the quantity of cable which has been used to anchor the craft and is measured in multiples of the depth of water. It is usually considered to be the length of cable from the stem to the anchor.

There are conflicting recommendations on the correct length of cable needed to anchor safely and securely. Three times the high water depth is probably the most common recommendation for chain, and 5 times the high water depth is suggested for rope in normal weather and current conditions. Some proponents advise adjusting the length of the cable so that the ratio of the scope to depth is constant as the tide rises and falls, but this solution is so obviously impracticable that it is better to use an optimum length which will be correct at high water. My preference is for 3 times the depth of chain on the bottom, which therefore dictates that the total scope needs to be 4 times the high water depth and the scope for rope should similarly be increased by 1.

The sentinel

There is one way of aiding the efficiency of ground tackle by improving the catenary despite prevailing weather conditions or because the anchorage is too crowded to lay out the full scope. It simply involves lowering an additional weight down the anchor cable to induce a greater curve than would otherwise be the case. It is particularly effective when rope is used and it is easy to rig. The weight should ideally be at least 50% of your bower anchor weight and never less than about 20 pounds (9 kg).

The sentinel is made fast to a large stainless steel snap shackle or bow shackle to which a tripping line is made fast so that it may be lowered after the anchor has been set and recovered before you weigh anchor. Once you are riding to the anchor lower the sentinel down the cable for about one-third of the scope, and make its line fast on the opposite bow to the anchor cable to aid recovery.

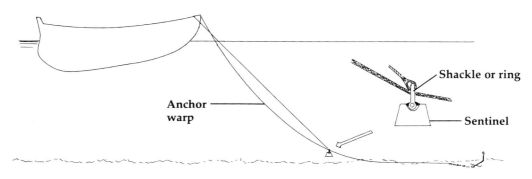

Anchor warp

Shackle or ring

Sentinel

FIG 28 A boat lying to a single anchor on a rope rather than chain cable, where the slightest increase in the wind will soon have the rope bar taut and risk breaking out the anchor. The addition of the sentinel weight causes the rope to sag and so induce a catenary, which will absorb and snatch loads and improve the holding power of the anchor.

Selecting the anchorage

Preparation is the most important aspect of all seamanship and anchoring is no exception; but it is not only a matter of having the ground tackle ready to let go. Some time needs to be spent in selecting the anchorage itself. The proposed anchorage needs to be as close as reasonably possible to a weather shore so as to obtain the best protection. The desire to get as close as possible and derive the maximim shelter must be tempered by the risks should the wind change, which might turn a comfortable berth into one on an exposed lee shore.

The expected depth at high water governs the scope of cable, which in turn dictates how far off the anchor must be let go. Too close and there is the risk that, should the wind change, the yacht could go aground at low water.

It is essential to work out the minimum depth of water required to stay afloat as well as how much cable to pay out. There may be no clear charted information on the depth of water so either the echo sounder or lead line will have to be used to make sure there is no risk of going aground at low water. In order to ascertain whether there is sufficient water to lie afloat at all states of the tide, first work out the minimum depth of water required below your keel to include a safety margin of about 1 m (3 ft). Depending upon the intended time of anchoring, calculate how much the tide has to drop until low water and subtract this from the depth indicated on the echo sounder. If the resulting figure is less than what you draw, find another spot as you will be aground at low water.

It is a great mistake to pick one spot on the chart in which you intend to let go, only to find another yacht already there or close by. The chart must be studied closely to confirm the quality of the holding ground and, if possible, select a number of simple transits or bearings for use on arrival because there will be no time during the final approach to sort these out. The ideal is a transit along the approach line with a cross-bearing – or, better still, a transit to indicate the point at which the anchor should be let go.

Anchoring under power

It is normal to anchor under power but there is always the possibility of engine failure or perhaps a fouled propeller. I once found myself moored by the stern after fouling a length of cheap polypropylene rope trailing from a mooring. In a fine piece of seamanship it had apparently been cut free and abandoned when the knot jammed. The task in the gathering gloom of going for a dip in order to clear the rope from the prop was one of those little events which make sailing so much fun!

An initial pass through your planned anchorage would be an advantage, checking that the position is clear and the direction in which you will lie at anchor. It's also worth confirming that the position has enough swinging room and that there are no anchor buoys to show an adjacent craft's ground tackle fouling the anchorage.

Before making the final approach the anchor must be ready to let go with enough cable on deck. The whole coil of an anchor warp should be to hand, but in the case of cable only have twice the depth of chain to start with flaked on deck: this is to prevent it running out of control and landing in a heap on top of the anchor! A pile of chain will hold nothing and, were this to happen, it must all be recovered to ensure that the anchor isn't prevented from digging in by becoming fouled in its own cable.

The yacht must be stopped over or just past the intended position for the anchor and either allowed to drift backwards or the engine put astern. As the yacht moves sternwards over the position the anchor is lowered to the bottom and the cable allowed to run or pay out so that it lies along the bottom in a straight line. Never let it go while the boat is stationary or you will pile the chain on top of the anchor.

The run of the cable or warp must be controlled around the sampson post and not be allowed to run out of control; but neither must it be checked too early as it will merely plough a furrow along the seabed. Once you have about two-thirds the scope on the bottom, friction can be increased to start digging the flukes in. If the tide is not strong enough to carry the yacht astern then short bursts of the engine must be used to give just enough stern way.

When the full scope of cable has gone over the side the cable can be made fast, to dig the anchor in, aided by the engine if necessary, taking it out of gear before the cable comes taut. Place a hand on the cable to see if it tautens, thus indicating that the anchor is holding. However, if the cable vibrates as it first tightens and then slackens, this indicates that the anchor is dragging. The choice now is to pay out more cable, if there is room, to see whether the anchor will dig in. If this does not work recover the anchor and see whether it has been fouled by its cable or weed before trying again in the same place. If neither of these options are appropriate, select another anchorage position and start again.

Anchoring under sail

The easiest anchorage approach is one that is made with a fair wind and tide, nevertheless anchoring under sail demands greater preparation than under power, not least because just enough sail has to be carried so as to reach the anchorage and then for the anchor to be quickly lowered. It must also be possible to raise sail again quickly if, for one reason or another, the anchor does not hold and a second attempt has to be made.

Whenever possible on the approach sail under mainsail jib alone and dispense with the staysail which will only get in the way; it is important to keep the anchor clear of the sheets. Nothing could be worse than a sheet snagging the anchor and tipping it over the side as the sail flies across in a tack! The halyards of those sails which are to be used for the approach must be laid on deck coils capsized and free to run when they need to be dropped, and the topping lift should be set up enough to take the weight of the boom without spoiling the set of the sail.

Wind and tide together

Once the preparations are complete, if you must beat against a foul into the anchorage, do so just a little to leeward before luffing up into position. Keep the sheets free as soon as the boat begins to gather stern-way, then let the anchor go. Pay out cable until there is enough scope before making fast to dig the flukes in.

If you have to run into the anchorage and the same conditions apply, haul your wind about a boat's length past the position and luff up into the anchorage, releasing the anchor as soon as she starts to gather stern-way.

Any attempt to sail across the anchorage dropping the anchor on the way is fraught with risks: not least that the yacht will be snubbed hard-round and the chain will chafe against the hull; or the boat will still be making way through the water once the intended scope is reached and made fast. The only way to avoid this is to continue paying out cable until the boat stops turning head-to-wind and heave it in again: this is another good reason for having a well-marked cable.

Wind against tide

Decide whether the boat is to be wind- or tide-rode and whether you have any freedom of choice as to your approach direction. When you are to be tide-rode the easiest route will be to lower the mainsail and run to the anchorage under headsails alone. Lower or furl the headsails as soon as you have just enough headway to reach your anchoring position. Lower the anchor to the bottom as soon as you have started to gather stern-way and then bed the anchor in the same way as before.

If you can only reach your anchorage beating to windward, then sail a short way past and lower the mainsail while gybing round to run into position. Stow or furl the headsails as soon as she will carry enough way before letting go as soon as she starts to drop back on the tide. When you are running downwind to a wind-rode anchorage, then just before you reach it stow or douse the headsails while hauling your wind and rounding up into position. Again wait until she starts to drop astern before lowering the anchor and paying out the cable. Beating up to the anchorage with a fair tide under you only requires that you luff into position before letting go as before.

When the wind is blowing across the tide and the only approach is a beam reach, the yacht's speed and how to reduce it is the biggest worry. The preferred option therefore is to approach against the tide. This may mean sailing past the anchoring position, turning round, perhaps even lowering the main and reaching back under headsails alone. When all is ready furl or drop the sails and let go the anchor as soon as the boat gathers way astern.

Yachts that handle well under main alone could make the same approach, but in this case lower the main before dropping anchor to stop her sailing around. The experienced owner may leave the main until the anchor has been let go if he is sure that he can get the main down before the boat starts to become tide-rode.

Two anchors

The reasons for lying to two anchors are either to create additional security or to reduce the swinging room significantly in a restricted or congested anchorage. When it is a case of extra security this is only likely to be successful if the anchors are of the same or similar size, as otherwise while the yacht sheers around in the wind, the lighter anchor will be dragged until it no longer takes any weight. The only answer in this case is to lay them piggyback or in tandem.

Two anchors in tandem

This is a tactic to be used when strong winds are expected and there is sufficient time to take precautions. Start by laying the lighter of the pair with at least a scope of 1½ times the depth between them. The reasons are firstly to allow it to settle ready to dig before the second is lowered over the side, and secondly so that when they are being recovered you don't have to try to lift the weight of both of them.

The first anchor is likely to be the kedge with a short length of chain and perhaps 60 m (196 ft) of rope. Make the anchor warp fast to the crown of the bower and then marry the remainder of the rope with the main cable until its end is reached and you have to make it fast. Do this with a rolling hitch which is then seized back on to the cable to avoid it undoing. Now continue to pay out the bower until you have sufficient scope and are satisfied that both are dug in.

The running moor

To moor a vessel strictly means that she is anchored midway between two anchors, thus restricting her swinging circle to little more than her overall length. The limited space to be found in most yacht anchorages has resulted in this method of anchoring almost becoming extinct due to the much greater risk of fouling other anchor cables. However there are still occasions, principally in narrow, fast flowing rivers or channels, when using two anchors is the only way to ensure a safe berth.

The safest and more usual method of mooring is first to lay the bower anchor in the normal way so that the yacht will be lying to the larger anchor when wind and tide are together. Then, provided the yacht has more than twice the scope needed to ride to her bower anchor, the kedge can be laid without too much difficulty. It is also essential that she is lying in the direction in which it is intended to drop the kedge and does not sheer to one side or the other.

The cable on the bower is slacked away until slightly more than twice the total riding scope has been paid out, not forgetting that the kedge warp will be longer than chain. When vessels are moored between two anchors it is usual for the cables to be led from opposite bows to reduce the possibility of twisting the cables around each other when the tide turns. Despite lashing the tiller over it is unlikely that the wind and tide will allow the boat to swing round the same way on each tide. Consequently the cables will not only foul each other but also the bowsprit. The solution as we will see later is to lead the cables from the same bow and once the yacht is brought up between the two anchors to marry them together.

Once the kedge has been lowered to the bottom, its warp is gradually paid out while the bower cable is hauled in. Before all the kedge has been paid out make it fast, while still heaving on the bower cable to dig the kedge in and check that it is holding. If there is any doubt about the quality of the bottom, it's as well to check if the anchor will hold before the whole scope has been paid out.

Finally, if the yacht is to remain moored over several tides, or the wind is expected to change, then the two cables must be married to each other. The slack warp must be made fast, usually with a rolling hitch around the riding cable, and then both cables lowered so that the hitch is clear of the bowsprit and below the keel. The two cables must then be made fast again on deck. Although the cables may still twist with each turn of the tide, they will be easier to recover on the same side and will not foul the bobstay.

Yachts with insufficient bower cable will either have to bend on an additional warp to temporarily lengthen the cable or will have to run the kedge further out in the tender. The tender will also have to be used when the yacht is not lying along the desired line and it is not possible to induce a sheer with the rudder. Using the tender to lay the kedge has probably resulted in more capsizes than any other operation and requires great care. The modern GRP tender is not more stable than many of its clinker forebears, while the inflatable – although safer in this respect – is never easy to row.

Although it might at first appear more difficult, don't be lulled into believing that it's best to have just the anchor in the tender while the crew pay out the warp from the cockpit. Under these conditions the stern of the tender is effectively made fast to the yacht and therefore its freedom to manoeuvre limited. Instead, coil the warp into the bottom boards and, keeping it underfoot, allow it to pay out gently as you row. The anchor is best hung over the stern on a slip-rope so that there is no need to stand up to throw the kedge over the side. As soon as the full extent of the warp is reached the anchor is slipped and the warp hauled taut to dig the anchor in.

It is possible to moor a yacht while still under way; usually under power, although with experience it can be achieved under sail. In this case the kedge is dropped first and consequently must have a warp which is equal to the total length of both cables.

Under power the anchor position is approached stemming either the wind or tide, whichever she will lie to. The kedge is let go over the stern while the boat continues to make towards the second anchor position. As the yacht should still be moving slowly ahead when the limit of the warp is reached, the bow will be snubbed round as the kedge anchor digs in, at which time the bower anchor should be let go. The bower cable is then paid out as the slack on the kedge is brought back on board. It is safer to allow the wind or tide to bring the yacht back towards her kedge, so reducing the risk of fouling the propeller. Once the yacht is brought up lying between both anchors, the cables must be married as above and the warp must be made fast around the chain.

Attempting to moor under sail is only really practical when running downwind under headsails, or with a beam wind in a tideway. In either case the principles are the same, although great attention has to be paid to the sails so that they don't fill with wind at the wrong moment.

When running downwind there is some merit in setting not only the headsails but also the main, because it will help the yacht to round up into the wind. As the end of the bower cable is reached and the boat snubbed round, the headsails must be let fly and the main sheeted hard in, while the kedge anchor is quickly let go. As soon as the yacht comes head-to-wind the sails can be stowed before the bower cable is hauled in and the kedge is paid out until the craft is moored between her anchors.

Sailing across the wind should be done with as little sail as possible because it must be doused very quickly once the second anchor is let go. If this isn't achieved it may not be possible to keep the yacht tightly moored between her two anchors.

One final point on this subject: all anchored craft are required to indicate that they are at anchor by day and night. The merit of this is apparent when creeping up a familiar creek to a much loved quiet anchorage on a pitch black night and a silhouette looms ahead. It is possibly the drain on the battery which deters many people from hoisting a light at night, but a small hurricane lamp hoisted on the forestay will do just as well. There is less excuse for not showing the anchor ball by day. Owners with bowsprits should remember that they are very much in the minority and an anchor light well forward will cast some illumination over their projection, so avoiding unpleasant collisions!

Harbours

The congestion in many of our ports and harbours has limited the freedom to anchor wherever you wish; the demands of so many other water users, both commercial and recreational, have now to be met as well. Few of the smaller ports are able to offer the luxury of an anchorage; nearly all the available space is taken by private or visitors' moorings. The anchorage in a sheltered creek still exists but it is less likely to be either quiet or empty.

In order to save embarrassment or later problems it is always wise to seek advice on available moorings and anchorages when entering an unfamiliar port. Most harbours maintain some form of VHF radio watch even if it is only over high water, and details of the watch times can be obtained from almanacs, *Admiralty Lists of Radio Signals* or over the telephone in advance. It is the port which you didn't plan to visit that requires some care, especially when anchoring or making use of an unoccupied private mooring, and even more so at night.

Unless the harbour bye-laws specifically forbid it, there is nothing wrong with picking up a private mooring on a temporary basis provided one or two rules are adhered to. A tender left on a mooring frequently indicates that the owner is only on a day sail, but lack of a tender should not infer the opposite.

Boats of similar lengths and sizes are normally grouped together so don't moor your 35 foot yawl amongst a clutch of Hurley 18s because the mooring will neither be strong enough nor will there be sufficient space. At best the adjacent berths might be fouled and at worst the whole mooring dragged or parted. Remember the mooring has an owner who may return at any time from just a day sail or a very long overnight passage, so never leave the boat without enough crew to move it. The sight of another yacht on his mooring will not be welcome to the returning yachtsman whose only thought is of a large drink and a warm bunk. Neither will his temper improve if the yacht is discovered to be unoccupied!

If intending to use the mooring overnight, make fast with a bight of rope through the cable rather than the mooring bridle or pendants. This allows the owner who is inconsiderate enough to return while you are turned in to recover his own mooring and leave you sleeping undisturbed. Although with that sort of activity going on alongside I'd feel safer if I'd woken up instead of sleeping through it all!

CHAPTER 11

Heavy weather

The possible onset of bad weather should find the cruising yachtsman in one of two places: either as far away from dry land as possible or with his feet firmly on it. It's a fool or a ferry passenger who puts to sea from choice when a gale is blowing or forecast, and it is an equally dubious decision to try to reach port when the wind and sea have already started rising.

When a safe harbour is out of reach there are a number of reasons for staying well out to sea, not least the risk of being trapped on a lee shore. A summer gale usually blows itself out in a matter of a few hours. However, the coast is never far away, so if the gale continues from the same direction for a day or more, then problems can arise.

The coastal sea conditions which most yachts experience are modest, lacking the enormous power found in the open ocean. Waves are a direct result of the wind blowing upon the surface of the water and therefore their height is relative to the speed of the wind causing them. Swell, which is more recognisable in mid-ocean, is a wave which has travelled many hundreds of miles away from the wind that generated it.

The height of inshore waves and whether their crests will break largely depends upon the depth of water rather than sustained high wind speeds. The wave approaching shallower water starts to heap up until it reaches a critical height when its crest either breaks or tumbles down the face. Coasts exposed to the ocean are likely to face these critical conditions much sooner as waves build on to the existing swell.

Yachts are built to cope with water across their decks, but there is a limit to just how much weight of water a small boat can withstand. In deep water the approaching wave train has a rhythm on which the yacht will rise. In shallow waters, off headlands and in contrary currents, the waves may rise in height out of all proportion to the wind speed.

The seaworthiness of the yacht and the experience of its crew will determine the tactics employed to cope with heavy weather. The wind strength and wave height which constitute heavy weather will differ from yacht to yacht. The seaworthiness of similar craft should be the same, but judging the moment at which the limit is reached will vary from owner to owner depending upon their experience. When deciding just how seaworthy his yacht is, the owner must examine all the factors which make up a sound vessel. It is not just a question of strong hull, sails and rigging; there are other, less obvious components which go towards the making of a safe and seaworthy yacht.

Bad weather naturally increases the stresses that are imposed upon a yacht and her equipment. Reducing the risk of gear failure is therefore an essential part of maintaining seaworthiness. When small cruising yachts mirrored their larger sisters they tended to be over-sparred, with long booms, heavy topmasts and very long running bowsprits. It was a difficult task handling these spars in a seaway and required great care to avoid injury from the boom in particular, especially when taking a reef. The solution, which continues even in these days of modern light-weight materials and construction techniques, is to use a boom gallows. Reefing with the sail set is much safer if the boom can be held fast in a boom gallows or crutch. Otherwise, as the yacht rolls, if the boom is not secure, the crew could lose their footing and end up in the water.

Gallows are usually mounted across either the after end of the coach roof or the cockpit, and will hold the boom on each quarter or amidships. The crutch, on the other hand, is usually mounted along the centreline; it is therefore much harder to settle the boom into it. Scissor crutches should not be used as they are liable to collapse, with the potentially disastrous consequences of the crew going over the side.

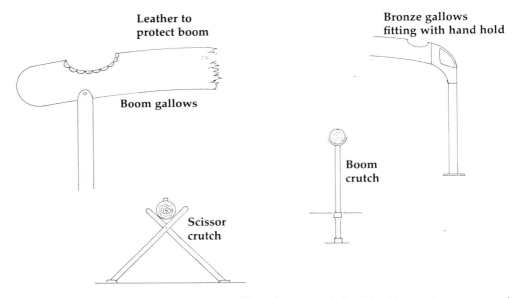

Leather to protect boom

Boom gallows

Bronze gallows fitting with hand hold

Boom crutch

Scissor crutch

FIG 29 Examples of various boom supports. The scissor crutch should not be used as a means of supporting the boom when reefing in a seaway; it only remains upright through the weight of the boom, and may topple over while the crew are struggling with the sail.

Gallows aft of the cockpit support the full length of the boom and stop it being bent if the mainsheet is hauled down too hard. When the gallows are across the coach roof the boom does not have to be sheeted so far inboard but the outboard end of the boom remains unsupported. Coach roof gallows also provide extra handholds when leaving the cockpit to go on deck; some even have handgrips cast into them. However, I prefer the gallows mounted well aft.

The added weight of topmast and long bowsprit meant that both would have to be reefed in bad weather. The bowsprit may have been brought inboard in stages depending upon conditions but the topmast usually came all the way down with its heel on the deck.

It is not only the boat and her gear which are at risk in heavy weather; eliminating the risks to the crew are just as important. Humans are probably the most fragile

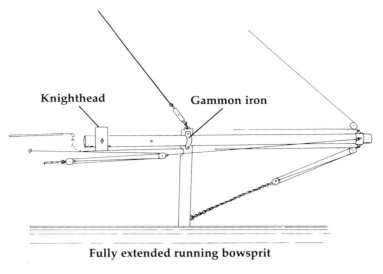

Fully extended running bowsprit

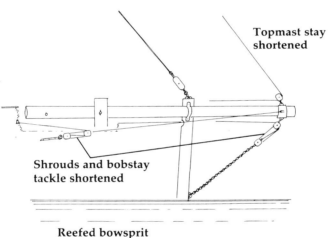

Reefed bowsprit

FIG 30 Some older craft are able to reduce the size of the sail plan by reefing the bowsprit. This also has the advantage of cutting down mooring fees and improving freedom to manoeuvre in congested harbours. The inboard end of the bowsprit is usually housed between the knightheads. The pin must be removed and the spar slid inboard through the gammon iron on the stem. Once it has been resecured the standing rigging must be set up again.

element on board a yacht, and can quickly lose their efficiency if they are hurt or suffering from fatigue. Stopping the crew from being injured is perhaps easier than ensuring that they don't become too tired. Secure stanchions, safety lines and toe rails, plus ample life jackets and lifebuoys, are all basic safety aids. Other precautions that need to be taken may require more effort to discover – for example the importance of well-planned accommodation is often forgotten. Unless the crew is free from the risk of injury by badly sited sharp objects, the yacht can hardly be said to be seaworthy. The cabin of a small yacht can contain any number of hazards for its crew when they are being tossed around in seas much smaller than the races off Portland Bill or the Lizard.

When the crew are moving around the accommodation they should have one or preferably two grab handles always within arm's length. The older yachts have narrow coach roofs so that, by reaching out on either side, the drip channels beneath the ports can be pressed into service as hold-fasts in poor weather. The junction between coach roof and deck is an ideal point for locating grab rails, even on board modern craft. Handles either side of the main companionway and forehatch must be suitable for use when going below or coming on deck. There will be occasions when a sudden lurch will throw you against an unexpected corner, so all edges should be well rounded and any equipment with projections – like switches and knobs – need to be recessed. Don't forget the heads either, as without a pair of strong points the occupant can feel very vulnerable here too.

The crew must be able to rest and sleep on either tack; much of the time in the cabin will be spent either sitting or lying down. The simple solution to remaining in the bunk when the world about you is leaping around is to use either lee-boards or lee-cloths. The former are probably the best choice, but it isn't easy to make a neat job of fitting them after the yacht has been built. It is not always possible or practical to fit lee-cloths for the full length of the bunk, but provided they support the torso from shoulder to mid-thigh this should be sufficient. They need to be about 45–60 cm (18 ins to 2 ft) high to prevent the bunk's occupant from rolling out over the top if the motion gets violent. I think that it is best to fit all the single bunks and divide doubles into singles with a lee-cloth if possible.

Double bunks on cruising yachts are a fine way of increasing their apparent capacity, but they are not very practical at sea. Few modern designs make provision for some form of lee-cloth on a double bunk, hence not only is considerable space wasted but the occupant may have a very rough night being pitched from side to side. If a lee-cloth cannot be fitted then one way of improving the situation is to fill out the vacant space with cushions or even sail bags, provided that the sail bags are dry and the watch on deck won't demand them 30 minutes after you've fallen into a deep sleep!

Many traditionally built wood yachts lack a self-draining cockpit, which is found on nearly all their modern counterparts. Some owners may question the need for the cockpit to be self-draining, particularly if it demands significant alterations to an otherwise original Edwardian yacht. The solution adopted by some owners was to construct a false deck covering the whole cockpit which could be removed during fine weather or in port. Any water coming on board could not get below and therefore drained back over the side; although the crew, lacking anywhere to put their feet, had to stretch their legs out in front of them. Self-draining cockpits are often not found aboard smaller yachts especially, because there is not enough depth within the hull to construct the cockpit sole above the waterline. The solution adopted by some owners is to install cockpit drains anyway and suffer water spurting up one side or the other – although as soon as a wave filled the cockpit all but the last few inches would drain quickly away. In such cases it is probably better just to make the cockpit well watertight and as small as reasonable, perhaps by including a bridge deck at the fore end. Then when it fills up unexpectedly a large capacity pump which can be worked by the helmsman on either tack should soon clear the water.

The self-draining cockpit may be questionable on yachts which, due to their size or from choice, spend most of their time in sheltered waters and are unlikely to encounter conditions bad enough to bring seas aboard. Remember, however, that it doesn't have to be a rough sea which fills the cockpit; just heeling over in a sudden, unexpected squall, or even a heavy rain storm on the mooring, could be enough. My experience is that such occasions tend to be rather hectic, what with freeing sheets and perhaps calming the crew, so when possible I would prefer the water to drain or be pumped out of the cockpit over the side, rather than see quantities of water disappear down into the cabin bilge.

Heaving-to

Heaving-to should not be considered solely as a tactic of last resort, only to be used when the last reef has been snugged down. Heaving-to is a valid precaution to take when conditions have finally reached a point when it is neither safe nor sensible to continue trying to sail.

When sailing single-handed or with a crew, provided the wind is just strong enough to drive the yacht forward, heaving-to is the safest way to leave the helm unattended. Whether slipping below to make a hot drink or plot the position, or going on deck to take in a reef or shake one out, it takes just a moment to heave-to. Not only will you not be making headway, but yachts approaching will understand your actions and keep out of the way.

So what is heaving-to? It simply means that the yacht's sails and rudder are trimmed in such a way that she lies with the wind and sea off the bow. Different hull forms will react differently when lying hove-to, and some of the more extreme modern designs probably won't even attempt it, preferring to run off. The traditional hull with a straight stem and long keel will fare best lying between 4 and 5 points (45–56 degrees) off the wind, fore reaching steadily to leeward, neither making headway nor falling astern.

It is important when heaving-to that there is plenty of sea room to leeward as ideally the yacht can then be left to her own devices. The crew needs only to keep a good lookout and check that none of the sails or rigging are being chafed – especially the staysail and its sheets which will be hard against the weather shrouds.

The helmsman has two choices; he can either heave the yacht to on the same tack or the opposite one. Heaving-to on the opposite tack is in many ways simpler but can cause havoc below if the boat has been on the same tack for some time or the crew are turned in without lee-cloths! In order to heave-to on the opposite tack the yacht must be sailed close hauled and then tacked, leaving the staysail on the weather side while the main is sheeted over the lee quarter.

Heaving-to on the same tack without hauling the staysail across against the wind depends on the prevailing sea conditions being reasonable. It is a manoeuvre more suited to strong winds but in the shelter of the weather shore, and requires some care from the helmsman. Start by freeing the sheets, bearing away and running down-wind until the staysail can be gybed across on to the opposite side. Provided things haven't been left until the last moment, this should not be too difficult as the apparent wind will be less than the true. Sheet the main hard-in and put the tiller to leeward to bring the bow up until the yacht is lying 4 or 5 points off the wind.

The helm will have to be lashed. The best position will be found by trial and error, most yachts heave-to best with the tiller slightly to leeward. How far the helm is lashed over and how much the mainsheet is eased will differ from yacht to yacht, but the thing to avoid is any tendency to sheer about.

The principle of heaving-to is that the yacht lies balanced between the opposing forces of wind in the staysail and main. As the wind fills the staysail when the bow rises to the crest of the wave the yacht will start to pay off; when the bow falls into the trough the main will fill, bringing her up into the wind again to repeat the cycle. If the balance is not right, the yacht will lie beam-on, head-to-wind. It is important that the yacht doesn't lie too broad on to the wind and sea, however; this will be risky if the crests start breaking and will be very uncomfortable. Neither must she gather too much headway because she will risk surging head-to-wind and even tacking if a sea catches the leeward bow.

A yacht which attempts to lie beam-on to the sea may ride better if her main is sheeted a little harder. If this does not work, then flatten the staysail so that it does not fill. If neither of these solve the problem, the helm can be brought close amidships or even to weather.

Yawls and ketches should follow the same rules, but should not set sail at both ends as the result makes matters worse. Yachts with a small storm jib set on the bowsprit and a reefed mizzen aft will adopt a most unpleasant motion in the slightest swell. When one sail is down in the shelter of the trough they will be on the crest, catching the full force of the wind. A ketch or yawl will have a much more comfortable time if a well-reefed main is set with a reefed staysail: this keeps the centre of effort in the middle of the boat instead of the ends.

Sloops setting a tightly furled headsail or a smaller storm jib move the centre of effort of both sails closer to the bow with equally uncomfortable consequences. A small storm jib from a short inner forestay will balance the yacht better, and incidentally will be much easier and safer for the crew to set, close to the security of the mast.

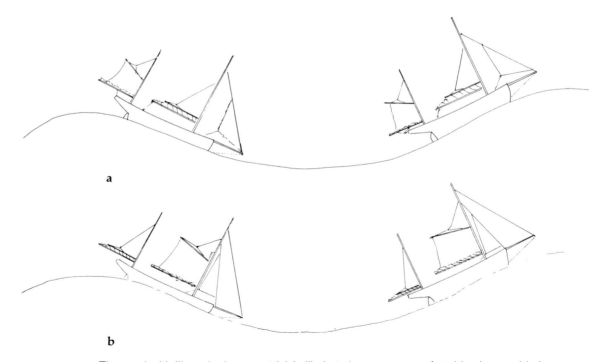

a

b

FIG 31 The yawl with jib and mizzen set (a) is likely to have an uncomfortable zig zag ride in a heavy swell, with first the bow blown off course and then the stern forced downwind. The wind will blow on the sails alternately as each is exposed to the full force of the wind on the crest of each wave. A well reefed main and small staysail (b) moves the centre of effort closer to the middle of the boat, so that the wind is more likely to blow with equal force on each sail.

Preparation for heavy weather

The best way to deal with heavy weather is to be ready, even if it means starting off being under-canvased or perhaps even delaying departure. In the same way that it is easy to take clothes off when the weather gets hot, so is the opposite true for your yacht's sails. I can think of nothing more demoralising than swapping shorts for oilskins and boots and reefing the sails as soon as the harbour entrance is cleared; it seems to place a dampener on the whole passage.

Initial preparations should be made on the mooring or pontoon, checking that deck gear is secure and stowing away all loose items down below. No matter how secure it looks wedged into a corner, unless it is all properly stowed the first roll will see it all on the floor.

Check the galley and make sure that basics for hot drinks, soups, etc, are easy to reach and that any snack foods and biscuits are where the crew can find them. The galley crash bar should be in place if it is not a fixture, and the cook's safety harness must be rigged ready for use. Make sure that the contents of all the lockers will not spill out if they have to be opened in a rough seaway and that their doors and lids have been secured.

Every seacock should have a quick once over and any that don't need to be kept open, like the galley sink and heads washbasin, should be closed to prevent the risk of flooding when heeled over. Make sure that the crew know which seacocks have been closed, especially if the heads inlet and outlet are shut as a precaution.

Each crew member must have their safety harness on, preferably before you leave the berth. It won't do any harm to check as well that the safety lines are rigged properly on deck, and that life jackets and flares are in their proper stowage.

Poor weather seems invariably to be accompanied by large quantities of flying water; but making sure that it stays outside the boat is not just a question of keeping the hatches and ports closed. While it is important to keep the water out, plenty of fresh air is essential to the well-being of the crew. All the ventilators must be plugged or covered unless the yacht is fitted with a type that doesn't allow water down below.

The large cowl ventilator is very efficient at funnelling air into the accommodation, which is why it is seen aboard large commercial ships. On yachts it is usually highly polished brass and works well in rain or spray but may not be man enough to cope with large amounts of water. Ships fit a canvas cover over the cowl until the going gets rough, when the vent is removed and a wood plug inserted. Yachts should adopt the same practice, as the cover traps air within the vent which makes it very buoyant when surrounded by water, and the resulting hole is bound to be above your bunk. The best solution is one of the dorade-type vents which, though not quite as good as a cowl in light airs, do stop the water in all but the most extreme conditions.

The amount of water washing down the decks will not only be due to the strength of the wind or height of the seas; the angle at which the yacht is heeled is just as relevant. Carrying too much sail is not a sign of experience; it is more than likely to slow the boat and result in a very uncomfortable trip, so setting the right amount of sail is very important. The choice can either be one of setting fewer sails or of reducing the area by reefing those that are hoisted.

Reefing systems

Reefing used to be achieved simply by bunching or rolling a portion of the sail into itself and tying it neatly. The same method was used on all types of craft from square riggers to the headsails on small cutters. Then came Major du Boulay's introduction of a headsail roller, which comprised a wood luff batten to which the jib was secured; this was later replaced by the more advanced Wykeham-Martin roller-reefing gear.

Well found and well reefed during a summer gale off the Dutch coast. Note that all the crew are in harnesses and that the hatches are all closed. Despite the poor conditions the crew reportedly enjoyed themselves! *Photograph: Martin Tregoning*

Headsail furling has now turned full circle with modern furling systems adopting the same principle as du Boulay by fitting a rigid tube on to which the sail is rolled.

Still in use today, Wykeham-Martin is ideal for small gaff rigged craft where the character and appearance of the boat would be spoiled and standing rigging tensions are perhaps too slack for a modern aluminium headsail foil. The system is very good for furling the sail at the end of a day's sailing but is less efficient for reefing, especially if the standard lightweight luff wire is retained in the sail. The upper portion of the luff will lag behind and not roll up as quickly as the bottom part, spoiling the set of the sail. The answer is to replace the usual flexible luff wire with a heavy gauge rigging wire which will resist the twist but is more difficult to handle when the sail comes down.

The two principal mainsail reefing systems are slab-reefing – usually found on gaffers – or roller-reefing, more commonly used on bermudian mainsails. Each has its own staunch exponents. The reason that roller-reefing is not used aboard gaffers is because it works best when the sail is held against the mast with slides in a track; if lacing or mast hoops are used they have to be cast off whenever a reef is taken in.

There are a number of methods for rotating the boom for roller-reefing. The most common is either a ratchet or worm gearing fitted by the gooseneck. The problem that has to be overcome with roller-reefing is the method of attaching the mainsheet. Short booms are not a problem, but when the boom extends over the transom a claw ring has to be used and this is the usual source of difficulty. The claw ring allows the boom to revolve within it and has a large enough diameter to permit the sail to be wrapped around when taking a reef. The difficulty arises when the claw ring tries to wrap itself up inside the sail; the whole process then has to be begun all over again.

Wooden spars are usually tapered towards the ends, and this is also a hindrance to neat and efficient roller-reefing, because the sail is gathered unevenly around the boom. The belly of the sail is taut while the luff and leach are slack, which distorts the set of the sail. Instead of the flat sail essential to heavy weather sailing, the mainsail ends up with a mass of creases and wrinkles.

If the boom terminates inside the transom and the mainsheet can be made fast to its end, then roller-reefing is quite simple. The weight of the boom is first taken on the topping-lift, then the peak and main halyards are slowly eased away while the reef is wound in.

The size of the mainsail on a gaffer will dictate whether all the reef earings can be left rigged, but it is normal in all but the smallest yachts for a gaff mainsail to have three reef points. The earings are used to haul down and secure the clew or outboard end of the sail, while the tack or inboard end is either lashed or secured on hooks by the gooseneck.

A large main usually needs the assistance of a reef tackle which is kept rigged and hooked on to the first reef earing, under the boom ready for action. The tackle has in some instances been replaced by small mast mounted winches, but these lack the versatility of a tackle whch can be pressed into service all round the boat if necessary. When a reef tackle is used the clew must be lashed to the boom so that the reef tackle can be slacked off and hooked on to the next reef earing. Each earing should just be long enough to reach from the bee block on one side, through the leach thimble and down to the bee block on the other so that the reef can always be taken in on the weather side of the boom. Don't attempt to hook on to the leeward earing and heave down, because the sail can easily foul and jam the bee block stopping the reef being taken in.

It was once normal for the earings or reef pendants just to have whipped ends with a figure of eight knot to stop them unreeving. I prefer each end to have an eye splice which makes the task of hooking on the reef tackle much simpler.

This method of reefing does have one limitation which is that the length of pendant hauled down will be twice the distance from boom to thimble. Consequently although there is ample earing to make fast the reef, there will be plenty of slack on the second and third earings which must be tidied up. Some smaller yachts have even done away with the gooseneck hooks and rely simply upon long earings to heave down the luff and leach of the sail. The long earings are led from the bee block on one side of the boom, up through the reef cringle, down through the opposite bee block, and then forward along the boom to a cleat.

When to reef

The decision on how soon to reef can be a difficult one because there are a number of factors to be considered in deciding when the moment has arrived. It is also necessary to decide whether a reef is what is required, or whether a reduction in sail will be sufficient – changing one of the headsails for a smaller one or dropping the topsail, for instance.

Sailing single-handed in particular calls for early action, rather than leaving things until the last moment when the wind is really piping. The lone sailor will tend to set smaller sails when conditions are marginal, because there is a limit to the area of flaying sail cloth which one body can smother. Assuming that the sails have been reduced and that further reductions in sail area are required, what factors must be taken into account?

Firstly there are the elements, the forecast and present weather conditions, together with the general trend over the previous few hours and the time of sunset. Secondly, consider the crew's experience, and finally the type of reefing system. All must influence the timing of reefing.

If the forecast indicates that there is to be a wind increase overnight which will dictate that a reef is taken, then seriously consider taking it in early, before it gets too dark to see clearly. The weather always looks worse at night because the imagination comes into play; it feels as if the wind increases by force 2 on the Beaufort Scale and wave heights double! Always remember that if the weather conditions have changed enough for you to be thinking about taking in a reef *then do it now*! It is much worse to take in a reef which you should have taken in two hours previously, because the conditions will have deteriorated just that bit too much.

The way the yacht responds to the helm and how comfortably she steers are probably the best indications of when a reef is needed. As we discussed in earlier chapters, a yacht is designed to sail at her best when she is upright, so although sailing along heeled well over may be exhilarating, it is not efficient. If weather helm has increased to the point when freeing the sheets has no effect, or the boat is showing signs of starting to broach, then a reef is definitely indicated. A vanishing lee rail, or water rising halfway across the cockpit, are other sure signs that it was time to get things on a more even keel long ago!

The basic suit of sails on a cutter comprises the mainsail, jib headed topsail, jib and staysail, so when a reef is required you must decide where to start. The objective must be to keep the centre of effort of the sails as close to its normal position as possible, which means close fore-and-aft of the mast. If the main is reefed and too much sail is set forward of the mast, the yacht is very likely to suffer from lee helm, whereas by lowering a headsail, weather helm could result.

Much depends on the shape of the mainsail and the way the topsail is rigged above it. When deciding what to do first, either reef the main or strike the topsail. A high-peaked main is usually a sign of good windward performance and so it is easier to drop the topsail as a first reef. The low-peaked main lacks drive above and needs the additional length in the luff given by a topsail, and so the main is reefed first. The reason for retaining the topsail and taking in the main, rather than the reverse, is that a more measured and less sudden reduction in sail area can be achieved. However, while older sailing trawlers and smacks were able to retain the topsail in this way, more recent craft lack the rigging to set the topsail satisfactorily.

Mainsail roller-reefing, while a boon, can present problems, because the sail has to be hoisted all the way up before it can be reefed. A simple example is when lying partially tide-rode to a mooring amongst a number of other craft. Once the main is raised the yacht will come head-to-wind, risking collision with neighbouring craft which are still tide-rode.

Some of the smaller gaff sloops and cutters had long booms which extended several feet over the counter, making reefing the main very difficult. The reef cringle may have been hauled down but tying the reef points, which are outboard, would be very difficult – not to say dangerous when balancing over the stern. The sensible length for the main boom on a cruiser is one which ends at the transom, with little or no overhang. When there is no alternative to a long boom the only safe way to reef the main is for the boat to be hove-to and the main sheeted hard down into its crutch or boom gallows. Yawls and ketches have little alternative but to hang out over the stern, although those yawls with a loose-footed lug mizzen are much easier to reef.

Sailing well balanced under reefed mainsail with working jib and staysail, the luff of the jib is set taut with only minimal sag. It looks as though the crew have only just taken in the reef, as the topping lifts look as though they are only just slack and the leeward running backstay is still on.

Note the lazyjacks which gather the mainsail when lowered and the jackyard topsail stowed neatly under the boom. *Photograph: Peter Chesworth*

The working jib may be the smaller of the two headsails, but this does not mean that it should be carried in preference to the staysail – in fact quite the reverse. Leaving the jib set at the end of the bowsprit spoils the flow across the back of the main and ruins the yacht's balance. Lower the jib and replace it with a storm jib set halfway along the bowsprit; or just carry the staysail alone. Either option will bring the combined centre of effort more amidships. A jib set at the end of the bowsprit increases the risk of the bowsprit being broken. When the boat buries her head into an oncoming wave and fills the sail with water the added weight can easily snap a long bowsprit.

Taking a slab reef

When the options of simply reducing the sails have been exhausted, the only alternative is to further reduce sail area by making the sails smaller; taking a reef. Roller-furling or -reefing apart, only two sails are normally reefed: the main and, aboard some older yachts, the staysail as well, while two-masted craft will be able to reef the mizzen.

The safest way to work on deck even in good weather is with the yacht hove-to, which will calm down what can be a violent motion. It will also free the helmsman to lend a hand smothering the sail and putting in the reef ties. The yacht will make slow headway while drifting steadily to leeward so, in harbours and rivers especially, take care that there is plenty of sea room to leeward for the job to be completed whilst hove-to without tacking. If the yacht is to be reefed not hove-to then both headsails will have to be lowered so that she will ride head-to-wind; just releasing the jib and staysail sheets is likely to damage them. The mainsail will still catch some wind when hove-to so it will be harder to haul the reef, but the crews' job should be safer.

Although slab reefs can be taken standing close against the mast, all the reef points will have to be tied, working along the full length of the boom. The boom should therefore be sheeted hard over the quarter and landed in either the gallows or crutch before it can be reefed. This reduces the risk of the boom moving and the crew, standing on the coach roof, being pitched over the side.

Once the boat is hove-to, sheet the boom into the gallows and clear away the main and peak halyards ready for lowering. When there isn't a gallows or crutch, the weight of the boom must be taken on the topping-lift before sheeting the boom inboard. If two topping-lifts are rigged use the weather one so that it is clear of the sail. Clear the reef pendants or, if a reef tackle is used, hook it on to the weather earing. Everything is now ready to take in a reef.

Start by easing away on the two halyards until there is enough slack to take in the reef, but be careful not to have too much slack as the peak will be hard to set taut again. Heave down on the tack cringle if it doesn't run freely, until it lies on top of the boom, and then make the halyards fast temporarily. The tack cringle is either passed over a hook (fitted or seized on to the gooseneck) or its earing or pendant made fast to a cleat on the boom. Lowering the tack of a large mainsail may require a tack tackle to bring it down against the pressure of the wind, as well as setting the luff taut once the throat halyard has been secured.

Once the tack has been made fast the clew earing is hauled down on to the boom. It is essential, for the sail to set properly, that the foot is bar-taut, so the lead of the earing through the bee block must bisect the angle between foot and leach. This is why the boom's weight is taken by the topping-lift or gallows. The clew cringle is then lashed to the boom if a reef tackle is used, or the earing is made fast around its cleat. The reef tackle must be hooked on to the next reef earing so that, if the weather deteriorates further, the next reef can be taken in quickly.

Finally, before the sail is raised again, the reef points must be tied, so roll or gather up a loose-footed sail and tie off the reef points. Loose-footed mainsails must have their reef points tied only around the sail and not the boom, because the points are not strong enough to bear the weight of the boom and may tear the sail. However, when the foot of the sail is laced to the boom the ties will be long enough to encircle both sail and boom. The only exception to this arrangement is when the sail is laced to a rail fitted along the top of the boom, when the ties should only pass round sail and rail. When a reef tackle is used, do take care to avoid tying the points around the tackle as well as the boom on sails with a laced foot.

An alternative to tying reef points is to pass a lacing through each reef thimble followed by a marlin hitch along the full length of the sail. This will work equally well with loose-footed or laced sails. It is more satisfactory when the sail is likely to remain reefed for some time as modern synthetic reef ties can shake themselves loose; but of course it takes longer to lace or unlace.

When the last reef has been tied, raise the main (throat) halyard, and bowse down the tack if a tackle is rigged. It may be necessary to ease the mainsheet and free the boom from the gallows or crutch before the peak halyard is finally made fast. When a topping lift is rigged set up the peak halyard before letting go the lift. Still lying hove-to, ease off the sheets so the headsails cross over to the opposite tack, unlash the tiller and get under way.

Reefing a staysail is a simple task, although likely to be a wet one on the exposed foredeck. If the jib is still set and it is possible to heave-to then do so, otherwise it means coming head-to-wind. Working on a pitching foredeck requires care so use the safety harness and stay clip-on. While working forward, don't be tempted to open the forehatch as a means of passing gear because the moment you do the bows will bury themselves!

Some headsails may have a set of heavier sheets for use in poor weather, so this must be rigged prior to reefing. The sail will have only one set of tack and clew cringles with reef points so the halyard is eased until the new tack can be made fast and the sheets changed over. Should the upper part of the sail start to flog, lower it to the deck and smother it, as a cringle can inflict a nasty gash. Tie off the reef points and rehoist the sail before returning to the cockpit to sheet in and get under way again.

Setting a topsail above reefed mainsail

Although the topsail will have to be lowered with the gaff, it should be possible, depending upon the way it is rigged, to reset the topsail above the reefed main. The type of topsail and the way it is rigged will determine if and how it can be set above a reefed main.

The basic jib headed topsail is usually set hanked on to a jackstay running from the truck to the pin rail, or an eye on the deck, and it is this jackstay which prevents the luff from sagging. It is therefore a simple matter to lower the topsail before reefing the main and then hoisting it again. Some yard topsails also have the lower part of the luff hanked on, and these can be set in a similar way. The only difference is that the top of the yard, which is normally set flying above the truck, will benefit from also being hanked on to the jackstay.

The West Country yard topsail with a full-length yard is more difficult to set as it relies solely upon the tension in the halyard to keep it close against the mast. Once the main has been reefed the topsail can be rehoisted and the tack bowsed close against the gaff through the timinoggie before the halyard is set taut. Unless this is done, the peak of the topsail will sag off to leeward with little effect, with the risk of the yard banging against the mast as it rolls back and forth. Finally the sheet is hauled out through the end of the gaff.

Sea anchors

The sea anchor seems to have slipped from favour with yachtsmen, yet the RNLI still equip their lifeboats with them and a small one is packed into every liferaft. The reason for its loss of popularity is mainly as a result of the changes in yacht design from the heavy, long-keeled hull to the light displacement one.

Look at any anchorage when the wind is blowing, and watch the behaviour of all those craft which are riding to anchor warps rather than chain. The deep displacement hull will lie relatively steadily while the modern fin-keeled yacht will probably be sheering all over the place, an indication of how lively she might be at the end of a sea anchor.

The recommended tactic for most of the modern designs in bad weather has been to run off downwind or stream warps astern – which is fine provided there is the sea room. The older hull can lie hove-to and, if prudence requires that the drift rate needs to be slowed, then streaming a sea anchor is the best way.

Recent research has resulted in significant improvements being claimed over the basic sea anchor design, replacing the conical bag made from heavy canvas with a much lighter para-anchor. The problem with any type of sea anchor is the tripping line becoming entangled with the riding line and so inhibiting recovery after use. The anchor should be streamed from the weather bow, with the warp well protected against chafe in the fairlead, and the yacht will lie fairly comfortably just off the wind. The tripping line should be streamed from the weather quarter to avoid it fouling and twisting around the main warp.

CHAPTER 12

Disaster, or when the worst happens

A very daunting title for the chapter of a book, but it is a tale of preparedness rather than what to do after the event. Most disasters are the consequence of a whole series of small events, which in themselves are not problems but in combination and if they get out of control become more serious.

The scope of potential disasters that can be meted upon a traditional craft should be no greater or smaller than a modern yacht. In fact the construction and equipment carried will make some of the possible difficulties harder to contend with and others easier. Hopefully, most owners will experience nothing worse than grounding for a few hours, or fouling the anchor or propeller. It is by being prepared that the skipper will prevent the succession of mishaps that can prove so disastrous.

On a blustery autumn evening a single-handed yachtsman is motoring his way up-river to the winter mud berth, but has to anchor a few hundred yards short to await the last of the tide. Just before high water, efforts to raise the anchor are thwarted because the anchor has become fouled and is slipped. During hasty attempts to recover this expensive piece of gear, the floating warp fouls the prop and the yacht becomes anchored by the stern before drifting on to the mud. In preparation for the winter lay-up, all the sails are below, and in no time at all the boat is hard-and-fast. An extreme example perhaps, but still a valid illustration of how matters can get out of hand, and a comparatively simple problem becomes potentially disastrous.

The important lesson is always to be prepared, never taking anything for granted. Don't stow gear away until it is certain that it will no longer be required. Never leave emergency equipment ashore just because it's never been needed in the past; that's a sure sign that you'll want it next trip. Most yachts carry gear whose only reason for being on board is 'just in case' and, sensibly applied, it's a very valid reason for carrying it. Merchant ships have a heavy Insurance Wire to be used for mooring in extreme conditions when all else might fail. I have about 50 m (164 ft) of 3-stranded 25 mm (1 in) nylon at the bottom of the cockpit locker to be used as a tow rope or emergency anchor warp. Various other spares are there scattered around the boat, but who knows where they are? None except he who stowed them in an assortment of places. It would be an ideal world if every item and its stowage was listed for the information of those new to the boat – it might be a reminder for the skipper too! (Who hasn't turned out a locker only to remember in the end that the missing object was restowed the previous week?)

It's amazing just what will come in handy one day. Early on a very calm summer morning I left Falmouth in company with a number of yachts heading for France. Only a few hundred yards from the mooring we discovered that the key on the prop shaft had sheared; the spinning shaft then slid aft out of its coupling and jammed the rudder! Nothing daunted, we freed the rudder, then lashed ourselves alongside one of the other yachts and continued on our way while the problem was assessed. My sole crew member, who is a first class engineer, proceeded to make a new key from a brass bolt. It's strange but there were no brass fittings on board, yet I carried a couple of bolts and set-screws.

A mile or so further on, the rudder of the yacht alongside parted company with its bottom pintle, so until that could be manoeuvred back in place I steered while he provided the motive power! The new key was soon made, put back in place and the shaft reconnected for us to resume a normal and uneventful passage. The failure to complete that crossing would have been no more than an upset to our holiday plans, but the same incident on another occasion might not have been rectified so easily.

The first duty of any skipper is to ensure the safety of his crew, and the principal items of emergency equipment must be directed towards this end. It is equally important to remember that until – for whatever reason – the yacht starts breaking up beneath you, the safest place is to remain on board her. The oft quoted 1979 Fastnet illustrated that a number of yachts were abandoned much too soon – occasionally with tragic consequences – only to be discovered still afloat many hours later.

If the yacht is the best form of lifeboat, then make sure she stays afloat by being able to stop water entering the hull and removing any that does manage to get below. The maintenance advantages of fibreglass over wood are well known, but GRP is not so easy to repair in a hurry. A patch can be quickly nailed or screwed into wood and, even if it does continue to leak, the flow of water will at least be considerably reduced.

Not all holes can be patched however. A friend was cruising the Brittany coast when they struck a submerged rock while under power. The quick inspection down below revealed water flooding in but, despite a desperate search, no sign of a hole. The coastline nearby consisted of sandy beaches protected by off-lying reefs, so there was no sanctuary to be had in that direction. A red flare followed by a VHF broadcast quickly brought the assistance of a local fishing boat which soon had the yacht in tow.

The problems, rather than subsiding, increased, because although the fisherman rightly assessed that their need was great, he worsened the situation by heading at full speed for the local port. The yacht was now being towed at greater than her design speed which forced more water through the still invisible holes. The flow of seawater now increased well beyond the capacity of the pumps, or my friend's ability to bail with buckets.

The port was only three miles away and could not have arrived soon enough, and the reception could not have been more efficient or kinder. Awaiting their arrival were the fire brigade, complete with pumps and a diver; the harbour master and police were also there to lend a hand. The underwater inspection disclosed that there were no obvious holes, and although the big diesel pump soon emptied the hull, water continued to flow in. So the pump was left on board while the fisherman towed the yacht a further mile to a safe drying berth alongside a quay wall. The blow had only been a glancing one on the stempost, but was hard enough to loosen all the caulking along the garboard and lower planking. All that was needed to make good the damage was for the remains of the old caulking to be scraped and replaced with new. Repairs were completed over the next two days.

The lesson of this story is that if enough pressure is applied even small holes can let in more water than the best hand bilge pumps can cope with. Had the yacht just cracked or sprung one plank it would have been easier to locate the source of the water and perhaps to plug it.

The average yacht is usually equipped with no more than one hand pump which is really only good enough to deal with a small leak, such as from an engine cooling pipe. Skin fittings, like logs and transducers, are fitted low down in the hull near the keel and vary in size, but 40 mm (1½ in) would be a reasonable average. A hole that size, if it is not stopped, will overwhelm the most efficient yacht handpump. A 125 mm (5 in) hole just 60 cm (2 ft) below the water line will flood a boat with a ton of water in less than a minute, which illustrates how important it is to reduce the flow as quickly as possible.

The old adage that 'nobody can bail a boat quicker than a man in a panic with a bucket' may hold good for a swamped open boat but doesn't hold good for a yacht. Passing 2 gallon buckets up through the hatch and on deck spills half the water on the way. It will take a 2 gallon bucket every 15 seconds to keep pace with the rising water from a little 13 mm (½ in) hole 60 cm (2 ft) below the waterline.

A pump alone is not enough, neither is a chain of buckets unless there are unlimited crew members and buckets. The answer is to cut down the flow of water with anything that can be forced into or held over the hole, even if it's just your hand holding a bundle of rags in the hole, while the crew devise a more lasting method. If the hole is on the lee side, then – unless there is a very good reason for remaining on the same tack – change tack so that the hole is closer to the surface. This may even raise the hole above the water level, but if not it will certainly reduce the pressure and therefore the flow.

Many yachts now keep their headsails on furling gear, so there is little chance of rigging a sail on the outside of the hull to cover the hole, but the spray dodgers, cockpit cover, or canopy might serve just as well. Provided the hole isn't on a concave curve near the keel, the cover can be held flush against the hull by lashings led under the hull from each corner of the cover. This will work only so long as there is a differential between the water level inside and outside which will press the material against or even into the hole.

The external cover will not be enough in itself and must be helped by further work inside the boat. Bunk cushions will help, either slid between the canvas and hull on the outside or braced very firmly over the hole on the inside. The cushions must be placed over the hole and then backed up with locker doors, bottom boards, etc, which sandwiches the cushion between the locker fronts and the hull, improving the efficiency of the plug considerably.

Panic bag

Hopefully, panic is the last thing that will occur in the event of a serious incident, but the term 'panic bag' conjures up an image of its use and possible contents; emergency pack is probably a far more suitable name. The emergency may not even be your own, of course; it may be that of another yacht to whom you are rendering assistance. The pack is not intended to replace the flares, liferaft and other emergency equipment which should be carried by a seaworthy yacht; it is only a supplement, although it may duplicate some items. Never be lulled into thinking that only long ocean voyagers need to take this sort of precaution; if you are on your own then any extra help is vital.

The bag must be stowed under cover where it is easy to reach and will not have other items of equipment piled on top. This tends to exclude one of the cockpit lockers and suggests somewhere in the accommodation, close to the main companionway. The bag should be waterproof and reasonably buoyant so that, whether it is for your own use or that of another yacht close by, it can be thrown over the side. Consequently it must not weigh too much; preferably it should be a plastic container rather than a bag, with a watertight, resealable lid. The standard Department of Transport grey and red flare containers are ideal although a bit small; if all else fails two will have to do.

The selection of items that are to be carried will depend to a great extent upon the range of cruising that you will be doing. Be realistic: it is, for example, 50 miles to the nearest land midway between Cornwall and Brittany, which would take a long time drifting at perhaps 1 knot.

A basic liferaft will carry very little: a sea anchor, rescue quoit, pump and repair kit for the raft, paddles, bailer and a knife. No flares, no first-aid kit, no water or food; in fact nothing to aid survival or attract attention. The quantity of equipment is calculated on the basis of being rescued within 24 to 48 hours.

The emergency pack therefore needs to contain all the missing items, plus one or two more, if it is going to be of any use. The importance of the ability to signal or attract attention, especially at night, can not be stressed enough.

I once spent 2½ hours in a liferaft as part of an exercise on a relatively calm day. The search area in which I was left was small but the search vessel was given the incorrect coordinates and started searching outside the intended area. They commenced the search pattern only 1½ miles away on the other side of a low lying rocky reef, yet still within full view of my bright orange liferaft. They failed to see me. It was only after the search area had been extended that the liferaft was sighted at a range of three-quarters of a mile. Those searching were well-trained and knew that they were looking for a liferaft or similar; yet because I was not in the expected area, the raft was missed. What chance would you have of being seen if you are not being searched for and there is no means of attracting attention?

There is a well-documented case concerning a yacht to the west of Ushant, in distress and unsure of her exact position. She had established contact with a potential saviour by means of a small VHF hand portable, which has a very limited range. Still the ship could not find them because it had no idea in which direction they lay. Just one red parachute flare could have made all the difference in such circumstances.

A similar event, presumably, occurred on a liferaft which was recovered in the Western Approaches about 50 miles off the Isles of Scilly. The raft contained two bodies and from the log book on board it was assumed that they had been adrift for about 10 days, and had both died the day before being found. The Western Approaches are one of the busiest shipping lanes in the world, yet the liferaft, which was lacking stores but otherwise in good condition, had not been sighted. A very sad story but it serves to illustrate how important it is to have the right sort of equipment on board.

A torch plus spare batteries is essential, not only for signalling but for finding other items in the dark; so is a full pack of in-date flares for day and night use. They are expensive but it is false economy to keep them beyond their expiry date. Flares occasionally misfire while they are still within date and the chances of malfunction increase with age, not to mention the risk to you or your raft. I have seen the bottom plug of an expired parachute flare fly out downwards at great speed when it was fired. Not only could it damage some lower part of the anatomy but it would also punch a very large leaky hole in the liferaft. So flares, no matter what type, should always be prepared and fired by holding them outside the entrance flap of the raft.

Following the 1979 Fastnet Race Disaster there was considerable criticism of yachts which had been allowed to take part without any form of radio. This reflected upon the RORC as they set the standards at the time. However, they do represent their members' thinking: it soon became apparent that a significant number of RORC's members were against the compulsory fitting of radio, one stating that he'd never had a radio in the past and saw no reason to start now! The blinkered attitude of that yacht owner (he was certainly not a seaman) fortunately didn't represent the majority view, and attitudes soon changed.

There is a limit to the amount of equipment that can or should be bought, but proven equipment which is designed to alert others to your predicament or improve your survival chances should be seriously considered. I am not suggesting that every new item that comes on to the market should be bought, but the gear that you already have on board can be upgraded.

The liferaft is an expensive item both in terms of intitial cost and servicing, and as a result owners may buy rafts more suited to sheltered inshore waters rather than coastal or offshore because of cost. These basic rafts only usually have single flotation tubes plus paddles, pumps and bailers, but when it comes to attracting attention they are only equipped with a few hand flares, a whistle and perhaps a torch. So why not consider upgrading such a raft on the next service by increasing the variety and quantity of equipment packed. Always remember that this could dictate a larger canister or valise so stowage may have to be altered.

If it is not possible to upgrade your existing raft then look at the various options available. It is well worth checking to see whether the raft has an inflatable floor. A crew which has just abandoned their craft are liable to be wet and the insulation from a double floor will reduce the risk of hypothermia.

The majority of yachts are now fitted with VHF radio even if it is only used to contact the marina for a berth. The increasing numbers of small, hand-portable VHF radios which are on the market are often intended by the owner for use between the tender and yacht. Why not consider them as a standby for the main set, and also to take in the liferaft should the worst happen. They vary in output from a modest 1 watt with only 6 channels, to much more sophisticated multi-channel sets like the ICOM M11 radiating 6 watts.

A cheaper solution to the portable VHF is a small EPIRB (Emergency Position Indicating Radio Beacon) operating on 121.5 and 243 MHz, the civilian and military aeronautical distress frequencies. The signals can be received by high-flying aircraft, which increases their reception range to 100 miles from a set only 4 inches high with a long life sealed battery. The EPIRB is limited in that it lacks a two-way communication facility; while very efficient as an alerting device, further information cannot be passed so it is an all-or-nothing alarm. Once the signal has been picked up and verified a full-scale aircraft search should commence, as merchant ships cannot use their direction-finding equipment on these frequencies. The arrival of satellite communications has improved the system but, as yet, the cost does limit these more sophisticated EPIRBs to mainly commercial shipping and fishing vessels, and their special radio frequencies prevent general alerting of other shipping.

Unless long ocean passages are envisaged, food is of minor importance, although it is a terrific morale booster and therefore small survival packs with glucose or boiled sweets are a good idea, plus any chocolate or biscuits which can easily be grabbed from the galley. Water is a much more important commodity: when cruising European waters the quantities needed are more modest than in the tropics but additional fresh water in gallon or 10-litre cans would be a sensible precaution.

The liferaft will offer some protection from the elements but wear as much protective clothing as possible because hypothermia is more likely to cause death than lack of water or food. Make sure that the boat's first-aid kit is handy, that it is always topped up before each voyage, and that it includes sea sickness tablets. We do have some sun during the summer months, so although it may not be top of the list, don't forget the sun cream amongst the medical supplies.

Grounding

Going aground is probably the most common of the minor mishaps which can befall the yachtsman. It can either be a matter of a few moments working the engine to get off, or several tense hours waiting first for the tide to fall and then rise to bring you upright again.

The first few moments following a grounding are the most important and can make all the difference between resolving the problem or not. Going aground under power shouldn't demand too much effort to get clear again as it will hopefully just be a case of going astern to get clear. Under sail the rules are governed by whether the tide is ebbing or flooding, which point of sail you are on, and if you have grounded on a weather or lee shore.

Check the compass heading as soon as you realise that you are stuck, so that you leave the same way you came in; in that direction at least must lie deep water. Even when making the very first attempts to pull clear, get one of the crew to sound around the boat with the boat hook if a lead line isn't readily available.

If it isn't immediately clear in which direction the deep water lies, use the tender to sound further afield. The tender may not be over the side or inflated, so a quick way of extending the reach of your soundings is to make the lead fast to a short length of line suspended from the end of the boat hook. The crew can then give a clear picture of how the bed is sloping and in which direction escape hopefully lies.

Unless you are very confident about getting off, because the tide is rising, for example, and the yacht will refloat very soon, always assume the worst and react accordingly. If the tide is ebbing and you have not come off immediately, start preparing to dry out – partially or wholly. In the worst cases – on a rocky shore with the sea breaking, or when your soundings show that the boat is likely to topple right over when the tide is out – get ready to abandon. A flooding tide has its own problems, especially if you are aground on a lee shore and the yacht risks being driven further on to the obstruction.

The headsails must be backed and the mainsheet eased immediately after grounding close hauled on a weather shore; if the wind is abaft the beam, gybe to get off. The object is to spin the boat as quickly as possible before she is driven harder on to the ground. A lee shore doesn't offer any quick answers to getting off. Instead the most important task is to stop her being driven further ashore. All sail must be dropped or luffed to cut down windage, and only then can you start trying to get her off.

Reducing the draft is the obvious answer to freeing yourself from the mud; doing so is not always easy. It may sound silly but first be certain exactly where and how you have gone aground. A large ship spent many days being towed by tugs who tried to pull her all the way across the reef on which she had grounded. A little time spent checking the position and she would have been towed into deep water in the opposite direction. Remember that the deep keels of traditional yachts are a number of shapes: the plumb bow, curving to a long flat keel which is just about the same draft for its full length; the rockered keel which is deepest amidships; or the sloping keel, which reaches its maximum draft by the rudder pintle.

The method of reducing the draft will depend upon the keel and therefore

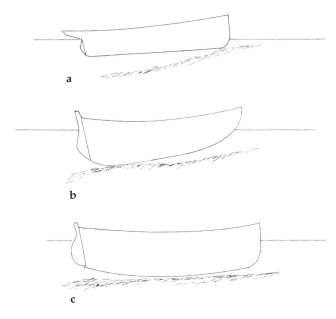

a

b

c

FIG 32 The various traditional hull shapes present different problems should they be unlucky enough to go aground. (a) A level keel will take the ground forward, and only a small alteration in trim by the stern will raise the bow and free the boat. (b) The more traditional yacht hull is usually much deeper aft, so the reverse applies provided the trim can be changed quickly. If the shore is steeply shelving and the bow has touched, a smart burst of astern should free the boat. (c) The rockered hull on a falling tide has little hope of freeing itself and it is doubtful whether it can be listed fast enough to free her from the predicament. Any other alteration in trim will just ground a different portion of the hull.

whether listing or trimming the yacht will free her. The long, level keel requires only that her draft is increased aft for the bow to lift and so float free, while the long, sloping keel has to be trimmed by the bow. The rockered keel requires the same action as the modern fin keel; she must be listed in order to reduce her draft, as trimming will merely alter the part of the keel which is touching.

The quickest way to trim by either bow or stern is to move the crew right forward or aft, even if it means sending them out to the end of the bowsprit to get the maximum leverage. Listing to one side or the other can be achieved in the same way, although the reduction of draft will not be so great. Swinging the boom out over the side and getting one or more of the crew to crawl out on to it takes even greater powers of persuasion!

Laying out the bower or kedge anchor and using this as a means of hauling off is the action you can take when initial efforts have proved fruitless and refloating must take place on the next tide. It is a particularly good ploy when on a lee shore, and some means of preventing further progress up the bank must be devised as the yacht lifts fleetingly with each wave on the rising tide. Lay out the anchor on the longest possible length of warp in the direction of deep water and then heave it taut, if necessary taking it to a winch or bending a tackle on to it. The warp should be led from either bow or stern, whichever ends up closer to the channel. If lying broadside-on then bend on another warp so that equal tension is applied fore and aft. When the bottom is soft sand or mud and the anchor will not bite, a pair of anchors laid in tandem may gain enough grip.

When your best efforts have failed or the water level is falling too fast even to contemplate refloating on this tide, prepare to list heavily or even dry out. First, attempt to heel over so that the yacht is listing towards the high side of the bank. This is of course the opposite direction from that in which the boat was heeled while trying to get free, so don't leave the decision too late or you may not be able to reverse the list.

Many older craft are equipped with legs, and these should be used if the bottom is fairly level; but if there is any danger of only one leg finding a secure footing, don't fit them, as toppling over on to the leg could cause greater damage. Making temporary legs from poles or spars is all very well if there is enough time, but this is usually the one commodity that you are short of.

Pump out the bilges while the boat is still nearly upright because it will be impossible once she is heeled well over, and the water will be liable to reach all sorts of places that it shouldn't. Water in the bilges may also be the first sign that things are not as they should be, once the tide starts to come in.

Check that all loose gear is lashed below, lockers and their contents secure, that tanks will not spill through vents or breather pipes and that all overboard discharges are closed. Protect the side of the hull which is going to settle on the bottom with fenders, sail bags, mattresses if necessary, and even a partially inflated dinghy.

Make sure that there are no obstructions projecting above the bottom; and, if there are any, cover them with gratings or the cabin sole to spread the load. Then wait for the inevitable while taking advantage of the chance to clean the bottom before laying out the kedge as far as it will reach.

The period over low water should be used to sort out a number of things and prepare for the incoming tide. First, clearly work out your passage to freedom and move the anchor if it hasn't been laid in the best position to bring you clear. Expose the inside of the hull where it is resting against the bank and check for cracks or any signs of movement in the frames and planking. There is probably little that can be done at present, but if water does start to seep in later the most likely spots will already be visible. It might be possible to brace any areas which look as though they are being pushed inward, but suitable lengths of wood are unlikely to be readily available.

Cockpits which aren't self-draining must be protected as well as possible in case the rising tide laps over the side. This is particularly important when she is heeled towards the weather. A sail or cockpit cover lashed down securely will help to keep a lot out before she starts to lift on the tide.

Once the tide begins to creep around the hull, start checking that there are no further signs that any of the planks have sprung. The worst part of refloating is when there is any wave action which starts the hull bumping against the bottom. One way of reducing the effect is to keep all the crew on board until she starts to lift, and then get them all into the dinghy if it is no longer trapped under the hull. This should lighten her enough so that the hull will only pound occasionally.

Towing

The need to tow or be towed is a relatively common situation for yachtsmen, yet it's not as easy as it looks. Unlike a car, the yacht astern has no means of stopping, and unless the correct precautions are taken the tow will charge into her salvor's stern. It may sound obvious but in order to complete a successful tow both yachts must have some basic equipment between them. One needs a heavy line to tow with, both must have strong points around which to make the towline fast, and the craft towing requires an engine sufficiently powerful for the conditions.

RNLI coxswains have complained loud and long about the strength and quality of the sampson posts fitted to modern pleasure craft. Some yachts have disintegrated before their stricken owners' eyes as foredecks and then coach roofs have been torn out by well-intentioned, though unskilled, offers of help. One small boat came home with a barrel hitch right round the hull, while another lost all her strong points on the foredeck and reached port with a large anchor hooked through the forehatch!

Older yachts were built to meet the problems faced during a lifetime afloat by men influenced by practicalities rather than budgets and aesthetics. Don't accept everything at face value, however; a 50 foot Colin Archer design, built at the turn of the century, was taken in tow by a small coaster after she suffered a series of serious gear failures, including a chainplate which pulled out of the hull during a gale. The events which had led up to the call for assistance and then a tow should have warned the skipper that all was not well on board. He made fast the first towline that came aboard around the knightheads, each 6 inches square and passing through the deck to the keel. Unfortunately, because the coaster couldn't or wouldn't tow at a very slow speed, they had covered only a few miles before one of the knightheads snapped off flush with the deck. The towline disappeared over the side taking part of the bulwark with it, because the stump of the knightheads wouldn't pass through the fairlead!

The windlass was employed as the next holdfast, but only for a short while before the bolts started to pull through the deck planking under the strain. The final and successful choice was the mast, which should perhaps have been used in the first place, bearing in mind the earlier problem with the chainplate.

It would be very difficult on board a modern craft to strengthen the sampson post or cleats on the foredeck but, because of the construction, older yachts should be easier. Unless the boatyard is willing to give advice and even check the work it is not really a DIY job so get a yard to do the work. If nothing can be done then accept the fact that the mast, provided it passes through the deck or has a very subtantial tabernacle, should be your emergency towing post. When the mast is not suitable on its own the tow rope may have to be passed all round the deckhouse and backed up on after cleats and winches. Do make sure though that they all take the strain evenly, otherwise each will pull out in turn.

When one yacht is towing another, engine power shouldn't be a problem, although yachts with folding propellers have difficulty making the best use of the power available. The important point to remember is that the speed must be governed by the conditions, the length and type of tow rope, and finally the ability of the yacht being towed to steer herself and, if necessary, slow down.

Towing too fast in a heavy sea will impose excessive strains upon the various links in the tow and risk something parting. Trying to connect a tow in a rough sea is difficult enough once, so having to repeat the exercise through lack of care would be rather stupid. Use a heavy three-stranded nylon warp of at least 14 mm, although 16–20 mm would be a better choice as a suitable towline if any distance has to be covered in the open sea, whereas a sheet or mooring warp should be strong enough on a short, sheltered tow. The warp carried for this type of emergency can never be too long, but I would suggest that a minimum of 50 m (164 ft) will suit most cases, including those when the other vessel has nothing to be towed with. Most modern synthetic ropes do have some stretch, but be careful not to use Kevlar or similar fibres which, although strong, won't absorb the snatch load. Do check what you are being offered as it is amazing how many owners invest in cheap polypropylene for their painters which, after a season in the sun, are worse than useless.

The length of the towline will depend upon the weather conditions, especially if there is a significant sea or swell running. The effective towing length should equal

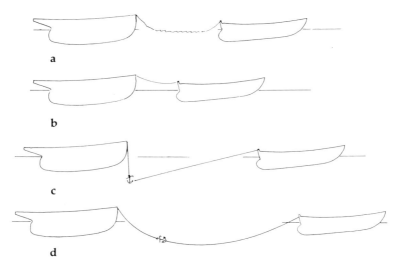

FIG 33 Starting to take a tow not only requires careful seamanship but also an understanding of the mechanics of what is happening between the two craft. (a) A messenger or heaving line is passed between the two vessels before the towline can be passed (b). The towing vessel moves slowly away and stops when the full extent of her towline is reached; the stricken vessel then pays out her line as well as some form of sentinel (c) which is often the anchor. The weight of the anchor hanging down will draw the two craft towards each other. As this happens the towing craft moves away (d) and the tow will follow. Never try to bring the line taut as this will court disaster.

the distance between crests so that both yachts rise and fall at the same rate to prevent excessive loads on the towline. Ideally, the weight of the anchor or sentinel will keep it under water even when the yachts are on their respective crests.

Just as the catenary in an anchor cable absorbs any shock loads from snubbing, so a bight of towing warp hanging down will soak up the occasional snatch or jerk which might otherwise cause it to part. However, it is unlikely that the cordage carried on board the average yacht will be heavy enough, so a weight must be rigged in the middle to make it sag. The quickest and safest way to achieve this is for the towing vessel to pass across a warp which is then made fast to the tow's anchor especially if it has a chain cable. Although a knot will weaken the towline and make it more vulnerable to parting, unless too much speed is tried or the sea conditions are horrific there should never be enough weight on the line to approach its breaking strain.

The chain serves two purposes: the extra weight increases the catenary as well as reducing its vulnerability to chafing on the fairlead or stemhead fittings. When, for one reason or another, the towline is all rope, a weight or sentinel can be used to induce a catenary. A close watch must then be kept on the nip as it passes through the fairlead forward, to see that it neither chafes nor comes out of the fairlead.

Preparing the foredeck

Before the towline comes on board, do all the preparation that you can. This will mean getting your own warp on deck if you have one and covering the foredeck fittings which the towline might rub or wear against. If you are the yacht being taken in tow then prepare your own line if you have one so that it can be made fast as soon as your rescuer passes his line across. The size of the towing warp determines where and how it is made fast on board the tow, so a little time spent deciding this, and how the towline is led over the bow, will be well spent. For example, if the forward sampson post is strong enough then make fast there, but ensure that it is backed if you have any doubt. Securing to the mast is often the safest option but it is a long way back from the bow and may be unsuitable if it is stepped in a tabernacle. Unless there are bitts, or a sampson post where the warp can be turned up properly, the line will have to be made fast round the mast with for example a round turn and two half hitches with the end seized back on itself.

Start preparing the foredeck with the forestay and its bottle screw, which is invariably close to the bow roller or fairlead and in a direct line for the towline to chafe against. Using a split plastic pipe or a length of painter wound round the stay from the deck to a point a foot or so above the deck should do the trick.

The pair of fairleads forward are not always close to the point of the bow, which will make the disabled craft difficult to tow, because unless the towline is led from the centre, the tow will sheer to the opposite direction. Fairleads or bow rollers are frequently incapable of holding a towline in place as the bow pitches up and down; neither are they big enough to take a large diameter rope or one bound with rope or cloth parcelling.

Once a warp escapes there is greater risk of it parting against the edge of one of the foredeck fittings, or bearing hard against the forestay where it is likely either to wear through or part the stay and cause a dismasting. The towline must be bowsed down with a lashing made up from the heaviest rope that can be used into the fairlead or bow roller; alternatively a large snatch block might work if it is shackled to a strong fitting on the bow.

Cutters with bowsprits have additional problems as it will be almost impossible to prevent a warp towline from rubbing against the bowsprit or topmast stay if one is rigged. If it is at all possible the bowsprit should be reefed in so that the towline has a clear lead. Craft using chain and a sentinel should avoid this problem, provided the tow starts slowly and there isn't a heavy sea to cause the snatch in the towline.

Protecting the towline

Remember that the method of protecting the towline against chafe will depend upon how quickly you have to be under tow and how safe it is to work on the foredeck. If you are drifting down close to a lee shore then just haul the towline on board and make it fast: worry about chafe later when there is sea room to stop and work in greater safety.

One way of protecting the towline itself is to split a length of plastic pipe from one end to the other. This can then be slid over the rope in the same way that owners protect their mooring warps in a marina. A pair of small holes should be made, one either side of the split, for some lashing to hold the pipe in place on the rope. When no suitable pipe is available and there is time, the towline must be parcelled with material or heavy rope binding where it is liable to rub against fairleads or fittings. The part of the line which passes through the fairlead should be covered with grease or similar lubricant, again to reduce friction.

Work on the towing craft

Towing with a gaffer should be simpler because there is no backstay to foul the towline, but as most yachts lack a fairlead on the centreline aft, a bridle led from each quarter will be the answer. This will not be so easy to make fast as the cleats and bollards are usually less substantial on the after deck. The bridle may have to be passed through the after fairleads and then made fast on the foredeck. The vessel

towing should pay as much attention to safeguarding the towline, as she will not
have the option of towing with chain cable.

The yacht requiring the tow will usually wallow broadside-on to wind and sea,
setting steadily down to leeward. If she has been dismasted any debris and loose
ends will be streaming up to windward of her. The approach, whether under power
or sail, should therefore be from astern and to leeward of the drifting yacht, Fig 34, so
as to avoid fouling the propeller. As the disabled yacht is closed, free off the sheets
and bear away to run close down her leeward side before luffing up ahead and
passing the heaving line across followed by the towline.

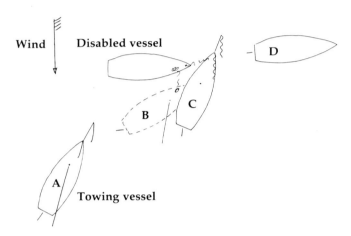

FIG 34 Picking up a tow under sail demands a high level of seamanship by both vessels. The
disabled craft will normally wallow in the troughs across the wind, so the approach should be
made upwind (A) before reaching slowly down her leeward side with sheets free to pick up the
towline (B). The towing boat should luff up close to the bow while the towline is made fast (C),
before again slowly reaching away until the towline is fully extended (D).

Once the towline has been made fast on board the tow, back the jib to bear away
and slowly draw ahead. The towing craft will manoeuvre clear while the tow's cable
or warp is paid out 3 or 4 m (10–13 ft) so that it hangs vertically to prevent it becoming
entangled or twisted around the towing warp. The towing vessel then pulls away
slowly to stretch out the towline and, once there is no further risk of anchor and warp
fouling each other, pay out more from the tow. Ease the sheets to reduce speed
before the weight of the tow can snatch and part the towline.

The proportion of towline paid out by each craft will depend upon whether chain
or rope is used: about a third for cable because of its greater weight or mid-way when
only warp is available. The sea conditions may force a longer length of warp
than necessary for towing to be used initially to establish connection. If this needs to
be shortened, it should be hauled in while the cable is paid out. When only warp is
used the towed craft should use some form of sentinel, even if it's only her anchor;
this should be lowered down the towline on a tripping line. The sentinel should be
positioned about one-third of the distance between the tow and the craft towing.

Starting the tow in a seaway will require patience, as trying to go too fast or
altering course too quickly is liable to part something. Gather way across the sea very
slowly, trying not to bring the towline up taut, leaving the weight of the anchor or
sentinel hanging between the two yachts. In still water and warps of equal length the
weight of the anchor hanging between two yachts would draw them close together
until they almost touch. This is the principle of all towing, so try to use this effect to

move the tow by just drawing slightly ahead and allowing the weight to start the tow moving rather than relying upon the power of your engine to pull her at the end of a bar-taut towline.

Start moving ahead very slowly, and the tow will soon move as the weight of the chain hanging down overcomes the resistance of the tow to moving and pulls her forward. It will be possible to build up quite a healthy speed, but don't forget that slowing down will have to be done in the same way. Normally the middle third of a towline will be under water, more if a heavy anchor or sentinel is used. When approaching port keep an eye on the charted depths, or use the echo sounder and shorten in the towline if there is any risk of it fouling on the bottom.

Following seas make towing very difficult as those who keep their dinghy astern on passage will know. The only solution to preventing the tow from overtaking her saviour is for the tow to stream a warp, heavy bucket or similar drogue astern.

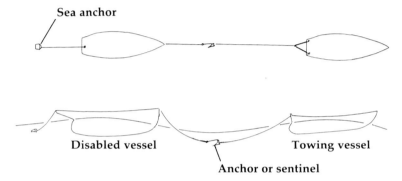

FIG 35 There is always the risk that the tow may attempt to surf down the face of a wave and ram her tug in the stern. A sea anchor or warp streamed astern will help prevent this, but take care not to impede the tow.

Returning the tow to her mooring can be done with her still close astern, but unless there is plenty of clear quay space, getting her alongside will not be so easy. The safest way is to secure the tow alongside and complete the last part of the journey together. Obviously it is important to fender both yachts well, but don't fall into the trap of using the largest inflated fenders you can find. The most important aspect of towing with the other craft secured alongside is that both vessels behave as near as possible as one, and not as two tied together. This means that all the lines must be as tight as possible, which is very difficult if there are large fenders in between. The fenders must be large enough to prevent the two hulls coming together, but that is all. To cushion the curved shape of two hulls, fenders of different sizes could be used; fatter ones forward and aft and thinner ones amidships.

Position the yachts alongside each other so that the maximum beam of the boat towing is just abaft that of the boat towed. When the towing boat goes ahead the combined width of the two boats will try to increase, so tightening the lines further. Make fast the bow and stern lines so that the bows are slightly in towards each other, with centrelines which are not quite parallel. If the craft are made fast in this way there should be no problems, but do keep an eye aloft if spreaders are rigged and make sure they don't tangle. Next run springs from forward and aft; these must be bar-taut to stop one boat surging ahead or astern against the other. Some people consider that only one spring is required between the bow of the towing boat to the stern of the tow. This works if no astern movements are needed, but unless a backspring is used there will be a tendency for the combined beam to reduce, so slackening the other lines. Finally go round and tighten everything again so there is no chance of movement.

Manoeuvring with another yacht lashed alongside will not be easy first time, so try a few simple evolutions before getting into close quarters with the quay or pontoon. Remember that just because the yacht is disabled in some way, this does not mean that all her gear is out of action. If it is only the rudder or steering gear which has failed, for instance, using one yacht's engine ahead and one other astern will turn you round in the tightest of corners.

Decide which craft is going alongside, as this will dictate who will be in the best position to give the manoeuvring directions for both craft. Once you are both happy with the way the boats handle, get under way. Meanwhile it would not do any harm to notify the harbour or marina that you are bringing in a disabled craft so that staff and even boats could be on hand to help on arrival. The harbour may be better able to handle the boat with their own craft so do not be surprised if they seek to take over from you prior to entering the congested harbour area.

CHAPTER 13

Life aboard

The crew's comfort would appear to be easy to provide, although it requires far more than just food, drink and a bunk to sleep in. These are of course important, but so are all the other less obvious details necessary for safe, enjoyable sailing.

For the crew's comfort a yacht requires just as much attention as they do, and if her needs aren't met, then the crew's life can be unpleasant and miserable. Insufficient fresh water capacity – one cup per person per day perhaps – can spoil life! Equally, an unreliable engine or battery charging system will be a nagging worry and should be rectified immediately.

Few of us are likely to spend more than two or three weeks of a holiday aboard at one stretch, but that is no reason for failing to ensure that the accommodation is practical. Stowage may look limited but a little careful thought will establish a place for everything. Lockers aren't always available, since space under the bunks on older yachts frequently wasn't suitable for more than basic items. Neither are they the complete answer to stowage problems, especially when it's not possible to build them into the limited space available.

Clothing has to be kept aired and dry, so provided that condensation isn't a problem, netting slung from either the deckhead or a bulkhead helps to keep the cabin tidy. Nets suspended from the yacht's side make a soft back rest when filled with a sleeping bag.

It is important that the accommodation is safe as well as comfortable. While neither of these factors is entirely within the owner's control, there is a lot which he can do to improve things. Safety must be of paramount importance; not only preventing the obvious gas and water leaks, but also ensuring that movement by the crew is not hazarded by sharp corners. The original interior design – if there ever was one – will usually have ensured that all wood surfaces and edges have been rounded off. However, once the owner gets to work, starting to add modifications, all the best intentions can go by the board. Equipment is usually fitted where it can best be seen – at eye level – which by coincidence also happens to be head height!

In order to move around the cabin safely in a seaway, there have to be plenty of strong handholds within easy reach on either tack. It must be possible to move about without ever having to let go with one hand before taking hold with the other. It is much easier to fit extra grab handles to wood-built yachts than to a boat with fibreglass decks. The coach roof can be particularly difficult, as there are few strong points on to which they can be mounted without removing the lining and bolting through to the deck.

The crew are not the only contents of a boat which suffer from being tossed around in seaway. The contents of a locker can achieve a remarkable speed across the cabin if the locker door is opened at the wrong moment. The sliding doors made from clear acrylic allow examination of the contents before opening the doors, but while clear plastic may suit today's cruiser, it is out of place amid varnish and burnished brass. One answer with a wooden locker-door is for it to be hinged at the bottom instead of the side, so that by peering over the top the risk of the contents flying into the opposite bunk is reduced. All shelves need high lips as another means of stopping the stores from blending together on the cabin sole.

The selection of publications for the navigator are produced in such a variety of sizes that just stocking the bookshelf can be a lengthy task. Finding somewhere to stow a small library of light reading material for a short cruise can tax the best nautical brain. Paperbacks can frequently be found in the booze locker as they are ideal for packing between the bottles to stop them crashing together. Hardbacks are more difficult however; their storage requires more thought.

A light and airy cabin with a skylight and plenty of opening ports, including one at the forward end of the coach roof in lieu of ventilators. Paraffin lighting is enhanced by the strategic mirror fitted behind the lamp over the galley.

The cooker has a substantial crash bar for safety, and this plus the stanchion and deep mahogany rail under the ports provide plenty of handholds for moving around in rough weather. Locker ventilation is improved by the holes drilled through the bulkheads. Note the deep fiddles around all the working surfaces. *Photograph: Peter Chesworth*

The crockery, if it's not to clatter and rattle every time the yacht pitches or rolls, needs sensible storage. The problem is that it is very difficult to clean shelves which are a maze of racks or fiddles, intricately constructed to hold a variety of galley items. Plates may be round, but four pegs forming a square will hold them in place and can be removed for washing. Cups and mugs are safer stacked, but glasses really need their own individual recess, otherwise they jam inside each other.

Searching the cutlery drawer when the yacht is rolling can be a hazardous task, which risks small sections of finger being left behind. Table knives and kitchen knives should be separated when possible – wood blocks with individual slots for a selection of sharp knives is a simple answer.

Unless there is no alternative, I never carry glass containers for sauces, seasoning, jams, etc. The possibility of breakage is great, which risks losing the contents and spreading sharp slivers of glass into unseen corners.

Ventilation

Whatever the climate, boiling sun or cooling winds, good ventilation is essential. The free passage of air through the cabins will improve the situation for those who have a slight tendency towards sea sickness, be it caused by heat, cooking smells or just stale air. The problem with some modern ventilator designs is that while they are very efficient at stopping water from finding its way below, they don't assist the air flow. The reason for this is that low sweeping sails have forced the ventilator to lie almost flush with the coach roof to avoid being fouled by either the sail or sheets. In port the ventilation can be improved by rigging canvas wind scoops over the hatches.

Aboard the small yacht, a cowl vent fitted to a dorade box is by far the best answer to ventilation as it prevents water from going below while funnelling wind down into the cabin. Whenever there is the risk of either sails or running rigging snaking their way around the vent it can be moved from one side to the other.

The problem of damp in the accommodation, crew's clothing, etc, is difficult to solve, and while good ventilation should cure condensation, it is not the only answer. Inevitably the galley attracts water; but apart from this and rain or spray being blown down the companionway, the only other way that salt or freshwater can reach the cabin is on the crew and their clothing. The best way of preventing this ingress of unwanted water is to establish a mental if not physical barrier which stops wet clothing and boots being worn beyond a certain point. Although it isn't practical for the navigator, who may be up and down constantly plotting positions, to take off his foul weather gear, the rest of the crew should be able to alleviate the problem by stowing their gear as they enter. I have seen a number of yacht interiors which boast a separate oilskin locker or suggest that the heads may be used for the same purpose – unfortunately they are located forward! A small locker located alongside the engine, under the main companionway, is an ideal position. It restricts the progress of water through the yacht and derives heat whenever the engine is used.

The galley

There are some aspects of the accommodation which cannot be easily changed. It is usual for cruising yachts to have the galley on the port side, for example. The reason for this convention is that a yacht should be hove-to on the starboard tack when it is not the give-way vessel under the Collision Regulations. Consequently when hove-to the galley is on the low side which makes it much easier to cook and prepare food, even under the most arduous conditions.

Improving the galley area can be a problem, especially on an older yacht which still has her original equipment – grease included! The preferred fuel was often paraffin, which was later changed for an early gas appliance which is now long out of date. How and with what to replace it? On board older yachts I think that it is important to choose something which will remain in keeping with the interior. Consequently a modern oven will usually look totally out of place. One manufacturer that immediately springs to mind is Taylor, who have been creating traditional style ovens and stoves for many years. The cookers are very efficient, and although the brass construction may demand time spent keeping it clean, the appearance is well worth the effort. They are available in three versions to suit most yachts, from a simple two-burner plus grill to a full oven.

Heating and lighting

Whilst paraffin has a number of advantages over gas, not least the problem of finding a space to provide a gas-tight locker on board a wooden yacht, convenience is not necessarily one of them. One of the worries so often quoted by those who do not like gas is that it can escape unheard or smelt, thus posing a serious fire hazard. Paraffin certainly will not do that. It also gives a comforting hiss when it is being used. Should it catch fire for whatever reason, water will put the fire out. The principal disadvantage of paraffin as a cooker fuel is that it is hard to light; the usual method is to preheat the burners with methylated spirit. To save time and inconve-

Opposite of the normal cabin arrangement with galley stove to starboard and the sink together with the chart table to port; all signs that the accommodation has been carefully planned to make the best use of limited space. Note in particular that work surfaces for galley and chart table are the tops of trotter boxes, thus increasing working area without restricting berth.

The grating at the foot of the companionway helps reduce damp being carried through the cabin, as it allows water to drain immediately into the bilges. *Photograph: Peter Chesworth*

nience, use a small propane blow lamp for just a few seconds with the flame playing over the burners. This will bring them up to heat and they should light immediately.

Cabin heaters were for many years solid fuel affairs and could be very attractive, but stowing the fuel and cleaning up next morning is a chore I would rather leave at home. The selection of a replacement heater is more difficult, not because of possible fire risk but because of its potential efficiency in drying out the hull. A ducted air heater may be ideal for the GRP hull but is really not suited to a classic yacht; instead look for a heater resembling the small fuel stove that is being replaced. Although there are any number of gas-fired ones available on the market, diesel or paraffin are preferable fuels. Your choice of heater will depend to some extent upon your choice of cooker. Employing the same fuel for heater and engine reduces the need for a multiplicity of fuels and means that their tanks can supplement each other if the worst comes to the worst.

While on the subject of fuels it should be remembered that some form of secondary lighting is necessary for use on a long cruise if batteries provide the primary source. Paraffin comes into its own here, and should not be viewed with distrust, even though it is not as convenient as switching on a bulb. Remember that a lamp will smoke if the wick is not trimmed – a task which must be attended to every day if paraffin lamps are to be used. Pressure lamps provide a better light, but require pre-heating and, unlike the paraffin cooker, the delicate lamp mantles do not take kindly to blow lamps.

Older yachts have often lost their original oil lamps, which were superseded by electric ones, now reaching the end of their life. Until recently, returning to oil lamps required lengthy searches at boat jumbles or waterside antique shops. Davey & Co, who have supplied chandlery to ships for many years, carry a very comprehensive stock of traditional yacht fittings – including proper brass oil lamps rather than coated imitations.

The chart table

Standing at a chart table is difficult unless it is mounted athwartships because of the vessel's motion. The navigator must either spend his time wedged under the side deck or trying to read a chart from 4 feet away – depending upon which tack the yacht is on. The advantage of the standing chart table is that it tends to be large, but it has probably fallen out of favour for this very reason and because of the quantity of electronic equipment now fitted on modern yachts. The navigator is usually seated, and whether the chart table should face forward or aft depends upon the size of the yacht and the space available. Facing aft makes communication between the helmsman and navigator much easier during pilotage but increases the risk of water getting on to the chart.

The chart table should be on the starboard side because the galley should be to port for the reasons explained earlier. Sailing on the starboard tack, the navigator has to lean in towards the hull, and unless some form of safety strap is fitted he can end up on the deck during more violent motions. On the port tack he is much more secure.

Sleeping and living quarters

Sleeping on board should be no less comfortable than at home, although I doubt that a double bunk has many serious supporters at sea. The idea of being able to roll slowly 4 feet towards a bulkhead only to reach it with a crash does not fill me with enthusiasm. The traditional varnished lee-board is probably the best way of keeping the slumbering crew in their bunks, but boards that are high enough make the bunk uncomfortable to use as a settee. The usual alternative is a lee-cloth, fixed below the level of the cushion and stowed flat beneath it when not in use. A simple lacing or series of strops are then used to keep it and the occupant in place. Provided that a double berth has single cushions then a lee-cloth can be used to turn it into a very serviceable single bunk for either tack, or if berths are in demand, to separate a pair of sleepers at sea. The problem of two occupants is that unless they are both keeping the same or opposite watches, one will disturb the other.

The bunk and settee cushions have a hard life, and one way of keeping up their appearance is to fit removable fabric covers so that they can be washed. It is better if the cushion is covered in a hardwearing waterproof material, with the loose cover over the top. During wet weather when everything below easily gets damp, the fabric covers can be removed leaving a protected cushion which is easily dried with a cloth. Cushions covered in this way can be used in the cockpit as well, either when sunbathing or for a quiet afternoon lounging with a book. Button cushions may look attractive, but add nothing to the comfort of the occupant, who emerges looking as though he has early symptoms of bubonic plague.

The main hatchway is usually very good at keeping water out of the accommodation, unless that water is falling vertically in the form of rain! At sea a small canopy over the hatch keeps the spray at bay and offers limited protection to the crew on deck. In port, rigging a small cockpit cover or more refined tent increases the living space and keeps the elements at bay. When it is hot the cover helps lower the temperature on deck and keep the cabin cool, while in the rain it will ensure that it remains dry down below. The Cornish Crabber has a very good tent which compensates for the lack of standing headroom below, and creates a very snug and dry living area in the foulest of weather. It is surprising how warm it can become, provided the cover or tent is closed at the ends. A simple sheet rigged over the cockpit or just by the hatchway will do a lot to improve living conditions, in particular when only a fine drizzle is falling.

It is important to remember after you have created your dream craft that at some point in the future you will have to sell her. Selling your pride and joy might come as a nasty shock because the items and changes that were essential to you may be the first things that a prospective purchaser will rip out. The moral is not to overdo things and turn a yacht into something that she is not.

Do not be misled into believing that yesterday's ocean or offshore racer will make a good cruising yacht. It might be cheap but it is also likely to be uncomfortable. She may even have all the very latest equipment, umpteen sails and other goodies, but her accommodation will be very spartan and it will not be an easy job to improve. Her motion in a seaway will be quick and lively, lacking the steady gait of a more traditional and heavier cruiser.

The accommodation aboard yesterday's yacht does not compare well length for length with today's version in a number of areas, unless it has been subject to fairly recent total refit. Unless buying a yacht based upon a working boat design or conversion, then headroom is often lower and the internal volume less than in a modern yacht. It is not uncommon for yachts as long as 30 feet to sleep only 2 and devote the whole of the forepeak to a sail locker and heads compartment. However there are exceptions and there is no substitute to looking around rather than just relying upon brokers' advertisements for making a shortlist.

The cockpit

Do not forget the cockpit when assessing general onboard comfort. The crew of smaller yachts will spend far more time, in port especially, in the cockpit rather than the restricted conditions of the cabin. At sea there seems little point spending most of the time below decks unless it is to shelter from the weather. A cockpit should therefore be able to seat the crew without obstructing the helmsman.

One of the great joys of sailing is meeting and talking to other crews in new or foreign ports – a pleasure which often includes some form of entertaining. A large cockpit may seat upwards of 6 or 7, and I have a photograph of a 24 footer whose cockpit is playing host to 10 without too much discomfort. She was trimmed very well by the stern, to the consternation of neighbouring yachts!

The tender

Not all the time will be spent on board and unless the whole of a sailing career is spent voyaging between marinas, then some form of tender will be needed. The rubber inflatable is undoubtedly very practical, in particular for a small yacht which lacks the space to carry her tender on deck when making an open sea passage. Parents feel much safer allowing their offspring to make their first solo efforts in an inflatable tender, even though it does little for their rowing style and is vulnerable to windage.

Probably the most enjoyable tender is a small clinker dinghy with a simple lug rig, which will also carry a low horsepower outboard. Instead of being a means of transport between the foreshore and the moored boat, such a tender becomes an extension of the yacht and her sailing and adds much to the enjoyment of cruising. On days when the weather prohibits passage making, the crew can now be occupied exploring the less accessible limits of the harbour estuary. Clinker or carvel forms of construction are equally practical, and the dinghy doesn't have to have been built for sailing either. A centreboard case isn't necessary, as simple lee-boards can be rigged for windward sailing, the mast can be stepped against the forward thwart and a rudder can be easily hung.

The standing lug is the most practical rig for a tender as it steps the mast right forward and is usually unstayed, permitting the greatest use of the internal volume. The dipping lug is also suitable and probably performs slightly better, but requires more attention from the crew when going about. The sail requires only a simple halyard traveller and single sheet, which in all but the strongest breeze can remain in the hand.

Small open boats, especially those used as tenders which have to be rowed, frequently lack space to provide sufficient cleats or belaying pins. Doubling up halyards on the same pin does not create too many problems, but all too often the helmsman is seen with one hand clinging desperately to the mainsheet and the other grasping the tiller. The simple solution is a pin which projects downwards, fitted under a thwart or the gunwale.

Sailing a small boat which is standing lug rigged is easy, but some new lessons must be learnt. The sails cannot be flattened and must be set fuller than a small gaff or bermudian equivalent. Unless she is allowed to ramp on so that she can carry her way through from one tack to the next, she may end up 'in irons'. To get under way again, try to back the sail by leaning or poling the clew of the sail out to windward. When the dinghy is small or children are in command, use a single on the windward side to row or paddle round with the rudder blade.

It is not uncommon for the yard to be dipped round the mast on to the new lee side, when the sheets are slack, by hauling down on the luff. This is not strictly necessary, but does improve the set of sail as it is not girt against the mast.

A dinghy with a dipping lug has her sailed lowered each time she tacks, unless each board is to be a short one, when with the sail on the wrong side the boat will not sail as well. The boat is brought close to the wind and the sheet is freed off before the halyard is eased, the yard partly lowered and the halyard resecured. The tack is released and the sail doused or brailed in before the forward part of the yard is hauled or pushed aft around to the other side of the mast. The tack is secured on to the windward hook before the halyard is released and transferred to the windward side also, when the yard is raised. The boat is likely to be stopped in the water unless the crew are very slick, so the sail may have to be backed in order to pay off on the new tack.

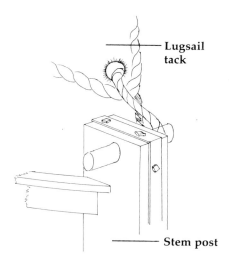

FIG 36 A simple method of securing the tack of a dipping lugsail on the stem of a small lugger. The rope grommet is passed over the pin and the weight of sail and yard keep it in place. Whenever the boat has to be tacked it can be easily unhooked, passed round the mast and secured again.

A good tender can provide endless hours of enjoyment, but it must not be forgotten that it is a small boat and safety precautions should not be allowed to slide. Whenever the tender goes away for any length of time out of earshot or eyesight of the parent craft then she must have some flares aboard in addition to bailers, life jackets, etc.

When the tender has to be towed astern, because for one reason or another it cannot be stowed on the deck, take care that it does not take charge and start nudging the stern. A following sea will give the dinghy a mind of its own, so that it tries to overtake the parent craft. This can be eliminated by streaming a bight of rope astern of the tender to stop her picking up speed on the face of a following sea.

The dinghy can also cause concern when at anchor; it may bump gently against the side when the tide turns, or when the yacht is tide-rode and the dinghy tries to lie to the wind. Yachts with long, high bowsprits can haul the painter out to the end with the traveller and allow the tender to swing, or else secure its stern painter to the traveller before securing the bow painter forward. The reason for hauling the stern out is that the reduced width of the dinghy's bow is less likely to collide with the yacht's stem.

A clear anchorage may permit the boom to be swung over the side and the tender moored to its end, or for some other form of boat boom to be rigged. The congestion of modern harbour moorings and popular anchorages limit the opportunities for this solution to be put into practice. Another solution is to moor the dinghy on a slack painter to the anchor cable and then make fast the after painter over the yacht's bow. The painter must be slack enough to allow the cable to sag without interference and the cable must be brought on board to release the painter.

CHAPTER 14

———

Maintenance and repair

If all the blandishments of salesmen were to be believed, no yacht would need anything more than the occasional wash and polish to keep it looking like new. Modern craft with modest wood trim may be close to this ideal, but the classic wood yacht requires far more attention to keep it in prime condition.

The idea that modern materials require less attention is correct but that does assume that some ageing is acceptable. By contrast, unless a wood hull has suffered very serious deterioration or has been damaged, it can be brought back to a near pristine appearance with paint or varnish much more easily than a GRP hull.

The whole process of cleaning after one season and preparing for the next probably absorbs more time than that spent actually sailing. It is an essential task so try to minimise the effort needed and gain as much satisfaction from it as possible.

Winter lay-up and fitting out

The sailing year is so often divided into three seasons which are separate and distinct from each other. In truth, laying up and fitting out should be one continuous period of planned maintenance work. Lists allow some planning when circumstances prevent more productive work being carried out. In addition, they will serve as a check because it is certain that the weather and other factors will prevent many of the jobs being carried out in their logical sequence.

In order to get the most from a not inconsiderable investment, most owners will start sailing as soon as they can around Easter, and not finish until family or crew mutiny. When the sailing season finishes there is a period of winter lay-up, which is usually undertaken with almost indecent haste, and is separated from the fitting out season by as much free time as possible!

The weeks just before Easter see a rush of eager owners – the lucky ones will be accompanied by their crew – hauling the cover off the yacht that hasn't been touched since the previous autumn. The purposeful and ordered progress of the work turns to desperation as the crane works its way towards them down the line of laid-up yachts. The wiser, often retired, owner watches it all with a smug satisfaction; he will have been working away on fine days all through the winter.

The end of one season should merge into the other, so that before sailing finally ceases, work has already started in preparation for laying up. Equally, it seems pointless to duplicate work, so try to complete some preparation work for the following season that can be done when the yacht is being laid-up. Sails and running rigging are the best examples. Any signs of wear to the running gear can be put right over the winter months and their replacements bought at the best prices rather than the highest. Other work has to be completed as the opportunity and weather conditions present themselves.

Although wood-built yachts are the better for remaining in the water, they have to be taken out at some time for routine maintenance. Unfortunately, the most suitable weather for painting and varnishing also happens to be the best weather for sailing, so the yacht has to be maintained under less than ideal conditions.

The end of the summer holidays also marks the end of sailing for many yachts-men, but boats still remain on the mooring or marina berth. An unexpected Indian summer can provide enjoyable sailing right through until early November, and the pressure to stay in the water can be great especially if the summer's weather has been foul.

The sooner painting and varnishing are started the less likelihood there is of having to rush the job in unsuitable conditions. The fine days of autumn and approaching winter may be shorter but much of the painting and varnishing work can be started even if the final coats can't be applied. The sails can be aired and stowed away or taken for repair and valeting at the sail loft, and the winches and other running gear stripped down, cleaned and serviced ready for next season.

Cleaning the hull inside and out

Once the yacht has been lifted out, start work at once to clean her down. The best way to remove slime, weed and the general muck that accumulates on the under-water surfaces is to wash it off as soon as the boat is lifted from the water, before it dries and solidifies on the hull. The quickest way is with a pressure washer, but take care on wood hulls that the power isn't too strong and it starts to remove the caulking for you! The other more gentle way to remove the season's weed is with a scrubbing brush, but as this will take longer use a hose or buckets to keep the surface wetted down.

The time spent cleaning the hull while it is still wet will save hours of effort if it has been allowed to dry hard. Barnacles can also be more easily persuaded to release their grip at this stage without a telltale ring of shell left when they are dead. While the underside is being cleaned, check the condition of the anode; if it needs replacing note it on your list.

The decks must be washed off before the boat cover is lashed in place. Take the opportunity now to scrub any bare teak such as cockpit gratings. Oxalic acid will remove bad rust stains while one of the proprietary cleaners will reduce, if not wholly lift, grease and oil.

The anchor and cable should be ranged along the decks to be washed or hosed off with fresh water. The chain locker, which is a great harbinger of salt crystals, needs to be cleaned very thoroughly before being washed down. When the yacht is laid-up ashore and it is safe to do so, leave the anchor and cable laid out under the boat. If the cable has to be left on board then flake it out on polythene to prevent rust stains along the deck, or stow it in a couple of well-covered buckets. One tip to remember for the next season is cover the threads of all shackles with plumber PTFE tape. I have found that this keeps the threads clean and free of rust for a full season, even on the lower bobstay shackle.

Once the exterior is clean it is time to go below and clean the interior thoroughly as soon as possible after the boat comes ashore. Start by going through all the lockers and stowage spaces to make sure that nothing has been left behind, especially the odd items of food – they will look and smell horrible next spring if they are missed!

Provided there is enough space at home remove all the soft furnishings, including the bunk mattresses and cushions, so that they can be cleaned and aired. Pump or sponge out any salt water from the bilges and then sweep the cabins clean; remove any dirt and fluff which may have escaped into the bilge. Check that the limber holes under the frames are clear of dirt and that water will drain freely aft to the bilge pump. Wash down all the cabin surfaces, lockers and under the bunks before bailing out the bilge a final time and drying it out.

The galley and heads require special care. Make sure that nothing is left in any of the overboard discharges and finish off by pouring some disinfectant (well-diluted) down the basins and toilet bowl. Once all the cleaning has been completed, empty the fresh water tanks; bring a gallon can of water to make tea during the winter months.

All hatches and vents should be left open, so should the locker and cabin doors to allow the air to circulate during the winter. The deck boards on the cabin sole must also be lifted.

Follow the manufacturer's instructions carefully and winterise the engine; don't forget the tender's outboard while the spanners, oil and grease are about. All seacocks must be shut to help stop frost damage; the exhaust should also be plugged with something highly visible so that it will not be forgotten before the engine is started next season. The electronics ought to go ashore along with the main batteries; and dump the dry-cell batteries from torches and equipment.

Mast and rigging

Wood masts will have suffered from wear and or chafe during summer months and, if it isn't possible to keep the spars under cover during the winter, they will need to be treated now. Whatever wood treatment is used, at least complete the initial preparation and apply at least a couple of coats to protect exposed wood over the winter.

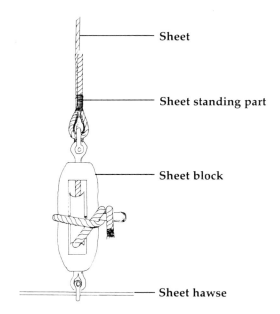

— Sheet

— Sheet standing part

— Sheet block

— Sheet hawse

FIG 37 A traditional means of securing the sheet fall to a pin on the side of a wood block. The arrangement is commonly used when the sail is self tacking and the lower sheet block runs on a hawse. A cutter's or schooner's foresail is a good example.

Older, more traditional boatyards will have undercover storage for wood masts, but the advent of aluminium spars has resulted in reduced demand for this facility. The mast must be supported at frequent intervals on trestles clear of the ground with lights, aerials and running rigging removed. Plugs and sockets should be protected with a smear of Vaseline and then be taped up to keep out the weather.

When the mast is to remain in place, either stepped or still on board, then remove as much of the running rigging as possible so that it will not suffer over the winter. Lash any rigging that is remaining on the mast to stop further chafe or wear. This is particularly important when the mast is to remain stepped; winter gales like nothing better than a loose end to play with.

Inspect all the standing rigging, shackles, blocks and bottle screws for signs that any will have to be replaced by next season. If the mast is coming down then grease the threads on the shackles, bottle screws and mounting bolts so that they will not seize over the winter.

Mast apron

Since a keel-stepped mast passes through the deck, this hole must be sealed if the boat will not be covered, so don't forget the wedges and apron when unstepping the mast. The wedges hold the mast in place while the apron keeps it watertight. Make sure that the wedges are safely stowed as they can easily be lost in the flurry of activity as the mast is lifted out. Probably the simplest way to seal the hole for the mast is with a short length of timber the same shape as the mast but with a flange on the top to seal against the deck.

The top of the apron is lashed to the mast while the bottom is sealed to the deck with either a wood or brass ring. Depending upon the size of the mast the ring may either be in sections or complete; if the latter, make sure that it's in place before the mast is restepped. If the sealing ring has been lost or damaged a new one must be made from a non ferrous metal like brass or stainless steel. The ring should be two equal half-circles of flat bar which have a greater inside diameter than the overall diameter of mast and wedges. The bar must be drilled for fixing screws every 50–75 mm (2–3 in).

Replacing the mast apron

The apron is made from canvas which will deteriorate in time; once it's beyond repair, use it as a pattern for its replacement before throwing away. When there is no original available to use as a pattern, use cardboard to make one. Start deciding how far above the deck the apron will be lashed and then measure the mast's circumference (A) at this point. Measure around the circumference (B) of the deck sealing ring and finally measure the distance (C) from the top lashing on the mast down to the inside of the ring.

Before cutting, add 50 mm (2 in) to both circumferences to allow for turning over to seam down the edge; add 100 mm (4 in) to C for turning under the binding at the top, plus at least double the width of the sealing ring for tucking under.

Wedges should be made from hardwoods like teak and iroko that will not shrink or swell too much. Provided they can be kept in the right order, small ones are just as good as preshaped ones.

A simple mast apron lashed and sealed with tape to prevent any water gaining entry to the accommodation. The mainsail, instead of having lacing or mast hoops, has parrel beads instead. *Photograph: Peter Chesworth*

The boat cover

The topsides must be covered over for protection from the ravages of winter, especially if they have been well weathered by a blazing sun during the summer months. Nothing can strip varnish or expose the weak points in the paintwork like an overdose of sun followed by a winter of wind, rain and cold.

Covering the yacht allows winter residents who are really intent upon gaining access to do so at their leisure under cover of a tarpaulin. The newer, industrial translucent sheeting will overcome this problem to some extent but may allow the harmful effects of sunlight to continue their work. There really is no substitute for regular visits for deterring uninvited winter crews.

It is best to use a purpose-made boat cover which is a snug fit, rather than a selection of cast-off lorry tarps which are difficult to tie down securely and invariably leak. A poorly tied down cover is liable to rip in the first real gale, while canvas and rope flapping in the wind may well add to the damage done during a season's sailing.

Some covers can be fitted with the mast still stepped and the choice of which type of cover is used will depend on how easy it is to unstep the mast and lift it out. The mast is often used as a ridge-pole for the cover; if it is, it must be well supported along its full length, otherwise it may become bowed as the lashings are tightened.

The boat must be covered from end to end and down as far as the waterline, but don't stop the free passage of air through the boat. It is especially important to cover a wooden hull to the waterline as this will cut down the risk of drying out and opening up. On fine sunny days when visiting to check that all is well, open the cover to dry out any condensation that may have accumulated.

Sails

Sails, like every item of equipment, require care and attention if they are to last as long as they should. The canvas and cotton sails were very susceptible to the ravages of damp because they frequently had to be stowed away after a thorough soaking. Modern materials don't suffer from the same problems, although they should not be stored wet at the end of the season; it is sunlight which ruins today's sail cloth. The effects of ultra-violet light break down the cloth and stitching quickly if the sail is exposed for long periods of time. The sail must never be left unprotected from direct sunlight when not in use, and must either be stowed away down below or be covered. The popularity of roller furling for headsails has dictated that a sacrificial blue strip of cloth is sewn along the leach and foot of these sails which is a simple if unattractive solution to the problem.

Sails that are kept below should be folded carefully and not allowed to crease; polyester is especially vulnerable to creasing if folded in the same spot repeatedly. I prefer to coil the luff wire so that the sail forms a long tube, before wrapping the sail around the coil. This method reduces – if not entirely eliminating – the number of creases resulting from sharp folds.

At the end of the season if the sails are not being taken to the sailmaker for attention or valeting they must be washed and aired before being put away. Lay each sail out on a flat surface clear of sharp projections; the lawn is better than a concrete or stony drive! Examine the sail closely for any signs of damage or wear and attend to any stains that need special treatment. The most difficult are either rust or oil marks. Oxalic acid is good for the former while neat Tufanega or Swarfega will usually shift oil and grease if applied early with a clean cloth. When paint or varnish gets on to the sail seek advice before using thinners or similar products as they might melt or damage the sail cloth. General dirt and grime can be removed with mild soap, warm water and a scrubbing brush.

The sail must be hosed off on both sides with fresh water to remove any salt crystals; it is these that do the damage if allowed to work their way into the fabric. Allow the sail to dry thoroughly before finally rubbing saddle soap into all the leather patches along the bolt ropes to stop them drying out and cracking. A single drop of light machine oil on the piston hanks of the headsails will keep them from seizing over the winter.

The best method of winter storage is to hang them from the rafters in a large barn or similar building; but as few owners can enjoy that sort of luxury, draping them across lines rigged in the attic is a satisfactory alternative. The last resort must be to put the sails back into their bags as there is always the risk that a family of mice will have taken up residence during the winter months.

Much of the attraction and charm of traditional designs has been their uniqueness, many changed or modified from their original specification. This can pose a major problem when it comes to ordering new sails as, unless the chosen sailmaker has the details on record, the sails will have to be made up from patterns or measurements. When it's not practical to send away the old sails as patterns, and they are unable to come and take the measurements themselves, you'll have to do the job with their guidance. There are one or two basic rules to remember in this respect. Start by making a list of each measurement and then drawing a plan as a means of checking that all measurements have been taken. When the halyard and perhaps tack downhaul pass through a block, make sure the measurement is between the bottom of the blocks and not the jaws of the sheaves.

A steel tape is better than a linen one because it doesn't stretch; ensure before reading off the length that the tape is bar-taut – a sagging tape will result in a sagging sail. Double check each measurement before writing it down as soon as it has been taken. There is a great truth in the saying 'mark twice and cut once'. When using the halyard to haul the tape aloft, make sure that there is a downhaul rather than trying to bring it back down by pulling on the tape.

Starting with a jib, the length of a luff rigged at the end of a long bowsprit is probably more easily measured alongside a pontoon rather than walking out to its end! Also measure the foot and leach of the existing sail; when one isn't available it will be necessary to take as many other measurements as possible. Starting from aloft, measure to the deck at the foot of the mast, then along the bowsprit to the stemhead if a staysail is set, and finally from the tip of the bowsprit to the mast. Measuring for a new staysail would follow similar lines, but don't forget to specify the size and type of hanks used.

Replacing a gaff mainsail should not be viewed with undue alarm but, like all sail measurement, mistakes can be costly. It will be simpler if the old main is available, not so much as an exact pattern, but to ensure that the height and angle of the gaff are taken correctly. Provided the old sail is still serviceable it should be used as the basis for all the measurements. If it's not, then seek advice from your sailmaker as he may prefer to take the measurements himself. A number of basic details can be recorded, however, while the sail is still laid out on the deck or harbour side. Record the number of reefs and reef points plus the distance between them. At the same time count the number of cringles or eyes along the luff for the lacing or mast hoops. Record any deviations from the normal cut of the sail or problems that you have experienced which the sailmaker could cure.

Bend the sail on to its spars as described in Chapter 5 and then raise it up the mast, setting it as near as possible to the ideal. The fact that a replacement is being considered indicates that the old main has reached the end of its useful life and therefore is probably full of creases. Nevertheless it will serve as a guide. The best way to measure a gaff sail is across the diagonals as well as along the sides, so make a tape measure fast to the peak and the throat.

Set the gaff and make sure that stretch in the sail doesn't allow the boom to sag down too much. If it does, raise it to the correct height by using the topping lift. There will be some stretch in a new sail so if this isn't done the boom could end up lower than the original one. Once gaff, boom and sail are set satisfactorily, the measuring can begin. Start with either the throat or peak and measure the distance from here to the clew and tack. Repeat the measurements from the other upper corner of the sail down to clew and tack.

When two vertical sides and diagonals have been measured, it remains only for the length along both gaff and boom to be marked for the job to be complete. Draw all the measurements on to a plan and check them at least twice; errors can be corrected provided they enlarge the sail, but when it's too small things may not be quite so simple. The same procedure applies to any gaff sail, so for ketches, yawls or schooners the task is identical.

Woodwork

Everyone likes the appearance of varnish but many dislike the work entailed in keeping it looking good. The sun tends to bleach unprotected hard woods like mahogany, while water creates dark stains; and oily woods like teak throw off varnish after only a few seasons. The two-pot polyurethane varnishes will give a tough, long lasting finish, but once the surface is damaged and water starts creeping underneath, it's difficult to restore without starting again from scratch.

In order to restore the colour to stained or faded wood the surface has to be removed by scraping, including the old varnish. One solution to the bleaching effects of the sun when bare wood is exposed is to apply an oil, stain or preservative before the first varnish coats are applied. The choice of colour and maker is a personal one; when no advice is available locally, it will just be a case of trial and error on a piece of scrap wood. Strangely, most owners consider they can achieve a good paint finish, but that a good finish with varnish is much harder. The truth is that mistakes become apparent quicker in poor varnishing because they start to show through, whereas paint covers all until it falls off or is stripped. The answer to either a good paint or varnish finish is in the preparation.

The old varnish can be removed in a number of ways, from simple scraping, through a heat gun, to using one of the modern chemical strippers. The choice will depend upon how big an area has to be stripped, whether it is flat or intricately carved and upon what resources, like power and water, are available. Whichever method is chosen for removing the old varnish, don't forget to remove all fittings and to work with the natural grain of the wood. Once the old varnish has been removed, go to work on any areas that have been discoloured by bolts or other metal fixings.

Whether starting with new or stripped wood, it's always very important to sand the surface well before applying the first coats. Fine wire or steelwool can be used to lightly abrade hard varnish, but be very careful not to leave any particles behind on the surface of the varnish and surrounding area. Remove as much dust as you can with a brush, wash off with spirit or thinners and finally wipe over with a clean rag soaked in whichever was used to wash off. If water is allowed to start reacting with the steel a fine rust sheen can blossom all over the brightwork.

Between each coat the surface should always be lightly sanded down and then wiped over with a lint free rag soaked in thinners to remove fine dust. Once any coats of stain or preservative oil have dried, brush on the initial varnish coats, which should be diluted 50:50 with the appropriate thinners so that it will soak deeply into the grain. These first three or four coats of varnish should be followed by a similar number of coats, diluted only to 75:25, before applying the final undiluted coats. The number of final coats will depend upon how well the wood has soaked up the earlier coats, but to achieve a really good finish expect to put on between 4 and 6 coats.

Varnish work on deck will require attention each year, and will probably have to be stripped back to bare wood every few years. The cabins down below are another matter; if they have had a very thorough coating with a good 2-pot polyurethane varnish, and provided the surface is not liable to damage, it should last for years.

Having spent all the time and effort on preparing the varnish work there can be nothing worse than the first chip or scratch. I have my own way of dealing with them without all the performance of keeping a varnish tin, brush and sandpaper on board or collecting it all from home. Instead I use an empty bottle of the type used for typists' or printer stencil correcting fluid, even a nail varnish bottle will do. The significant thing about them is that they have a small soft brush as part of the cap.

Clean the bottle and brush thoroughly before topping it up with the varnish and make sure that the cap is screwed well down before stowing it on board. I roll 2 or 3 strips of different grades of sand paper around the outside to rough up the surface before application.

Much of the effort spent at the end of a season when the weather may be finer will be well spent. The weeks before Easter are highly unpredictable and the weather is almost bound to change to endless wind and rain as soon as the crane has been booked to lift you back into the water.

CHAPTER 15

Glossary

This is a glossary of less common words used in this book. Where several words or phrases have the same meaning, the definition is given against the most common one.

aback   a sail is aback when the wind blows upon the reverse side to that on which it is sheeted. See **back, to**.

abaft   aft of or behind – part of a vessel that is towards the stern relative to a specific position: 'abaft the beam' or 'abaft the mast'.

abeam   usually abreast of the middle of the craft; at right-angles to the fore-and-aft line.

about   the status of a sailing vessel after it has tacked; 'she's gone about'; or the order prior to tacking; 'Ready about!'

above board   above the covering board, on deck; clear and visible; not obscured or hidden.

adrift   floating free, broken from its moorings; to cut adrift is to cut loose. Poorly stowed or lost gear is also adrift.

advantage   when a purchase is rigged so its hauling part leads from the moving block and gives maximum power available.

aft   generally the after portion (also after part) of a vessel; an order to go aft or to haul aft a sheet which means to pull it in the direction of the stern.

after   being aft; the after hatch – opposite of forehatch.

after peak   a small locker located in the aftermost extremities of a boat. The aftermost tank aboard larger vessels. See also **lazarette**.

ahead   anything which is in front of the vessel or her course; opposite of astern.

a'hull   See **bare poles**.

a'lee   on the lee side. The term is little used nowadays being strictly opposite to 'a'weather'.

all-standing   everything in its correct position; so to gybe all-standing is to do so unprepared. To be 'brought up all-standing' is to be stopped or checked suddenly by the anchor with too much sail set and probably going too fast.

amidships   the area midway between bow and stern; the middle part of the vessel. To have the helm amidships means that it and the rudder are lying in line with the keel.

answer the helm   a vessel answers the helm when she responds to the action of her rudder.

apostles   See **knightheads**.

ardent   the tendency to come to; fly up or gripe against weather helm.

arse   the bottom of a wood block opposite to the crown; also the space between sheave and shell through which the fall does not pass.

astern   behind; outside the vessel, the opposite of ahead. To drop astern is to be left behind or to drift sternwards.

athwart   across the vessel, the opposite of 'fore-and-aft'.

athwartships   See **athwart**.

a'weigh   when the anchor is clear off the ground when heaving in; you have the 'weight' of it.

back, to (1)   to back is to do the opposite, so to back the jib means to haul it out to weather and catch the wind on its lee side in order to blow the bow round. See **aback**.

back, to (2)   to give added or extra support to something under pressure.

back and fill, to   a series of short tacks by which progress is made up a narrow channel aided by a favourable tide against the wind. The helm is put slowly down until the craft almost luffs. While the tide pushes the craft back to windward, the headsails are backed and the boat gathers way again on the same tack. Also to remain in one place by backing and filling sails on the same tack. See **gilling**.

backing   the opposite of veering, usually meaning the alteration of the wind's direction in an anti-clockwise direction. More correctly the wind is moving back against the sun.

backstays   standing rigging which supports the upper portion of the mast, in particular when reaching with a beam or following wind. They are led aft to the sides of the craft.

baggywrinkle   short lengths of stranded rope frapped into bushy lengths, then served around the standing rigging at points where there is risk of damage to the sails from chafing.

balance lug   similar to a standing lugsail but with the addition of a boom.

balance reef   taking a reef which turns a gaff into a three-cornered sail. The reef crosses the sail diagonally from throat to clew. It is not common practice today.

ballast   weight which sinks a craft to her designed waterline, counters the heeling effect of the wind on the sails and provides a safe righting moment. May be either fixed or movable internally, or bolted externally to the keel.

balloon canvas   large lightweight sails which are used in light airs.

bare poles   a heavy weather tactic when conditions are too bad to sail or man the cockpit. No sails are set and the craft lies or scuds before the wind.

batten down, to   to ensure that all openings are secured, shut and watertight, especially when bad weather approaches.

beam, a   one of the timbers fitted athwartships which support the decks.

beam, the   the width of a vessel across her widest part. Also the stock of the anchor.

beam-ends   a ship is on her beam-ends when laid right over at almost 90 degrees – so that her deck beams are nearly vertical.

bear, to   the bearing or direction of an object from a vessel either relative to the ship (i.e., 30 degrees to port) or as compass bearing.

bear away, to   to sheer away from; to take action to avoid or to move away. To bear away is also to put the tiller to weather, free the sheets and move in a leeward direction.

bear off   to fend off or shove away.

bear up, to   logically to bear up should be the opposite of bear away, but in fact refers to the tiller being moved and so has the same meaning.

beating   to sail close to the wind, working to windward in a series of tacks; hence, beating to windward.

becket   the eye at the bottom of a block to which the standing part of the purchase is made fast. A loop usually spliced into a short length of rope which is then used for securing objects in their stowed position. See **lizard**.

becueing   See **scowing an anchor**.

bee blocks   sheaves or blocks for the reef earings to render through, fitted on either side of the boom end.

before   forward or in front of; before the mast.

belay, to   to make fast; a rope which has been hauled in will be made fast.

belaying pins   wood or metal pins fitted to a pin or fife rail to which ropes are secured; the pins are usually removable to aid release.

belly   the curve or arching of a full sail.

belly halyard   an additional halyard rigged to the middle of a long gaff.

bend, to   to secure one rope to another or to bend a sail on to its spar. See **hitch**.

berth   the place where a craft lies in harbour, either alongside or riding to her anchor – a safe berth. Also the bunk or bed where a sailor sleeps.

bight   the loop of rope hanging down in a coil, or that part between its two ends. Also the single coil lying on deck: 'Don't stand in the bight!'

bilge   the curve where the vertical side of the hull turns under and becomes the bottom. Hence 'bilge keels'; a boat is bilged when holed in this area. That part within the hull just above the keel where water collects; to pump the bilges.

bill   the point of an anchor or hook.

binnacle   the housing for the ship's compass, usually made of wood or brass.

bitter end   a corruption of Better End; the inboard end of the anchor cable or hawser. 'Better' because this portion of the cable was little used and therefore the better of the two ends.

bitts used for securing warps and cables; a pair of strong upright timbers rising through the deck around which the cable was wound. Aboard small craft bitts would also serve as the knightheads to support the bowsprit.

block a pulley. The number of sheaves indicate the capacity; a single block has one sheave, a double block two sheaves, etc.

block and block See **two blocks**.

block to block See **two blocks**.

bobstay standing or running rigging under the bowsprit to stop it lifting – usually a chain or heavy wire between the end of the bowsprit and the stem.

body hoop iron or metal bands fitted around to strengthen a built or made mast. Also to support a mast with shakes or a scarph joint.

bollard mooring posts usually on the quay, although may also refer to a single bitt aboard a boat.

bolsters hardwood cheeks or chocks bolted to the mast for the rigging to rest on and prevent chafing.

bolt rope the rope sewn into the edge of a sail to prevent wear to the sail by chafe. Also strengthens small heavy weather or storm sails which are often set flying, so lacking support from mast hoops or lacing to the spars.

bonnet extra sail area laced to the bottom of a loose-footed sail to increase the sail's size in light winds. If fitted to a square sail then it is usually no more than a third its area.

boom the name usually given to a spar with one end secured to the mast along which the foot of a fore-and-aft sail is set.

boom crutch a removable version of the boom gallows, usually mounted at the stern in which to stow the boom. See **gallows** and **scissor crutch**.

boomkin a small spar extending from the gunwale or ship's side to give the sheets a fair lead. See also **bumkin**.

boot-topping formally the paint or treatment used on the waterline area of a vessel's hull, in particular on those vessels with a significant difference between their loaded and light waterlines.

bouse See **bowse**.

bow the forepart of the vessel; 'on the bow' means anything visible or sighted between 4 points on either side of the bow.

bower anchors the normal working anchors. North of the Equator the 'best bower' is the port anchor. The wind usually veers in the northern hemisphere; consequently, if a second anchor is needed, the starboard can be dropped without fouling or crossing over the port cable.

bowse, to to pull on anything with a tackle; the luff of a sail is bowsed down to stop it sagging off.

bowsprit the spar which projects forward of the stem. It enlarges the fore triangle so enabling more sail to be set or the mast stepped further forward – a boon on cruising craft.

bowsprit cap See **crance**.

box haul to bring a vessel quickly round from one tack to the other when she will not tack through the wind – similar to wearing. When rigged fore-and-aft the vessel is brought up into the wind but, as the seas force her to pay off, the helm is put to windward and the mainsail scandalised. The full pressure of wind upon headsails brings the stern quickly up into the wind. Once the wind is on the opposite quarter, the main is reset as the craft gathers way on the new tack.

brails the ropes which gather up a boomless mainsail, spanker or spritsail. It encircles the sail via lead blocks on the mast and through the leach cringles to draw the sail towards the mast for stowing.

break out, to to unstow for use; to break out the sails from their lashings, also to break out the anchor from either its stowage or the seabed.

breast rope a short mooring line between vessel and shore at right angles to the fore-and-aft line.

bridle a length of chain, rope or wire, purpose-made for connecting two objects; a mooring bridle between ship and buoy.

bring-to to bring a messenger or warp to the capstan or winch.

broach-to, to to fly across the wind against the action of the tiller when running before it, usually in a heavy sea. It is often the result of poor steering or too much sail. To turn suddenly broadside on the face of a following steep sea – if the sea breaks then the boat can be swamped or overwhelmed.

broad reach sailing with the wind abaft the beam, between reaching and running.

broadside-on sideways-on to the sea

with the full weight of the wind and waves against the hull.

brought by-the-lee   an involuntary gybe, being caught with the wind suddenly on the lee side.

brought up   a vessel is brought up when she lies settled to her anchor. After dropping astern on wind and tide, tautening her cable, she then slowly works her way back up to ride to the cable.

bulkhead   either temporary or permanent divisions separating sections of the vessel, perhaps into watertight compartments.

bull rope   a rope used to stop a mooring buoy from fouling the bobstay and bow. A line secured to the buoy, led through a bull's eye at the end of the bowsprit which when hauled inboard keeps the buoy clear.

bull's eye   a round thimble made of hardwood through which a rope may render freely.

bulwarks   the sides of a vessel above the deck but of solid construction as opposed to rails.

bumkin   a wooden spar pointing aft over the stern of a yawl or even ketch to take the mizzen sheet and to help stop the boom lifting. See also **boomkin**.

bumpkin   See **bumkin**.

bunt   the middle of a furled sail or the belly of a full-cut one.

bunting   the material or fabric used to make flags, a strong but open weave. Slang for flags.

burgee   a signal flag with a swallow tail; a small triangular flag or pennant indicating membership of a particular yacht club.

burton   a tackle made up of two single blocks.

button   See **truck**.

by the head   a vessel trimmed so that her forward draft is greater than the after draft.

by-the-lee   sailing free with the boom on the same side as the wind.

by-the-wind   sailing as close to the wind as possible.

cable   the rope or chain secured to the anchor and by which a craft is moored. Also being approx one-tenth (100 fathoms or 600 feet) of a nautical mile.

camber   the upwards arch of ship's deck towards the centreline – the athwartships equivalent of sheer.

cap   an iron band shaped like the number '8' used for attaching the extension of a mast or bowsprit. The lower cap is sometimes called the yoke.

capsize   to turn over a boat or a coil of rope.

carry away   to break anything, usually rigging or cordage.

carry way   to continue moving forward due to momentum rather than any means of propulsion.

cast, to   usually to 'cast the lead' but also an anchor. To use the sails to pay off the ship's head when weighing anchor so that the sails start to draw.

cast off, to   to let go.

catch a turn   to take a turn around a capstan or bitts so that the strain may be held on a rope.

cathead   a timber or small davit projecting over the bow from which a Fisherman's or similar anchor is hung as the stock prevents it from stowing in the hawse pipe.

chafe   to rub or wear against.

chainplate   plates bolted outboard, taking the lower ends of the shrouds and other principal standing rigging.

channels   timber attached outboard between the hull and chainplate to give the shrouds a greater spread.

check, to   to steady or stop the rate at which a rope is being slacked away – even to take a turn and so use the friction to slow down.

check her, to   to stop or reduce the swing of the ship's head when altering course quickly.

cheeks   the sides of a wood block.

cheek blocks   a sheave fitted on the side of a spar; the topsail sheet passes through a cheek block on the gaff.

chock-a-block   See **two blocks**.

chock-up   a gaff or sail is chock-up when hauled up as far as it will go. The sails are chock when they are full of wind.

choke the luff   to prevent the fall of a tackle from rendering by putting the bight or end of the hauling part across the mouth of the sheave to jam the block.

clamp   See **bee blocks**.

clear, to   to clear the decks is to remove all unnecessary gear; to clear a locker is to empty it and to clear the land is to get away from it into open water.

cleat, a   a broad based 'T' made of metal or wood, around which ropes can be secured.

clew   the two lower corners of a square sail or the after corner of a fore-and-aft sail. The sheets of loose-footed sails are secured to the clew.

close hauled when sailing hard on the wind with all sails sheeted hard home.

close reefed with all possible reefs in.

coamings the sides or framework of a hatchway or cockpit above deck level.

cockpit the well in the after deck from which a yacht is steered.

coil, to to lay a rope or wire down on deck in a circle with one turn on top of the previous one. To coil up is to make a rope up into bights and hang from a cleat or belaying pin.

combe See **bee blocks**.

come, to to bring the craft nearer the wind.

companion the sliding hatch which gives access to the accommodation below via the companionway.

companionway a ladder or stairway.

counter the overhang of the hull abaft the sternpost.

covering board outboard deck plank which covers the top of the hull timbers.

crabbing going sideways; making a lot of leeway.

crance the iron band with eyes fitted to the outboard end of the bowsprit to which the rigging is secured.

crank a very tender craft that can be heeled easily and therefore potentially dangerous. See **tender**.

cranse/cranze See **crance**.

cringle an eye or metal thimble worked into the corner or edge of a sail.

crown the top of a block.

crutch a single removable support for the boom to rest in. See **gallows**.

cutter a single-masted bermudian or gaff rigged vessel with two headsails. Earlier cutters also carried a large yard and square sail on the mast.

dandy another name for a yawl (also Dundee and Dandis, Fr.) with the mizzen sail lug rigged rather than gaff but never bermudian.

deadeye a round block of hardwood with sheaveless holes which is seized into the eye of a shroud. A lanyard is rove through these holes and a second deadeye fastened to the chainplates so as to set the shrouds up taut.

dipping lug a dipping lug sail must always be set to leeward and so during each tack the spar must be shifted to the leeward side of the mast. Aboard large luggers this meant lowering the gear.

dog vane a small piece of bunting or yarn tied to the shrouds or topsail yard to indicate the direction of the wind.

dolphin striker spar, usually metal, projecting below the bowsprit to give greater spread to the bobstay. Sometimes called a **martingale**.

dorade vent a ventilator which traps water entering and prevents it from finding its way below decks.

double up, to to use extra, or to increase the numbers used, for reasons of safety; to double up mooring warps because of bad weather.

douse, to to stop using or douse the staysail is to lower it quickly and stop it drawing.

downhaul a line to haul down a sail; the opposite of a halyard.

down helm to put the tiller to leeward and so luff up into the wind.

drabbler a small light-weather sail laced on to the foot of a **bonnet**, itself additional sail area.

drag, to when an anchor has broken out due to the increased pressure of wind and sea, the vessel is said to drag.

draft the depth of a craft from her waterline to the lowest part of the keel; indicates the minimum depth of water needed for the vessel to float.

draught See **draft**.

draw, to a sail draws when it catches the wind – while a boat which draws 3 feet has a 3-foot draft.

drift, the the distance between the two blocks of a purchase or tackle. The direction of a current.

drive, to to be forced bodily to leeward when the wind is too strong to retain control with the sails and rudder. Also when the anchor drags is to be driven ashore.

drop, to to drop anchor is to let the anchor go, while to drop astern is to fall back or be left behind.

earings lines used to secure the outboard end of the head of a square sail to the yard – the earing cringle is at the top of the leach. Also reefing earings are the lines which haul down and secure the reef cringle to form the new clew of the mainsail.

ease, to to slacken off carefully; to relax the pressure on the helm when it is hard or nearly hard over.

ease up, to to come up handsomely.

end for end to change one end for the other, often when turning a working coil of rope over and starting to work with the new unused end.

even keel when a vessel is lying level in

the water, fore-and-aft as well as transversely. This does not mean that the forward and after drafts are the same but that the ratio between them is the same as when fully loaded.

eyes, the   the forwardmost part of a vessel, an allusion to the eye-like similarity of hawspipes, or perhaps making an oblique reference to the days when eyes were painted either side of the stem.

eyes of the rigging   the eyes spliced into the ends of the shrouds to pass over the mast.

fag end   the frayed out end of a rope.

fair lead, a   the straight unobstructed lead of a rope between two points.

fairleads   smooth grooves or channels of metal or hardwood through which rope is led to prevent chafing.

fake   a single circle of a coil of rope.

fall   The loose or hauling part of a rope or tackle.

falling off   when a craft tends to go away from the wind rather than come up into it.

fast   secured or belayed.

fender   (defender) Pads, cylinders, or balls of rope or canvas-covered material to protect the ship's side from wear or damage.

fend off   to push off, to prevent a craft touching the quay or another boat using fenders, a boathook or pole.

fid   a flat wedge of wood or iron used to keep the topmast or bowsprit in place. Also a round tapered piece of hardwood used to splice fibre rope. See **marline spike**.

fiddle   a wood or metal bar holding light sheaves to give a better lead for light running gear.

fiddle block   a block with a large sheave above a small one.

fiddles   the raised edges of work surfaces or the bars across a galley stove which stop pots falling off in a seaway.

fife rail   a curved rail around the foot of the mast holding the belaying pins. See also **pin rail**.

fill, to   to brace or trim the sails so that they fill with wind after they have been flogging or shivering. See **cast, to**.

fine   sailing so close to the wind that the sails are just at the point of shivering.

flake   to coil or lay out a rope so that it is clear and ready to run without kinks or risk of it fouling.

flat-aback   with the wind on the wrong side of all the sails.

flatten-in   when fore-and-aft sheets are hauled in as far as possible.

fleet, to   to haul apart or overhaul the blocks of a tackle which have been 'two blocks'; also to float.

flowing sheet   sheets eased off before a favourable wind.

fluke   irregular shifts in the wind.

flukes   the blades of anchor.

fly   to let fly is to release suddenly; also the part of the flag furthest from the halyard. May be used to describe the horizontal length of a flag.

flying   a sail set flying does not have its luff hanked on to a stay.

flying jib   a headsail set either from the jib boom or above the jib, provided it is not hanked on to a stay. Not to be confused with a **jib topsail**.

foot   the bottom or lower edge of a sail.

fore-and-aft   on a line with the keel; from stem to stern; also describes a vessel rigged without square sails.

forecastle   space under the foredeck.

fore-foot   the area at the bottom of the bow; exterior junction between keel and stempost.

fore guy   the guy from boom or whisker pole which is led forward.

forelock   the tapered pin holding the arm of a Fisherman's anchor in place.

fore-reaching   movement to windward when hove-to under sail.

foresail   the principal sail set on the foremast – the fore course.

fore staysail   the foresail set upon the forestay inside the jib; on a cutter often just called the staysail.

forward   in the fore part; on the forward side of.

forge ahead   to make strong progress ahead.

foul   opposite to clear: a foul anchorage, berth or bottom all have obstructions.

frap   tight binding around the parts of a rope lashing or tackle to draw them together and so increase their tension.

free   off the wind with sheets eased between 'full and by' and 'going large'.

freeboard   the distance between the waterline and the deck or the gunwale of an open boat.

French lug   See **balance lug**.

full and by   sailing close to the wind with all sails full but not as close as close hauled.

furl   to roll or gather up a sail into itself or on to a spar.

gaff   the spar which supports and extends the upper edge of a fore-and-aft sail; gaff rigged.

gaff saddle   a curved cup, leather lined to reduce friction, which locates the end of the gaff against the mast.

gaff topsail   a sail set above a gaff sail – it may be either four-sided and set on a yard or jib headed.

gallows   a permanent fixed support for the boom.

gammoning   a lashing securing the bowsprit at the stemhead, usually at the cutwater.

gammon iron   the modern alternative to gammoning; a metal hoop securing the bowsprit to the stem.

gantline   a single rope often rove through a block or sheave at the masthead by which all materials or gear are taken aloft. Also used to rig a boatswain's chair on the mast.

gasket   a length of rope used to make up and stow a sail; also describes the way a coil is secured on to a belaying pin by a short twisted bight.

gather way   to start moving through the water due to oars, sails or engine.

gear   rigging or tackle of any kind but in particular masts and sails.

gilling   to sail so close to the wind that steerageway is barely maintained – a tactic used in squalls or when waiting to take a pilot and not wishing to reduce sail.

girt   to loosely stow a sail into bellies or bags; also when a sail's shape is fouled by a taut line or crease.

give, to   to stretch or part; a new rope gives as it takes the strain or a lashing will give as it parts.

give way   can also mean to part or break; a boat's crew will give way as soon as they start rowing.

go about   to change tack.

gobstick   the light spar used as a boom for headsails.

gooseneck   the metal fitting or joint securing the boom of a fore-and-aft sail to the mast.

goose-wing   to sail downwind with headsails boomed out and set on the opposite side of the boat to the mainsail – schooner, ketch or yawl to have main and mizzen on opposite sides.

gorge   See **swallow**.

grapnel   a multi-pointed hook or anchor often used by small boats.

gripe, to   when a vessel has a tendency to keep coming up into the wind – countered by weather helm. A desirable feature provided it is not excessive.

grommet   a rope ring – like a quoit.

ground tackle   all gear relating to a boat's anchors and cables.

gudgeons   metal eyes mounted on the stern into which the rudder pintles ship.

gunter rig   a triangular sail laced to a yard which extends the sail's luff vertically above the mast; also known as sliding gunter.

gunwale   the top of the sheer strake or upper edge of a boat's side. Pronounced and sometimes written gunnel. See also **covering board**.

guy   a rope used to control a spar or derrick; often a preventer guy used in heavy weather to control the boom.

gybe, to   to bring the wind from one quarter to the other by passing the stern through the eye of the wind.

halyards   the ropes and tackles used for hoisting sails (also called halliards from haul-yards).

hand   a member of the ship's crew (always singular because one hand for himself and one for the ship – oft forgotten by modern skippers!) In hand, to keep hold and not make fast; or to hand a sail is to furl and stow it.

handsomely   steadily and carefully, but not necessarily slowly.

hand taut   making a rope as tight as possible without use of a tackle or swigging up.

hand-over-hand   a rapid method of taking in a rope – hauling with one hand after the other.

handy billy   a small purchase or jigger used for sweating up gear (made up with a double and a single block).

hanks   rings or clips for securing the luff of a sail on to a stay (staysails) or its own halyard (jib topsail); small stuff or line is made up in hanks rather than coils.

hard down   to put the tiller hard to leeward.

hard up   to move the tiller hard to weather.

harden in   to haul in the sheets and flatten the sail.

hard-and-fast   when a craft is well aground.

hatchway   an opening through the deck which can be made watertight with a cover (hatch).

haul   to pull.

hawser   a large diameter rope suitable for mooring or towing.

hawser laid   the normal left-hand laid three-stranded rope – laid against the twist of the strands.

head the upper edge of a sail laced to a gaff or yard; also the forepart of the ship.

head rope the rope sewn to the head of a sail.

heads an area of grating either side of the bowsprit on large ships used by the crew as a lavatory: hence the current use for a shipborne toilet.

headsails those sails set forward of the only or forward mast.

head sheets the sheets for the head-sails.

head stick the former name for a headboard – the wood at the top of a sail to stop it from twisting.

head-to-wind lying with the bow pointing into the wind.

headway movement forward or ahead.

heart a multi-stranded rope is laid up around a central strand called the heart; a deadeye with only a single hole.

heave-to, to to stop making headway or to lie with headsails aback so as to make only enough way to keep steerage in heavy seas.

heel to list or to lean over; the bottom of the mast.

heel rope a line which passes through a sheave in the heel of a topmast or bowsprit. By this means they can be raised or hauled out.

helm the means of steering craft whether tiller or wheel.

hitch part of a knot; 'a round turn and two half hitches'.

hog to clean or scrub very thoroughly.

hoist to haul or raise anything aloft; also another name for the luff of a sail. The side of a flag next to the mast or halyard.

home in its place; to haul the sheets home is to bring them in as far as possible.

hoops wood or metal rings which hold the luff of a sail close to the mast (also **mast hoops**).

horns the sides of the gaff which fit together to form the jaws either side of the mast.

horse the rail or bar across the deck along which the sheet block travels athwartships.

hounds a metal band, wood cheeks or even a thickening of the mast which locates and holds up the lower shrouds; formerly the support for the trestle trees. The portion of the mast where the shrouds are secured.

house, to to secure in its proper place of stowage; the upper mast is housed when lowered and made fast.

housing the part of the bowsprit or mast which is inboard or below decks.

hove-to See **heave-to**.

inboard inside the rails or bulwarks.

inhaul running rigging for hauling a sail inboard from the end of a spar or yard.

in irons a vessel unable to complete a tack and remain head-to-wind unable or reluctant to pay off on the new tack or resume the old one.

in stays the moment at which a vessel is head-to-wind, when tacking as the wind goes through the stays (see also **in irons**); formerly meant tacking.

Irish pennant a loose end of rope hanging free or blowing in the wind.

jackstays made from metal, rope or wire and rigged tautly between two points along which anything can travel or be made fast to. Also the rods along the tops of yards for securing the sails.

jackyard a length of wood laced to the foot of a topsail to extend it beyond the end of the gaff. Usually used in conjunction with a topsail yard which extends the luff above the masthead.

jackyard topsail a jib headed topsail – the luff and foot are extended beyond the masthead and gaff by two small yards; a light weather sail.

jaws the crutch at the end of the boom which fits around the mast.

jenny yard See **jackyard**.

jib the foremost headsail, set at the stem or bowsprit end.

jib-boom the extension of the bowsprit; not a boom for a jib. See **gobstick**.

jib headed any triangular-shaped sail.

jib header slang for jib headed topsail.

jib topsail a headsail set above the jib on the topmast stay.

jib traveller the metal ring fitted around the bowsprit, to which the jib tack is secured and by which the jib is hauled in and out.

jigger a small tackle similar to but smaller than a 'handy billy' often used as a luff tackle. Sometimes the name for a small mizzen sail set aboard yawls.

joggle a joint between timber to prevent movement.

joggle shackle use in anchor work – a long-jawed shackle.

jumper similar to a bobstay, this counters the upward lift of the jib boom and is led from the end of the jib boom, inboard over the dolphin striker. See also **martingale**.

junk old rope used to make baggywrinkle, fenders and similar.

kedge a small anchor, often referring to a spare anchor.

kentledge preshaped permanent ballast.

ketch a two-masted vessel which has the smaller after mast stepped well inboard forward of the sternpost or rudder head. See **yawl**.

kevel a length of timber often fitted horizontally inside the bulwarks and used as a large cleat for mooring ropes.

kink a sharp bend in a wire rope, liable to cause damage.

knee elbows of wood or metal for strengthening angle joints, usually between deck and hull.

knightheads the pair of vertical timbers, securing the inboard end of the bowsprit.

labour to roll and pitch heavily in a seaway.

lacing the line used to secure a sail to a mast or spar along one of its edges.

lanyard a lashing rove through a deadeye or thimble, frequently used to secure and set up standing rigging.

larboard formerly the left side, opposite of starboard, but changed because of the similarity of the spoken words. See **starboard**.

lay the lay of a rope is the direction in which the strands are twisted; to lay is to come or go in that direction, 'to lay aft'.

lazarette a small locker at the stern usually in the counter.

lazy usually means additional or extra and therefore not the principal – as in lazy guy, lazy sheet or lazy painter.

lazy guy the extra guy or preventer which stops the boom swinging inboard against the pressure of a light wind as the vessel rolls.

lazy jacks lines which help gather a gaff sail as it's lowered and control the gaff if vangs are not rigged. Secured to the topping-lifts, lazy jacks hang vertically either side of the sail and under the boom to catch the sail as it drops.

leach the aftermost edge of a sail whether gaff or bermudian (now also spelt leech).

lead the weight used for making soundings.

lead, to to pass or run cordage; e.g., to lead the jib sheets outside the shrouds.

leads See **fairleads**.

lee See **leeward**.

lee-board large boards fixed outboard, usually on barges and other flat-bottomed craft to reduce the drift to leeward; also a board serving the same purpose as a **lee-cloth**.

leech See **leach**.

lee-cloth canvas or other material rigged on the inboard side of a weather bunk which prevents the occupant from falling out to leeward.

lee helm a craft that naturally tends to turn to leeward (away from the wind) has lee helm; opposite of weather helm.

lee ho! the warning given by the helmsman as he tacks and puts the helm over to leeward.

leeward the opposite side to that from which the wind is blowing; the side on which the sails are set.

leeway the sideways drift away from the desired course line of a sailing craft caused by the action of the wind.

leg o'mutton the original name for a jib headed or bermudian sail.

legs wooden supports fitted either side of a craft to keep it upright and on an even keel when drying out or taking the ground.

let draw allow a sail to fill with wind.

let fly to let go or release – as let fly the sheets and allow the sails to spill their wind and flap free.

let run to allow a rope or cable to go out at its own speed without checking or slowing it down.

lift a rope or wire which takes the strain or raises one of the spars; the topping-lift raises the boom and takes the strain of the sails.

limber rope a length of rope fed through the limber holes and which, when pulled to and fro, keeps the limber holes clear of dirt or obstructions. Chain may be used in place of rope.

limbers holes or spaces beneath the floors or frames which allow bilge water to drain aft to the pump or sump.

linch pin See **forelock**.

line small ropes are usually called line, hambroline, houseline, etc.

list, to to lean or heel at a semi-permanent angle; not when rolling.

lizard a short length of rope with a thimble spliced into one end through which another rope may render freely, such as a boat's painter when used as an outhaul on a boom.

locker a cupboard or stowage compartment aboard a boat.

log   the instrument which measures the vessel's speed through the water and records the distance travelled.

long-jawed   when the lay of a rope has been straightened due to excessive or prolonged strain and has lost its elasticity.

loose-footed   a fore-and-aft sail either without a boom or, if set on one, then secured only at the tack and clew.

lose way, to   to reduce speed through the water.

lubber's line   the mark on the compass indicating the fore-and-aft centreline of the ship; used to steer by.

luff   the front or leading edge of a sail; to luff is to bring that edge up close to or even into the wind.

luff, to   to bring the ship's head nearer the wind.

luff tackle   a small tackle used to set taut the luff once the halyard has been made fast. Usually a single and double block and is often used to describe such a tackle regardless of its use.

luff-upon-luff   one luff tackle made fast to the hauling part of a second to give additional power.

lug   a small eye projecting from a spar for securing rigging; can also mean the spar upon which a lugsail is laced.

lugger   a lug rigged craft.

lugsail   the four sided fore-and-aft sail laced to a spar which extends some way forward of the mast, unlike a gaff with jaws. Either standing or dipping lugs.

main   the principal or most important, as in mainmast, mainsheet, mainsail, etc.

make fast   to secure or belay a rope or line.

man, to   standing ready to use; to man the sheets, the halyards or the dinghy.

manhandle   to move manually.

man-ropes   ropes rigged alongside a ladder to aid climbing.

marl   to bind together strands of rope by a series of half-hitches with spunyarn – as when making a selvagee strop.

marline   a small loose, two-stranded yarn or line which may be tarred; spunyard is an example.

marline spike   (Also marling spike.) a pointed, tapered tool used in rope work in particular when splicing wire. See also **fid**.

marry, to   to join together, to place two parts of rope alongside each other so that they may be hauled together; to merge the strands of two rope ends before joining them by splicing.

martingale   another name for the **dolphin striker**, used to spread the bobstay. Also stays from the jib boom to the dolphin striker.

mast coat   the waterproof cover around the mast which stops water getting down below.

masthead   the portion of the mast between the hounds and the truck.

mast hoops   the hoops around the mast, each lashed to the luff of the sail to keep it close in to the mast.

mast step   the notch into which the foot or heel of the mast slots, usually cut into the keelson.

messenger   any light line used to haul a heavier or larger one, aloft or out to a mooring buoy.

midships   the midsection or in the middle; 'Go amidships!' The tiller is amidships when on the fore-and-aft line.

miss stays, to   to fail to go about when tacking and so fall back on to the original tack.

mitchboard   a crutch-shaped wooden pad fixed to the rail or bulwark as an alternative to a free standing boom crutch.

mizzen   the smaller after mast or its sail aboard a ketch, yawl or any other two- or three-masted vessel; not to be confused with the **jigger** aboard a four-masted barque.

mizzen staysail   a sail set flying between the main and mizzen masts with its luff extending from the mizzen masthead down to the deck.

moor, to   strictly to anchor with two anchors but now often used to describe the act of making a vessel fast to a buoy.

mousing   a lashing or seizing of yarn or wire to close the jaws of a hook, or to prevent a shackle pin working loose.

muzzle   to smother a sail and stop it being blown over the side before it's hoisted or after it's lowered.

nail sickness   when many of the nails in a clinker-built boat have worked loose or the iron fastenings in a wood boat have corroded away; as a result the boat usually leaks heavily.

nip, to   to make fast with a seizing – usually large rope like hawsers.

nock   another name for the throat of a gaff sail or other quadrilateral sail (staysails); its upper fore corner or the weather corner.

nose   the band protecting the stem of a small boat; also any carved decoration on the stem above the gunwale.

nosebag   a jib that bellies too much or one that is too large for the mainsail.

oakum   a fibrous material usually made from unpicked condemned ropes. See **junk**.

off   abeam or abreast of.

on the beam   at right-angles to the fore-and-aft line of the vessel.

outhaul   a rope used to pull a sail or other gear out along a bowsprit or similar spar; also to heave a small boat out on a running mooring.

overhangs   the extremities of a craft which extend or overhang the water.

overhaul   when the parts of a tackle are slack and will not run, the parts are 'overhauled' through the sheeves so that the blocks can be stretched further apart.

over-peaked   when the peak of a gaff sail is hauled so taut that creases run diagonally across the sail from peak to tack. Provided this is not done to excess then ideal for setting sail.

over-raked   when seas break over the bows and run the full length of a vessel's decks, in particular when at anchor in an exposed position.

overreach   to stand on too long on a tack so that, upon tacking, the destination or mark is further to windward than necessary.

overrun   to be pooped by a following sea.

over stand   See **overreach**.

pads   the shaped wood inserts fitted between the deck beams and deck planking to create the camber necessary for water to run off.

painter   the rope by which a small boat is secured.

palm   the leather and hide tool which protects the sailmaker's hand and helps push the needle through the canvas.

parcel, to   to protect a rope by winding narrow strips of canvas around it with the lay (worm and parcel).

parrel   the gear used to close the jaws of a gaff and so keep the gaff close to the mast; also other similar spars.

parrel balls/beads   small balls or beads made from hardwood to reduce the friction of the parrel.

parrel line   the line holding parrel balls or beads in place.

part   a portion of a rope; the standing part, running part or hauling part.

part, to   to carry away or to break.

partners   the strengthening beams fitted around the opening on the deck where the mast passes through.

pass, to   to take a turn around or through an object.

pawl   the pivoted stop which falls into the ratchet teeth of a windlass preventing it running back.

pay off   to let the ship's head fall off the wind.

pay out   to slack or pass out, usually hand-over-hand.

peak   the top or outer part of a gaff sail secured to the end of the gaff. Also the narrow extremities of the ship's hull, forepeak or afterpeak.

peak, to   to set up a gaff sail by tightening the halyard until creases appear at the throat of the sail. See **over-peaked**.

peak downhaul   a rope led from the peak of the gaff to haul upon when lowering the sail.

peak halyard   the halyard for raising the peak of the sail, worked in conjunction with the throat halyard.

peak purchase   the tackle used to set up the peak – not usual on small yachts.

pendant   a length of rope with a thimbled splice at either end; multiple uses, e.g. joining spar to tackle.

pennant   a long, narrow, almost triangular flag; numeral pennants. (May be written pendant.)

pig   ballast pigs; pieces of cast metal for ballast.

pin   the spindle for the sheave of a block.

pin rail   a board pierced for belaying pins, at the ship's side, secured to or near to the shrouds.

pinching   to sail too close to the wind. See **squeeze**.

pintles   metal pins on the rudder which fit into the gudgeons allowing rudder to be unshipped.

pitching   the rocking or plunging motion of a vessel into head seas.

plain sail   all normal sail; neither the light nor heavy weather canvas. Aboard square riggers, the lower sails.

play   slackness in some otherwise fixed object; play around the fixings of a beam or joint.

plug   a stopper for a hole; the plug in the bottom of a boat.

point   compass point; is equal to 11.25 degrees (11 degrees 25 minutes).

pointing   a measure of a ship's closeness to the wind; 'How is she pointing?' or, 'How close are you to the wind?'

pole mast   a mast unbroken over its full length; not a lower and top mast.

poop   formerly the after castle; the raised deck at the stern of a vessel.

pooped   when a sea breaks over the stern or poop. See **overrun**.

port   the left-hand side of a vessel.

porthole   originally gun ports and therefore can only truly be applied to square openings in the ship's side for light and ventilation. See **scuttles.**

port light   a scuttle which does not open.

port tack   with the wind passing across or blowing from the port side; the sails are set on the starboard side and the boat heels to starboard.

preventer   a rope or wire rigged to give additional support; preventer guy to stop the boom crashing around when rolling in light winds.

prussik knot   a means of forming a quick jamming knot which holds under pressure but can be slid along a rope once the tension is off.

purchase   a tackle no matter how simple or complex a system of blocks.

put about   to tack.

quarter   four points (45 degrees) abaft the beam; midway between abeam and dead astern.

quarter fast   a mooring rope made fast on the quarter; a spring on the quarter.

queenie   a four-sided staysail set between the masts of a schooner, hanked on to the triatic stay.

rack   to seize two ropes together with a racking seizing.

raffee   a triangular-shaped light-weather sail set above the yard of a square sail.

rail   timber along the tops of the ship's side stanchions.

rake   the angle away from the vertical of a ship's mast, either raked forward or aft.

rakish   a fast, smart-looking craft, perhaps due formerly to being over-canvased and having over-raked masts.

ramp   sailing close hauled when hard pressed without easing the sheets as would be prudent.

ramping full   sailing with all sails full when slightly free of close hauled.

range, to   to haul up and flake down on deck enough slack anchor cable so that when let go it will run freely.

ratlines   the rope rungs rigged across the shrouds to give access up the mast.

rattle down   to make and rig ratlines; eyes at each end are seized on to the shrouds, with clove hitches around intermediate shrouds.

reach   to sail with the wind free.

ready about!   warning from helmsman before putting helm down to leeward (lee ho).

reef, to   to reduce or shorten sail; reef points, reef cringle, etc.

reef bands   strengthened sections of sail which are double thickness through which the reef points are rigged.

reef cringle   eyes sewn into luff and leach of sail through which earings are rove.

reef earing   pendants permanently reeved from one side of the boom up through the reef cringles and down to bee blocks ready for reefing.

reef pendant   See **reef earing**.

reef points   the short lines attached across the sail to tidy the slack sail when reefed.

reef tackle   the purchase hooked on to the reef earing to pull down the reef.

reeve   to pass or thread a rope through a deadeye or block.

relieving tackles   tackles set up to assist the helmsman during heavy weather.

rendering   yielding or giving way to a given force; rope renders through a block, or a lanyard through a deadeye.

ride, to   lying at anchor or a mooring.

rig   the general description of a ship's masts, sails and spars.

rig, to   to set up anything.

ringtail   a studding sail for a gaff; extra sail area fitted to the leach of a fore-and-aft sail (similar to a **bonnet**).

roach   the curve in the foot or leach of a sail which gives it shape.

robands   See **ties**.

rockered   a keel which is curved or rounded along its length.

rogues' yarn   a coloured yarn running through all Admiralty cordage to identify it and so prevent theft.

roove   the copper washer placed over the end of the copper nail before clenching when building a clinker boat.

rotten cotton   thin weak yarn used to stop up sails that can then be broken out by pulling on the sheets.

round in   to haul in on a warp or rope.

round turn   a complete turn around an object with a rope.

rove   a rope that has been passed through a cringle; the throat of a block, etc has been rove.

rowlocks   square sections cut from the gunwale or washstrake of a large open boat for the oars, instead of crutches or thole pins. Usual in boats used for sailing as well as pulling, which have a high freeboard that would make rowing with crutches difficult as the oar would be too high.

rubbing strake   a thicker, often half-rounded wood strake fitted outboard to protect the hull from abrasion.

run   the narrow after section of the vessel's underbody.

runners   a rope with a purchase on one end which is then rove through a single block on the end of a pendant.

running   sailing with the wind aft.

running backstays   See **runners**.

running boom   See **whisker pole**.

running bowsprit   a bowsprit that can be reefed by hauling inboard.

running rigging   that rigging which is used to haul and adjust the use or set of the sails. Not standing rigging which is set taut.

saddle   the protection on a spar where it bears against another. See **gaff saddle**.

sagging to leeward   when the whole vessel drifts bodily to leeward.

samson (or sampson) post   a strong post forward used for making fast mooring warps or anchor cable.

save all   a type of water sail set below a boom in light winds.

scandalise   to lower the peak of a gaff sail so as to spill the wind and slow or stop the boat. Sails with mast hoops could also have the tack triced up. It is necessary to lift or trice up the boom so as to take the weight of the boom off the sail.

scantlings   the size or dimensions of the boat's timbers.

scarphing   joining two lengths of timber together in a long tapered joint.

schooner   a sailing vessel with two or more masts all rigged fore-and-aft. A two-masted schooner will have a foremast and mainmast. However topsail and t'gallant schooners have yards on the foremast.

scissor crutch   a wooden 'X' which is pivoted off centre so that when erected it will support the boom when the mainsail is not set.

scope   the length of a cable between ship and anchor.

score   the groove around the cheeks of a wood block which takes the rope strop.

scowing an anchor   used in a small boat; make fast the warp of the anchor to the crown and then stop it back to the rig so that, if it fouls, the stopping will part and the anchor come clear. Instead of using a tripping line.

scud, to   to run before strong winds.

scull   to row a boat with a single oar over the transom.

scuppers   draining holes for water cut through the deck or toe rail.

scuttle   a round glazed hole for light and ventilation in a ship's side (not a porthole which is square).

seizing   a tight lashing around two parts of a rope to join them together along their length.

selvedge   the finished edge along a length of canvas.

sentinel   a weight lowered part way down a small craft's anchor wharp to induce a catenary and so reduce the risk of the anchor breaking out.

serve, to   to bind yarn or twine around a rope as protection; bound against the lay. The final stage after worming and parcelling.

serving mallet   the wood tool used to wind serving around a rope.

set, to   to hoist or make sail; also to 'set sail' is to leave or depart.

set flying   a sail not hanked or bent on to a stay.

set up, to   to tighten the standing rigging.

settle, to   to slack back a little, usually when a halyard or lift has been set up too taut, to settle the peak halyard on a gaff.

shackle   used to connect rope or wire to metal fittings; can only be used if the eyes have thimbles. Also a measurement of 15 fathoms of chain cable.

shake   a crack along the length of the mast in the grain.

shake out a reef   to release the reef points and reef earings and re-hoist the sail.

shank   the anchor's shaft.

sheave   the wheel within a block over which the rope passes.

sheer   the fore-and-aft or longitudinal upward curve of a ship's decks towards the ends.

sheer, to   the angle a vessel takes up across the tide when at anchor, rather than lying in line with the tidal stream.

sheer strake   the uppermost plank of the hull but below the bulwarks.

sheet anchor   a spare or extra bow anchor, the same or similar size to the working anchor.

sheet home   when the clew of the gaff topsail is hard against the cheek block on the gaff; so to haul the sheet so taut that the foot of the sail is as straight as it can be.

sheets   the ropes secured to the sail's clew to control the manner in which it is set.

shell   the outside of a block – usually referring to a wood block.

ship   a fully square rigged vessel of three or more masts.

ship, to   to take aboard; to ship oars is to bring them into the boat and lay them flat across the thwarts.

shiver, to   to luff or ease the sheet of a sail so that it spills its wind and shivers.

shiver the mizzen   to luff up until the mizzen sail shivers.

shorten   to shorten or reduce sail; the wind shortens when it moves more ahead.

shrouds   standing rigging supporting the mast on either side.

sister block   a block with two equal sized sheaves, one above the other.

skin fitting   any fitting which projects through the hull of the boat under water. A transducer is a unit used to transmit and receive information.

slack   loose, not taut; take in the slack; to pick up or haul in the bight until taut.

slack in stays   slow to go about, or tack.

slew   to turn or swing round (also written slue).

sliding gunter   See **gunter rig**.

slip, to   to release or let go; to slip the anchor and cable so as to put to sea quickly; the end to be buoyed off for later recovery.

sloop   a single-masted fore-and-aft rigged vessel with either gaff or bermudian mainsail, rigged with a single headsail.

slue   See **slew**.

small helm   when the sails are properly trimmed the helmsman may sail with little effort and only small movements of the helm.

snatch block   a block, the side of whose shell hinges open so that the bight of a rope may be reeved without the end being passed through.

snotter   a strop with eyes at both ends – used to support the sprit on the mast in a small boat. Either wound around and one eye passed through the other or with a rolling hitch on the bight before hooking on to the traveller.

snub, to   to stop or check suddenly.

snubbing her   to stop or bring up a vessel with her anchor or even turn her 'snubbing her round'.

sny   the toggle at the top of a flag.

span   rope which is middled and fixed at both ends, or has two legs for lifting or supporting, such as a gaff span.

spanish reef   tie a knot in a headsail to reduce its size; a rather dramatic last resort.

spars   all the masts, booms, gaffs and yards; in other words all the lengths of timber upon which sails are set.

spider band   See **spider hoop**.

spider hoop   a metal hoop attached around the mast into which belaying pins are fitted. (Not to be confused with fife rail which is self-supporting.)

spill   to empty a sail of wind so that it no longer draws.

spindle jib   See **jib topsail**.

spitfire jib   the smallest jib carried for use in very strong winds as a balance at the end of the bowsprit for a deep-reefed main.

splice   joining two parts of rope together by interweaving their strands.

split lug   a two-part lug sail, one forward, the other aft of the mast but both laced to the same yard. Both sheeted separately and the tacks are not released when going about.

spreader   a strut, a crosstree of wood or iron used to spread or widen the angle of leverage for a stay or shroud on a long spar; the dolphin striker is the spreader for the bobstay on a bowsprit.

spring   a warp led from forward to a bollard aft along the quay (or vice versa); checks progress, stops ranging ahead and along the quay; used to snub the bow or stern off when leaving.

sprit   the spar supporting a loose-footed, gaffless sail; fitted on the mast and running diagonally across the sail to its peak.

spritsail   the sail set upon a sprit common on Thames and other similar barges.

sprung   timber, planks, spars or even seams cracked or damaged by extreme pressure or strain; to have sprung a leak.

spunyarn   fibrous two-stranded tarred line used mainly for serving.

spurling pipe   the pipe through which the chain cable passes from chain locker and emerges on to the deck.

squeeze   the same as pinching; sailing

as close as possible to the wind in order to weather a mark, beacon or headland.

stanchion   a pillar or column supporting an overhead load or deck; also along the side of a hatch rove with safety wire, in place of bulwarks.

stand on   to maintain or hold your course and speed.

standing lug   a lugsail with the tack bowsed down to the mast or close ahead of it; once set, the lug or spar remains on the one side of the mast and is not dipped each time the boat tacks.

standing part   the part shackled on to the block in a tackle; in fact the part of any rope or tackle which is permanently made fast and is never hauled or rendered.

standing rigging   that rigging which is permanently secured by lanyards, bottle screws or shackles and not free to run.

starboard   the right-hand side; said to come from 'steerboard', the side on which the Vikings rigged their steering oar; therefore larboard or landward, the side against the land.

start, to   to loose or free; a rusted shackle pin starts when it first moves.

stay rope   the rope sewn down the luff of a jib or foresail, next to or in place of the stay; the bolt rope.

stays   standing rigging which provides fore-and-aft as well as lateral support to the mast; other than shrouds.

steer, to   to direct or guide the ship's course with the helm.

steeve   the angle by which the bowsprit is raised or cocked up above the horizontal.

stem   the principal or chief timber in the bow.

stem post   See **stem**.

stem, to   to just make way or hold position against the tide.

step   the seat or socket cut into the keelson in which the heel or bottom of the mast is located.

stern   the after end of the vessel.

stern board   to turn short round when in a confined space by making stern-way. Come up into the wind and then allow the vessel to drop or fall astern with the rudder in the opposite direction.

sternpost   the aftermost principal timber, opposite of stem.

stiff   describes the resistance (strong righting moment) of a vessel to heeling;

a too stiff ship whips quickly and uncomfortably from one side to the other as she rolls.

stock   the shank or principal member of an anchor.

stoop   dipping into the trough of the swell – an easy, comfortable pitching motion.

stopper   a rope lashing wound around a larger rope or warp to hold it while the strain is transferred between belay, windlass or hands.

stops   rotten cotton used to hold a sail set flying until it's hoisted and ready to break out.

stop water   the treenail or trennel driven through the keel and stem at their joint.

stow   to put away in its proper place; furl or roll up a sail.

strake   any length of planking.

strand   a number of small fibre yarns twisted together. A rope usually has three strands.

stranded   a vessel aground or ashore; also an unlaid rope no longer laid up.

stream, to   a rope or line trailed behind with one end still fast aboard; a log line trailed astern.

strike   to lower or bring down gear that is aloft; 'strike the topmast'; also to touch or encounter the seabed or strike soundings.

stringers   longitudinal members of a ship's hull joining frames or beams together and giving added strength to the joint.

strop   usually rope around a wood block to which thimbles, hoots, etc. were attached; also a rope sling for lifting cargo.

stuff   small line or rope used for lacings, etc.

surge, to   to allow a rope to pass or render round a cleat, belaying pin, capstan or winch drum.

swallow   the slot between the crown of a block and the sheave through which the rope passes. See **arse**.

swamped   a boat filled with water or a vessel overwhelmed by the sea.

sweat, to   to take up the last possible slack on a rope or tackle without resorting to additional mechanical assistance. After heaving taut, the hauling part has one turn taken on a pin or cleat – then, while the tension is maintained on the belay, the bight is pulled at right angles before quick release for the extra slack to be taken.

swift in, to   to tighten the rigging.

swifter the forward shroud on a lower mast.

swig off, to See **sweat**.

tabernacle the support for a mast stepped on deck; allows the mast to be lowered.

tabling the doubled thickness of canvas around the edges of a sail to which the bolt rope is sewn.

tack, the the forward lower cringle or corner of a sail.

tack, to change course, passing the bow through the eye of the wind and so bringing the wind from one bow to the other.

tack tackle the tackle used to bowse down the tack of a sail.

tackle rope rove through two or more blocks, each with one or more sheaves which combine to form a purchase.

tackle-fall the hauling part of a tackle or purchase.

taffrail the bulwark capping or wood rail around the stern of a ship – now used to refer to any similar capping wherever located aboard.

tail block a block with a length of rope spliced on instead of a hook, eye or shackle. May be tailed on to standing rigging to give a temporary lead.

tail tackle a purchase made up of a single and double block. The single has a hook, the double rope tails to be hitched on to a hauling part or standing rigging so as to provide additional power.

tail, to to secure one warp or hawser on to the end of another which is being veered out.

take charge to run out of control.

take in to furl and stow sail.

take off, to See **take in**.

take up, to when rope or canvas shrinks or tightens up; or as the planks of a dried-out wooden boat swell and close open seams when she is returned to the water.

telltale, a another name for a **dog vane**.

tender, a a small boat belonging to and carried by a larger craft as a means of getting ashore.

tender said of a craft which rolls easily – a dangerous feature in heavy weather.

tenon, the the square tongue cut in the foot of the mast that slots into the keel.

thimble a circular or pear-shaped, grooved metal ring, fitted into a spliced eye to stop wear.

thorough-foot, a a twisted or incorrectly rove part of a purchase; if twisted can be cleared by dipping on block.

thorough-foot, to to coil a rope down in figure of eight flakes.

throat the upper forward corner of a gaff sail next to the mast; and the jaws of the gaff. The inner or deepest part of the jaws of the gaff.

throat halyard the halyard secured to the jaws of the gaff which raises the sail in conjunction with the peak halyard (also called the main halyard).

thumb cleat a small wood horn mounted on a spar to prevent a strop or rope slipping along it.

thwartships See **athwart**.

tie the runner or halyard to which the tackle is hooked to raise a lugsail.

ties rope or canvas gaskets for securing the furled sail on its boom or yard.

tiers See **ties**.

tight does not leak; staunched; impervious to water.

tiller the wood or iron handle which fits into the rudder head for steering the boat.

tiller line rope secured to the tiller's weather side to relieve the strain on the helmsman's arms – in large craft a tackle may be used.

timinoggie a fixed wooden lead secured to the gaff close to the jaws through which a sheet controls the lower end of a topsail yard. Common to West Country gaffers.

tingle a patch of wood, copper or lead nailed to the outside of a wood vessel to cover a leak or small hole.

top hamper masts, spars, rigging; in fact anything above the decks.

topping lift a tackle or rope used to lift or support a boom or spar.

topsail a sail carried above the gaff or above a course on a square rigged vessel.

track the course or wake of a vessel through the water.

transom the planks or board forming the flat heart-shaped stern of a ship or boat.

traveller a hoop or ring which can be hauled along a spar or up a mast, taking a sail with it. See also **sentinel**.

treenails See **trennels**.

trennels wood pegs used to secure the planking to the frames – held tightly by small wedges driven in at either end.

trestle trees the fore-and-aft wood supports for the topmast fid and the crosstrees.

triatic stay the stay between fore and main mastheads onboard a schooner.

tricing line   a line rigged from the tack to the throat or hounds for raising the foot of a loose-footed gaff sail.

trick   the period that the helmsman spends at the wheel or tiller is his 'trick'.

trim, to   to adjust or alter; to trim the sails.

trim   the fore-and-aft set of a vessel in the water, on an even keel or trimmed by the head or stern.

trip, to   to free; to lift the anchor clear of the bottom; to raise a topmast just enough to free the fid before lowering.

tripping line   a line used to trip, secured to the crown of an anchor so as to break it free; not necessarily an anchor buoy-rope.

trough   the hollow or valley between wave crests.

truck   the circular wood cap on the top of the mast.

truss   the metal band binding a yard to the mast.

try   to heave-to.

trysail   originally a small gaff sail but now commonly applied to storm canvas whether gaff or bermudian.

tuck   the passing of one strand under another when splicing.

tumbler   the piece of wood fitted in the gaff jaws which is pivoted so that its face is always flat against the mast no matter the angle of the gaff.

turn, a   one complete circle with rope around a capstan, drum end or bollard. So 'to catch a turn' or 'take a turn'.

turn up   to make fast or belay a rope or fall; to take several turns.

two blocks   when the two blocks of a purchase are hard up against each other and no more rope can be hauled in without distorting or damaging the gear (same as block and block, chock-a-block).

unbend   to undo or release a knot or hitch; also to release sails from their yards or spars.

under-canvased   too little sail area set for the prevailing conditions.

under the lee   in the shelter of the land.

under way   strictly not at anchor, made fast to the shore or aground. More usually meaning moving through the water.

unreeve   to pull out all the parts of a tackle from the blocks.

unship   to remove; to unship oars from their rowlocks or crutches.

up helm   to put the helm to weather.

vang   the lines used to control the peak of a gaff or sprit – stops it sagging off to leeward. On ketches and yawls a vang may be rigged from the mainsail gaff to the mizzen mast and on schooners from the foresail gaff to the mainmast.

veer   to pay out or slack away.

veer and haul   to ease up a little in the hope that momentum will take in more slack when hauling; also to express opposing opinions.

wake   the eddy or disturbed water left astern of a moving vessel.

wallow   to lie rolling heavily in the trough of a swell.

warp   a heavy mooring rope.

warp, to   to heave or pull a vessel ahead or astern, using her mooring ropes by manpower or capstans.

wash   the waves thrown out from the bow of a vessel moving through the water.

washboard   a temporary or movable plank fitted on to the gunwale of an open boat to increase her freeboard. May be fitted to the lee side only.

wash stroke   See **washboard**.

watch tackle   usually a small tackle kept on deck for use by the watch for a variety of tasks – the same composition as a tail tackle.

watches   the periods spent on duty, on the bridge, keeping look-out or just on the helm.

water laid   a left-hand laid rope.

watersail   a sail laced on to and set beneath the boom of a gaff sail when running in fine weather; different from a bonnet which is laced to the sail.

way   motion or momentum through the water.

wear, to   to alter course from close hauled on one tack to the other, passing the stern through the wind rather than the bow. Normally applied to square rig. See **gybe** for fore-and-aft rig.

weather helm   the need to keep the tiller pulled to weather so as to sail a straight course is weather helm. A desirable feature provided the degree of helm needed is not excessive.

weather roll   a vessel is usually heeled to leeward and the booms are held there by the pressure of the wind. However, when the wind is light and a heavy swell is running the vessel may well roll towards the wind or weather side. This can be hazardous as, unless guyed, the booms may fall across causing damage or becoming backwinded.

weathering   a vessel that is weathering another is doing so because she is sailing closer to the wind.

weatherside   the windward side.

weeps   rust stains down a ship's side caused by the rusting of exposed metal fastenings.

weigh, to   to raise or lift the anchor.

well found   a vessel in good condition with the full complement of gear.

whelps   iron lugs fitted to the drum of a capstan to give a better grip heaving chain and rope.

whip   a single block often rove with an endless rope, as in a breeches buoy.

whip, to   to bind the end of a rope with roping or sewing twine to stop the strands from unlaying and fraying.

whipping   the binding on the end of a rope. See **whip, to**.

whiskers   struts or spreaders used to spread the bowsprit shrouds.

whisker pole   a spar used to boom out the clew of the jib or other headsail on the opposite side to the mainsail boom when running before the wind. Often a light pole with a short spike to fit into the clew cringle.

wide berth, a   to give plenty of clearance when passing.

wild   a vessel which is difficult to steer regardless of how her sails are trimmed.

wind-rode   an anchored vessel lying to the wind rather than the tide due either to the greater strength of the wind or the shallow draft of the vessel.

wind sail   a canvas chute rigged over a hatchway to encourage through ventilation.

wind shadow   the disturbed or dirty wind to leeward of a sailing vessel.

windward, to   towards the wind; the side on which the wind is blowing.

wing-and-wing   See **goose-wing**.

withe   a thin willow sapling used to make mast loops for mainsails.

work, to   to move, as in 'to work loose'; a vessel works when the various parts of her framework move in a seaway; if this working becomes excessive it may cause weeps and leaks.

worm, to   when the lay of a rope is filled in with small stuff to make a flat surface without ridges prior to parcelling and serving.

yard   a spar permanently rigged on the mast, which supports and spreads the head of a sail.

yard-arm   the end of a yard.

yard topsail   a jib headed topsail with the luff extended above the masthead by a yard, and the clew sheeted to the end of the gaff.

yarn   the twisted fibres which when laid up together form the strand of a rope.

yaw   the swinging movement of the ship's head when not steering a steady course, either the result of bad helmsmanship or poor balance of the sails.

yawl   a fore-and-aft rigged vessel having a mainmast and a mizzen mast which is stepped abaft the stern post.

Index

OTHER TITLES AVAILABLE FROM ADLARD COLES NAUTICAL

Gaff Rigg	£29.95 net
Spritsails and Lugsails	£30.00 net
Surveying and Restoring Classic Boats	£18.99 net
Laurent Giles: An Evolution of Yacht Design	£22.00 net
Effective Skippering	£14.99 net
Cruising Under Sail	£16.99 net
Cruising Mate's Handbook	£12.99 net
Heavy Weather Sailing	£30.00 net
Anchoring & Mooring Techniques Illustrated	£12.99 net
Modern Rope Seamanship	£ 8.95 net
Fitting Out: Preparing for Sea	£ 9.99 net
Boat Electrical Systems	£12.99 net
Laying Up Your Boat	£ 7.99 net
Rigging	£13.99 net
Knots in Use	£ 5.99 net

All these books are available or can be ordered from your local bookshop or can be ordered direct from the publisher. Simply tick the titles you want and fill in the form below.

Prices and availability subject to change without notice

Adlard Coles Nautical Cash Sales, PO Box 11, Falmouth, Cornwall.

Please send a cheque or postal order for the value of the book and add the following for postage and packing.

UK including BFPO: £1.00 for one book plus 50p for the second book and 30p for each additional book ordered up to a £3.00 maximum.

OVERSEAS INCLUDING EIRE: £2.00 for the first book, plus £1.00 for the second book, and 50p for each additional book ordered.

OR Please debit this amount from my Access/Visa Card (delete as appropriate).

Card Number

Amount _____

Expiry date _____

Signed _____

Name _____

Address _____

_____

Fax no. _____